Manifestoes of Surrealism

M A N

Translated from the French by

Richard Seaver and

Helen R. Lane

O F

André Breton

R E A

I F E S
T O E S

Ann Arbor Paperbacks   The University of Michigan Press

S U R
L I S M

First edition as an Ann Arbor Paperback 1972
Copyright © by the University of Michigan 1969
All rights reserved
ISBN 0-472-06182-8
Published in the United States of America by
The University of Michigan Press
Originally published in Paris, France, by Jean-Jacques
Pauvert editeur as Manifestes du Surrealisme
copyright © chez J.-J. Pauvert 1962.
Manufactured in the United States of America

Book design by Quentin Fiore

2000   1999   1998   1997   21   20   19   18

CONTENTS

PREFACE
FOR A REPRINT
OF
THE MANIFESTO
(1929)

It was to be expected that this book would change, and to the extent that it questioned our terrestrial existence by charging it nonetheless with everything that it comprises on this or that side of the limits we are in the habit of assigning to it, that its fate would be closely bound up with my own, which is, for example, to have written and not to have written books. Those attributed to me do not seem to me to exercise any greater influence on me than many others, and no doubt I am no longer as fully familiar with them as it is possible to be. Regardless of whatever controversy that may have arisen concerning the Manifesto of Surrealism *between 1924 and 1929—without arguing the pros and cons of its validity—it is obvious that, independent of this controversy, the human adventure continued to take place with the minimum of risks, on almost all sides at once, according to the whims of the imagination which alone causes real things. To allow a work one has written to be republished, a work not all that different from one you might more or less have read by someone else, is tantamount to "recognizing" I would not even go so far as to say a child whose features one had already ascertained were reasonably friendly, whose constitution is healthy enough, but rather something which, no matter how bravely it* may have been, *can no longer be. There is nothing I can do about it, except to blame myself for not always and in every respect having been a prophet. Still very much apropos is the famous question Arthur Craven, "in a very tired, very weary tone," asked André Gide: "Monsieur Gide, where are we with respect to time?" To which Gide, with no malice intended, replied: "Fifteen minutes before six." Ah! it must indeed be admitted, we're in bad, we're in terrible, shape when it comes to time.*

Here as elsewhere admission and denial are tightly interwoven. I do not understand why, or how, how I am still living, or, for all the more reason, what I am living. If, from a system in which I believe, to which I slowly adapt myself, like Surrealism, there remains, if there will always remain, enough for me to immerse myself in, there will nonetheless never be enough to make me what I would like to be, no matter how indulgent I am about myself. A relative indulgence compared to that others have shown me (or non-me, I don't know). And yet I am living, I have even discovered that I care about life. The more I have sometimes found reasons for putting an end to it the more I have caught myself admiring some random square of parquet floor: it was really like silk, like the silk that would have been as beautiful as water. I liked this lucid pain, as though the entire universal drama of it had then passed through me and I was suddenly worth the trouble. But I liked it in the light of, how shall I say, of new things that I had never seen glow before. It was from this that I understood that, in spite of everything, life was given, that a force independent of that of expressing and making oneself heard spiritually presided—insofar as a living man is concerned— over reactions of invaluable interest, the secret of which will disappear with him. This secret has not been revealed to me, and as far as I am concerned its recognition in no way invalidates my confessed inaptitude for religious meditation. I simply believe that between my thought, such as it appears in what material people have been able to read that has my signature affixed to it, and me, which the true nature of my thought involves in something but precisely what I do not yet know, there is a world, an imperceptible world of phantasms, of hypothetical realizations, of wagers lost, and of lies, a cursory examination of which convinces me not to correct this work in the slightest. This book demands all the vanity of the scientific mind, all the puerility of this need for perspective which the bitter vicissitudes of history provide. This time again, faithful to the tendency that I have always had to ignore any kind of sentimental obstacle, I shall waste no time passing judgment on those among my initial companions who have become frightened and turned back, I shall not yield to the temptation to substitute names by means of which this book might be able to lay claim to being up-to-date. Fully mindful, however, that the most precious gifts of the mind cannot survive the smallest particle of honor, I shall simply reaffirm my unshakable confidence in the principle of an activity which has never deceived me, which seems to me more deserving than ever of our unstinting, absolute, insane devotion, for the simple reason that it alone is the dispenser, albeit at intervals well spaced out one from the other, of transfiguring rays of a grace I persist in comparing in all respects to divine grace.

MANIFESTO OF SURREALISM
(1924)

So strong is the belief in life, in what is most fragile in life —*real* life, I mean—that in the end this belief is lost. Man, that inveterate dreamer, daily more discontent with his destiny, has trouble assessing the objects he has been led to use, objects that his nonchalance has brought his way, or that he has earned through his own efforts, almost always through his own efforts, for he has agreed to work, at least he has not refused to try his luck (or what he calls his luck!). At this point he feels extremely modest: he knows what women he has had, what silly affairs he has been involved in; he is unimpressed by his wealth or poverty, in this respect he is still a newborn babe and, as for the approval of his conscience, I confess that he does very nicely without it. If he still retains a certain lucidity, all he can do is turn back toward his childhood which, however his guides and mentors may have botched it, still strikes him as somehow charming. There, the absence of any known restrictions allows him the perspective of several lives lived at once; this illusion becomes firmly rooted within him; now he is only interested in the fleeting, the extreme facility of everything. Children set off each day without a worry in the world. Everything is near at hand, the worst material conditions are fine. The woods are white or black, one will never sleep.

But it is true that we would not dare venture so far, it is not merely a question of distance. Threat is piled upon threat, one yields, abandons a portion of the terrain to be conquered. This imagination which knows no bounds is henceforth allowed to be exercised only in strict accordance with the laws of an arbitrary utility; it is incapable of assuming this inferior role for very long and, in the vicinity of the twentieth year, generally prefers to abandon man to his lusterless fate.

Though he may later try to pull himself together upon occasion, having felt that he is losing by slow degrees all reason for living, incapable as he has become of being able to rise to some exceptional situation such as love, he will hardly succeed. This is because he henceforth belongs body and soul to an imperative practical necessity which demands his constant attention. None of his gestures will be expansive, none of his ideas generous or far-reaching. In his mind's eye, events real or imagined will be seen only as they relate to a welter of similar events, events in which he has not participated, *abortive* events. What am I saying: he will judge them in relationship to one of these events whose consequences are more reassuring than the others. On no account will he view them as his salvation.

Beloved imagination, what I most like in you is your unsparing quality.

The mere word "freedom" is the only one that still excites me. I deem it capable of indefinitely sustaining the old human fanaticism. It doubtless satisfies my only legitimate aspiration. Among all the many misfortunes to which we are heir, it is only fair to admit that we are allowed the greatest degree of freedom of thought. It is up to us not to misuse it. To reduce the imagination to a state of slavery

—even though it would mean the elimination of what is commonly called happiness—is to betray all sense of absolute justice within oneself. Imagination alone offers me some intimation of what *can be,* and this is enough to remove to some slight degree the terrible injunction; enough, too, to allow me to devote myself to it without fear of making a mistake (as though it were possible to make a bigger mistake). Where does it begin to turn bad, and where does the mind's stability cease? For the mind, is the possibility of erring not rather the contingency of good?

There remains madness, "the madness that one locks up," as it has aptly been described. That madness or another. . . . We all know, in fact, that the insane owe their incarceration to a tiny number of legally reprehensible acts and that, were it not for these acts their freedom (or what we see as their freedom) would not be threatened. I am willing to admit that they are, to some degree, victims of their imagination, in that it induces them not to pay attention to certain rules—outside of which the species feels itself threatened—which we are all supposed to know and respect. But their profound indifference to the way in which we judge them, and even to the various punishments meted out to them, allows us to suppose that they derive a great deal of comfort and consolation from their imagination, that they enjoy their madness sufficiently to endure the thought that its validity does not extend beyond themselves. And, indeed, hallucinations, illusions, etc., are not a source of trifling pleasure. The best controlled sensuality partakes of it, and I know that there are many evenings when I would gladly tame that pretty hand which, during the last pages of Taine's *L'Intelligence,* indulges in some curious misdeeds. I could spend my whole life prying loose the secrets of the insane. These people are honest to a fault, and their naiveté has no peer but my own. Christopher Columbus should have set out to discover America with a boatload of madmen. And note how this madness has taken shape, and endured.

It is not the fear of madness which will oblige us to leave the flag of imagination furled.

The case against the realistic attitude demands to be examined, following the case against the materialistic attitude. The latter, more poetic in fact than the former, admittedly implies on the part of man a kind of monstrous pride which, admittedly, is monstrous, but not a new and more complete decay. It should above all be viewed as a welcome reaction against certain ridiculous tendencies of spiritualism. Finally, it is not incompatible with a certain nobility of thought.

By contrast, the realistic attitude, inspired by positivism, from Saint Thomas Aquinas to Anatole France, clearly seems to me to be hostile to any intellectual or moral advancement. I loathe it, for it is made up of mediocrity, hate, and dull conceit. It is this attitude which today gives birth to these ridiculous books, these insulting plays. It constantly feeds on and derives strength from the newspapers and stultifies both science and art by assiduously flattering the lowest of tastes; clarity bordering on stupidity, a dog's life. The activity of the best minds feels the effects of it; the law of the lowest common denominator finally prevails upon them as it does upon the others. An amusing result of this state of affairs, in literature for example, is the generous supply of novels. Each person adds his personal little "observation" to the whole. As a cleansing antidote to all this, M. Paul Valéry recently suggested that an anthology be compiled in which the largest possible number of opening passages from novels be offered; the resulting insanity, he predicted, would be a source of considerable edification. The most famous authors would be included. Such a thought reflects great credit on Paul

Valéry who, some time ago, speaking of novels, assured me that, so far as he was concerned, he would continue to refrain from writing: "The Marquise went out at five." But has he kept his word?

If the purely informative style, of which the sentence just quoted is a prime example, is virtually the rule rather than the exception in the novel form, it is because, in all fairness, the author's ambition is severely circumscribed. The circumstantial, needlessly specific nature of each of their notations leads me to believe that they are perpetrating a joke at my expense. I am spared not even one of the character's slightest vacillations: will he be fairhaired? what will his name be? will we first meet him during the summer? So many questions resolved once and for all, as chance directs; the only discretionary power left me is to close the book, which I am careful to do somewhere in the vicinity of the first page. And the descriptions! There is nothing to which their vacuity can be compared; they are nothing but so many superimposed images taken from some stock catalogue, which the author utilizes more and more whenever he chooses; he seizes the opportunity to slip me his postcards, he tries to make me agree with him about the clichés:

The small room into which the young man was shown was covered with yellow wallpaper: there were geraniums in the windows, which were covered with muslin curtains; the setting sun cast a harsh light over the entire setting. . . . There was nothing special about the room. The furniture, of yellow wood, was all very old. A sofa with a tall back turned down, an oval table opposite the sofa, a dressing table and a mirror set against the pierglass, some chairs along the walls, two or three etchings of no value portraying some German girls with birds in their hands—such were the furnishings.*

*Dostoevski, *Crime and Punishment.*

I am in no mood to admit that the mind is interested in occupying itself with such matters, even fleetingly. It may be argued that this school-boy description has its place, and that at this juncture of the book the author has his reasons for burdening me. Nevertheless he is wasting his time, for I refuse to go into his room. Others' laziness or fatigue does not interest me. I have too unstable a notion of the continuity of life to equate or compare my moments of depression or weakness with my best moments. When one ceases to feel, I am of the opinion one should keep quiet. And I would like it understood that I am not accusing or condemning lack of originality *as such.* I am only saying that I do not take particular note of the empty moments of my life, that it may be unworthy for any man to crystallize those which seem to him to be so. I shall, with your permission, *ignore* the description of that room, and many more like it.

Not so fast, there; I'm getting into the area of psychology, a subject about which I shall be careful not to joke.

The author attacks a character and, this being settled upon, parades his hero to and fro across the world. No matter what happens, this hero, whose actions and reactions are admirably predictable, is compelled not to thwart or upset—even though he looks as though he is—the calculations of which he is the object. The currents of life can appear to lift him up, roll him over, cast him down, he will still belong to this *readymade* human type. A simple game of chess which doesn't interest me in the least—man, whoever he may be, being for me a mediocre opponent. What I cannot bear are those wretched discussions relative to such and such a move, since winning or losing is not in question. And if the game is not worth the candle, if objective reason does a frightful job—as indeed it does —of serving him who calls upon it, is it not fitting and proper to avoid all contact with these categories? "Diversity is so vast that every different tone of voice, every step, cough, every wipe of the nose, every sneeze. . . ."* If in a cluster of grapes there are no two alike, why do you want me to describe this grape by the other, by all the others, why do you want me to make a palatable grape? Our brains are dulled by the incurable mania of wanting to make the unknown known, classifiable. The desire for analysis wins out over the sentiments.** The result is statements of undue length whose persuasive power is attributable solely to their strangeness and which impress the reader only by the abstract quality of their vocabulary, which moreover is ill-defined. If the general ideas that philosophy has thus far come up with as topics of discussion revealed by their very nature their definitive incursion into a broader or more general area, I would be the first to greet the news with joy. But up till now it has been nothing but idle repartee; the flashes of wit and other niceties vie in concealing from us the true thought in search of itself, instead of concentrating on obtaining successes. It seems to me that every act is its own justification, at least for the person who has been capable of committing it, that it is endowed with a radiant power which the slightest gloss is certain to diminish. Because of this gloss, it even in a sense ceases to happen. It gains nothing to be thus distinguished. Stendhal's heroes are subject to the comments and appraisals—appraisals which are more or less successful—made by that author, which add not one whit to their glory. Where we really find them again is at the point at which Stendhal has lost them.

We are still living under the reign of logic: this, of course, is what I have been driving at. But in this day and age logical methods are applicable only to solving problems of secondary interest. The absolute rationalism that is still in vogue allows us to consider only facts relating directly to our experience. Logical ends, on the contrary, escape

*Pascal.
**Barrès, *Proust*.

us. It is pointless to add that experience itself has found itself increasingly circumscribed. It paces back and forth in a cage from which it is more and more difficult to make it emerge. It too leans for support on what is most immediately expedient, and it is protected by the sentinels of common sense. Under the pretense of civilization and progress, we have managed to banish from the mind everything that may rightly or wrongly be termed superstition, or fancy; forbidden is any kind of search for truth which is not in conformance with accepted practices. It was, apparently, by pure chance that a part of our mental world which we pretended not to be concerned with any longer—and, in my opinion by far the most important part—has been brought back to light. For this we must give thanks to the discoveries of Sigmund Freud. On the basis of these discoveries a current of opinion is finally forming by means of which the human explorer will be able to carry his investigations much further, authorized as he will henceforth be not to confine himself solely to the most summary realities. The imagination is perhaps on the point of reasserting itself, of reclaiming its rights. If the depths of our mind contain within it strange forces capable of augmenting those on the surface, or of waging a victorious battle against them, there is every reason to seize them—first to seize them, then, if need be, to submit them to the control of our reason. The analysts themselves have everything to gain by it. But it is worth noting that no means has been designated a priori for carrying out this undertaking, that until further notice it can be construed to be the province of poets as well as scholars, and that its success is not dependent upon the more or less capricious paths that will be followed.

Freud very rightly brought his critical faculties to bear upon the dream. It is, in fact, inadmissible that this considerable portion of psychic activity (since, at least from man's birth until his death, thought offers no solution of continuity, the sum of the moments of dream, from the point of view of time, and taking into consideration only the time of pure dreaming, that is the dreams of sleep, is not inferior to the sum of the moments of reality, or, to be more precisely limiting, the moments of waking) has still today been so grossly neglected. I have always been amazed at the way an ordinary observer lends so much more credence and attaches so much more importance to waking events than to those occurring in dreams. It is because man, when he ceases to sleep, is above all the play-thing of his memory, and in its normal state memory takes pleasure in weakly retracing for him the circumstances of the dream, in stripping it of any real importance, and in dismissing the only *determinant* from the point where he thinks he has left it a few hours before: this firm hope, this concern. He is under the impression of continuing some-thing that is worthwhile. Thus the dream finds itself re-duced to a mere parenthesis, as is the night. And, like the night, dreams generally contribute little to furthering our understanding. This curious state of affairs seems to me to call for certain reflections:

1) Within the limits where they operate (or are thought to operate) dreams give every evidence of being continuous and show signs of organization. Memory alone arrogates to itself the right to excerpt from dreams, to ignore the transitions, and to depict for us rather a series of dreams than the *dream itself*. By the same token, at any given moment we have only a distinct notion of realities, the coordination of which is a question of will.* What is

---

*Account must be taken of the *depth* of the dream. For the most part I retain only what I can glean from its most superficial layers. What I most enjoy contemplating about a dream is every-thing that sinks back below the surface in a waking state, everything I have forgotten about my activities in the course of the preceding day, dark foliage, stupid branches. In "reality," likewise, I prefer to *fall*.

worth noting is that nothing allows us to presuppose a greater dissipation of the elements of which the dream is constituted. I am sorry to have to speak about it according to a formula which in principle excludes the dream. When will we have sleeping logicians, sleeping philosophers? I would like to sleep, in order to surrender myself to the dreamers, the way I surrender myself to those who read me with eyes wide open; in order to stop imposing, in this realm, the conscious rhythm of my thought. Perhaps my dream last night follows that of the night before, and will be continued the next night, with an exemplary strictness. *It's quite possible,* as the saying goes. And since it has not been proved in the slightest that, in doing so, the "reality" with which I am kept busy continues to exist in the state of dream, that it does not sink back down into the immemorial, why should I not grant to dreams what I occasionally refuse reality, that is, this value of certainty in itself which, in its own time, is not open to my repudiation? Why should I not expect from the sign of the dream more than I expect from a degree of consciousness which is daily more acute? Can't the dream also be used in solving the fundamental questions of life? Are these questions the same in one case as in the other and, in the dream, do these questions already exist? Is the dream any less restrictive or punitive than the rest? I am growing old and, more than that reality to which I believe I subject myself, it is perhaps the dream, the difference with which I treat the dream, which makes me grow old.

2) Let me come back again to the waking state. I have no choice but to consider it a phenomenon of interference. Not only does the mind display, in this state, a strange tendency to lose its bearings (as evidenced by the slips and mistakes the secrets of which are just beginning to be revealed to us), but, what is more, it does not appear that, when the mind is functioning normally, it really responds to anything but the suggestions which come to it from the

depths of that dark night to which I commend it. However conditioned it may be, its balance is relative. It scarcely dares express itself and, if it does, it confines itself to verifying that such and such an idea, or such and such a woman, has made an impression on it. What impression it would be hard pressed to say, by which it reveals the degree of its subjectivity, and nothing more. This idea, this woman, disturb it, they tend to make it less severe. What they do is isolate the mind for a second from its solvent and spirit it to heaven, as the beautiful precipitate it can be, that it is. When all else fails, it then calls upon chance, a divinity even more obscure than the others to whom it ascribes all its aberrations. Who can say to me that the angle by which that idea which affects it is offered, that what it likes in the eye of that woman is not precisely what links it to its dream, binds it to those fundamental facts which, through its own fault, it has lost? And if things were different, what might it be capable of? I would like to provide it with the key to this corridor.

3) The mind of the man who dreams is fully satisfied by what happens to him. The agonizing question of possibility is no longer pertinent. Kill, fly faster, love to your heart's content. And if you should die, are you not certain of reawaking among the dead? Let yourself be carried along, events will not tolerate your interference. You are nameless. The ease of everything is priceless.

What reason, I ask, a reason so much vaster than the other, makes dreams seem so natural and allows me to welcome unreservedly a welter of episodes so strange that they would confound me now as I write? And yet I can believe my eyes, my ears; this great day has arrived, this beast has spoken.

If man's awaking is harder, if it breaks the spell too abruptly, it is because he has been led to make for himself too impoverished a notion of atonement.

4) From the moment when it is subjected to a method-

ical examination, when, by means yet to be determined, we succeed in recording the contents of dreams in their entirety (and that presupposes a discipline of memory spanning generations; but let us nonetheless begin by noting the most salient facts), when its graph will expand with unparalleled volume and regularity, we may hope that the mysteries which really are not will give way to the great Mystery. I believe in the future resolution of these two states, dream and reality, which are seemingly so contradictory, into a kind of absolute reality, a *surreality*, if one may so speak. It is in quest of this surreality that I am going, certain not to find it but too unmindful of my death not to calculate to some slight degree the joys of its possession.

A story is told according to which Saint-Pol-Roux, in times gone by, used to have a notice posted on the door of his manor house in Camaret, every evening before he went to sleep, which read: THE POET IS WORKING.

A great deal more could be said, but in passing I merely wanted to touch upon a subject which in itself would require a very long and much more detailed discussion; I shall come back to it. At this juncture, my intention was merely to mark a point by noting the *hate of the marvelous* which rages in certain men, this absurdity beneath which they try to bury it. Let us not mince words: the marvelous is always beautiful, anything marvelous is beautiful, in fact only the marvelous is beautiful.

In the realm of literature, only the marvelous is capable of fecundating works which belong to an inferior category such as the novel, and generally speaking, anything that involves storytelling. Lewis' *The Monk* is an admirable proof of this. It is infused throughout with the presence of the marvelous. Long before the author has freed his main characters from all temporal constraints, one feels them ready to act with an unprecedented pride. This passion for eternity with which they are constantly stirred lends an unforgettable intensity to their torments, and to mine. I mean that this book, from beginning to end, and in the purest way imaginable, exercises an exalting effect only upon that part of the mind which aspires to leave the earth and that, stripped of an insignificant part of its plot, which belongs to the period in which it was written, it constitutes a paragon of precision and innocent grandeur.* It seems to me none better has been done, and that the character of Mathilda in particular is the most moving creation that one can credit to this *figurative* fashion in literature. She is less a character than a continual temptation. And if a character is not a temptation, what is he? An extreme temptation, she. In *The Monk,* the "nothing is impossible for him who dares try" gives it its full, convincing measure. Ghosts play a logical role in the book, since the critical mind does not seize them in order to dispute them. Ambrosio's punishment is likewise treated in a legitimate manner, since it is finally accepted by the critical faculty as a natural denouement.

It may seem arbitrary on my part, when discussing the marvelous, to choose this model, from which both the Nordic literatures and Oriental literatures have borrowed time and time again, not to mention the religious literatures of every country. This is because most of the examples which these literatures could have furnished me with are tainted by puerility, for the simple reason that they are addressed to children. At an early age children are weaned on the marvelous, and later on they fail to retain a sufficient virginity of mind to thoroughly enjoy fairy tales. No matter

---

*What is admirable about the fantastic is that there is no longer anything fantastic: there is only the real.

how charming they may be, a grown man would think he were reverting to childhood by nourishing himself on fairy tales, and I am the first to admit that all such tales are not suitable for him. The fabric of adorable improbabilities must be made a trifle more subtle the older we grow, and we are still at the stage of waiting for this kind of spider. . . . But the faculties do not change radically. Fear, the attraction of the unusual, chance, the taste for things extravagant are all devices which we can always call upon without fear of deception. There are fairy tales to be written for adults, fairy tales still almost blue.

The marvelous is not the same in every period of history: it partakes in some obscure way of a sort of general revelation only the fragments of which come down to us: they are the romantic *ruins*, the modern *mannequin*, or any other symbol capable of affecting the human sensibility for a period of time. In these areas which make us smile, there is still portrayed the incurable human restlessness, and this is why I take them into consideration and why I judge them inseparable from certain productions of genius which are, more than the others, painfully afflicted by them. They are Villon's gibbets, Racine's Greeks, Baudelaire's couches. They coincide with an eclipse of the taste I am made to endure, I whose notion of taste is the image of a big spot. Amid the bad taste of my time I strive to go further than anyone else. It would have been I, had I lived in 1820, I "the bleeding nun," I who would not have spared this cunning and banal "let us conceal" whereof the parodical Cuisin speaks, it would have been I, I who would have reveled in the enormous metaphors, as he says, all phases of the "silver disk." For today I think of a *castle*, half of which is not necessarily in ruins; this castle belongs to me, I picture it in a rustic setting, not far from Paris. The outbuildings are too numerous to mention, and, as for the interior, it has been frightfully restored, in such a manner as to leave nothing to be desired from the viewpoint of comfort. Automobiles are parked before the door, concealed by the shade of the trees. A few of my friends are living here as permanent guests: there is Louis Aragon leaving; he only has time enough to say hello; Philippe Soupault gets up with the stars, and Paul Eluard, our great Eluard, has not yet come home. There are Robert Desnos and Roger Vitrac out on the grounds poring over an ancient edict on dueling; Georges Auric, Jean Paulhan; Max Morise, who rows so well, and Benjamin Péret, busy with his equations with birds; and Joseph Delteil; and Jean Carrive; and Georges Limbour, and Georges Limbours (there is a whole hedge of Georges Limbours); and Marcel Noll; there is T. Fraenkel waving to us from his captive balloon, Georges Malkine, Antonin Artaud, Francis Gérard, Pierre Naville, J.-A. Boiffard, and after them Jacques Baron and his brother, handsome and cordial, and so many others besides, and gorgeous women, I might add. Nothing is too good for these young men, their wishes are, as to wealth, so many commands. Francis Picabia comes to pay us a call, and last week, in the hall of mirrors, we received a certain Marcel Duchamp whom we had not hitherto known. Picasso goes hunting in the neighborhood. The spirit of *demoralization* has elected domicile in the castle, and it is with it we have to deal every time it is a question of contact with our fellowmen, but the doors are always open, and one does not begin by "thanking" everyone, you know. Moreover, the solitude is vast, we don't often run into one another. And anyway, isn't what matters that we be the masters of ourselves, the masters of women, and of love too?

I shall be proved guilty of poetic dishonesty: everyone will go parading about saying that I live on the rue Fontaine* and that he will have none of the water that flows therefrom. To be sure! But is he certain that this castle

*Breton's pun eludes translation: Fontaine=Fountain.—Tr.

into which I cordially invite him is an image? What if this castle really existed! My guests are there to prove it does; their whim is the luminous road that leads to it. We really live by our fantasies when we *give free rein to them*. And how could what one might do bother the other, there, safely sheltered from the sentimental pursuit and at the trysting place of opportunities?

Man proposes and disposes. He and he alone can determine whether he is completely master of himself, that is, whether he maintains the body of his desires, daily more formidable, in a state of anarchy. Poetry teaches him to. It bears within itself the perfect compensation for the miseries we endure. It can also be an organizer, if ever, as the result of a less intimate disappointment, we contemplate taking it seriously. The time is coming when it decrees the end of money and by itself will break the bread of heaven for the earth! There will still be gatherings on the public squares, and *movements* you never dared hope participate in. Farewell to absurd choices, the dreams of dark abyss, rivalries, the prolonged patience, the flight of the seasons, the artificial order of ideas, the ramp of danger, time for everything! May you only take the trouble to *practice* poetry. Is it not incumbent upon us, who are already living off it, to try and impose what we hold to be our case for further inquiry?

It matters not whether there is a certain disproportion between this defense and the illustration that will follow it. It was a question of going back to the sources of poetic imagination and, what is more, of remaining there. Not that I pretend to have done so. It requires a great deal of fortitude to try to set up one's abode in these distant regions where everything seems at first to be so awkward and difficult, all the more so if one wants to try to take someone there. Besides, one is never sure of really being there. If one is going to all that trouble, one might just as well stop off somewhere else. Be that as it may, the fact is that the way to these regions is clearly marked, and that to attain the true goal is now merely a matter of the travelers' ability to endure.

We are all more or less aware of the road traveled. I was careful to relate, in the course of a study of the case of Robert Desnos entitled ENTRÉE DES MÉDIUMS,* that I had been led to "concentrate my attention on the more or less partial sentences which, when one is quite alone and on the verge of falling asleep, become perceptible for the mind without its being possible to discover what provoked them." I had then just attempted the poetic adventure with the minimum of risks, that is, my aspirations were the same as they are today but I trusted in the slowness of formulation to keep me from useless contacts, contacts of which I completely disapproved. This attitude involved a modesty of thought certain vestiges of which I still retain. At the end of my life, I shall doubtless manage to speak with great effort the way people speak, to apologize for my voice and my few remaining gestures. The virtue of the spoken word (and the written word all the more so) seemed to me to derive from the faculty of foreshortening in a striking manner the exposition (since there was exposition) of a small number of facts, poetic or other, of which I made myself the substance. I had come to the conclusion that Rimbaud had not proceeded any differently. I was composing, with a concern for variety that deserved better, the final poems of *Mont de piété,* that is, I managed to extract from the blank lines of this book an incredible advantage. These lines were the closed eye to the operations of thought

*See *Les Pas perdus,* published by N. R. F.

that I believed I was obliged to keep hidden from the reader. It was not deceit on my part, but my love of shocking the reader. I had the illusion of a possible complicity, which I had more and more difficulty giving up. I had begun to cherish words excessively for the space they allow around them, for their tangencies with countless other words that I did not utter. The poem BLACK FOREST derives precisely from this state of mind. It took me six months to write it, and you may take my word for it that I did not rest a single day. But this stemmed from the opinion I had of myself in those days, which was high, please don't judge me too harshly. I enjoy these stupid confessions. At that point cubist pseudo-poetry was trying to get a foothold, but it had emerged defenseless from Picasso's brain, and I was thought to be as dull as dishwater (and still am). I had a sneaking suspicion, moreover, that from the viewpoint of poetry I was off on the wrong road, but I hedged my bet as best I could, defying lyricism with salvos of definitions and formulas (the Dada phenomena were waiting in the wings, ready to come on stage) and pretending to search for an application of poetry to advertising (I went so far as to claim that the world would end, not with a good book but with a beautiful advertisement for heaven or for hell).

In those days, a man at least as boring as I, Pierre Reverdy, was writing:

The image is a pure creation of the mind.

It cannot be born from a comparison but from a juxtaposition of two more or less distant realities.

The more the relationship between the two juxtaposed realities is distant and true, the stronger the image will be—the greater its emotional power and poetic reality . . . *

These words, however sibylline for the uninitiated, were extremely revealing, and I pondered them for a long

*Nord-Sud, March 1918.

time. But the image eluded me. Reverdy's aesthetic, a completely a posteriori aesthetic, led me to mistake the effects for the causes. It was in the midst of all this that I renounced irrevocably my point of view.

One evening, therefore, before I fell asleep, I perceived, so clearly articulated that it was impossible to change a word, but nonetheless removed from the sound of any voice, a rather strange phrase which came to me without any apparent relationship to the events in which, my consciousness agrees, I was then involved, a phrase which seemed to me insistent, a phrase, if I may be so bold, *which was knocking at the window.* I took cursory note of it and prepared to move on when its organic character caught my attention. Actually, this phrase astonished me: unfortunately I cannot remember it exactly, but it was something like: "There is a man cut in two by the window," but there could be no question of ambiguity, accompanied as it was by the faint visual image* of a man walking cut half way up by a

---

*Were I a painter, this visual depiction would doubtless have become more important for me than the other. It was most certainly my previous predispositions which decided the matter. Since that day, I have had occasion to concentrate my attention voluntarily on similar apparitions, and I know that they are fully as clear as auditory phenomena. With a pencil and white sheet of paper to hand, I could easily trace their outlines. Here again it is not a matter of drawing, *but simply of tracing.* I could thus depict a tree, a wave, a musical instrument, all manner of things of which I am presently incapable of providing even the roughest sketch. I would plunge into it, convinced that I would find my way again, in a maze of lines which at first glance would seem to be going nowhere. And, upon opening my eyes, I would get the very strong impression of something "never seen." The proof of what I am saying has been provided many times by Robert Desnos: to be convinced, one has only to leaf through the pages of issue number 36 of *Feuilles libres* which contains several of his drawings (*Romeo and Juliet, A Man Died This Morning,* etc.) which were taken by this magazine as the drawings of a madman and published as such.

window perpendicular to the axis of his body. Beyond the slightest shadow of a doubt, what I saw was the simple reconstruction in space of a man leaning out a window. But this window having shifted with the man, I realized that I was dealing with an image of a fairly rare sort, and all I could think of was to incorporate it into my material for poetic construction. No sooner had I granted it this capacity than it was in fact succeeded by a whole series of phrases, with only brief pauses between them, which surprised me only slightly less and left me with the impression of their being so gratuitous that the control I had then exercised upon myself seemed to me illusory and all I could think of was putting an end to the interminable quarrel raging within me.*

Completely occupied as I still was with Freud at that time, and familiar as I was with his methods of examination which I had had some slight occasion to use on some patients during the war, I resolved to obtain from myself what

---

*Knut Hamsum ascribes this sort of revelation to which I had been subjected as deriving from *hunger,* and he may not be wrong. (The fact is I did not eat every day during that period of my life). Most certainly the manifestations that he describes in these terms are clearly the same:

"The following day I awoke at an early hour. It was still dark. My eyes had been open for a long time when I heard the clock in the apartment above strike five. I wanted to go back to sleep, but I couldn't; I was wide awake and a thousand thoughts were crowding through my mind.

"Suddenly a few good fragments came to mind, quite suitable to be used in a rough draft, or serialized; all of a sudden I found, quite by chance, beautiful phrases, phrases such as I had never written. I repeated them to myself slowly, word by word; they were excellent. And there were still more coming. I got up and picked up a pencil and some paper that were on a table behind my bed. It was as though some vein had burst within me, one word followed another, found its proper place, adapted itself to the situation,

we were trying to obtain from them, namely, a monologue spoken as rapidly as possible without any intervention on the part of the critical faculties, a monologue consequently unencumbered by the slightest inhibition and which was, as closely as possible, akin to *spoken thought*. It had seemed to me, and still does—the way in which the phrase about the man cut in two had come to me is an indication of it—that the speed of thought is no greater than the speed of speech, and that thought does not necessarily defy language, nor even the fast-moving pen. It was in this frame of mind that Philippe Soupault—to whom I had confided these initial conclusions—and I decided to blacken some paper, with a praiseworthy disdain for what might result from a literary point of view. The ease of execution did the rest. By the end of the first day we were able to read to ourselves some fifty or so pages obtained in this manner, and begin to compare our results. All in all, Soupault's pages and mine proved to be remarkably similar: the same overconstruction, shortcomings of a similar nature, but also, on both our parts, the illusion of an extraordinary verve, a great deal of emotion, a considerable choice of images of a quality such that we would not have been capable of preparing a single one in longhand, a very special picturesque quality and, here and there, a strong comical effect. The only difference between our two texts seemed to me to derive essentially from our respective tempers, Soupault's being less static than mine, and, if he does not mind my

---

scene piled upon scene, the action unfolded, one retort after another welled up in my mind, I was enjoying myself immensely. Thoughts came to me so rapidly and continued to flow so abundantly that I lost a whole host of delicate details, because my pencil could not keep up with them, and yet I went as fast as I could, my hand in constant motion, I did not lose a minute. The sentences continued to well up within me, I was pregnant with my subject."

Apollinaire asserted that Chirico's first paintings were done under the influence of cenesthesic disorders (migraines, colics, etc.).

offering this one slight criticism, from the fact that he had made the error of putting a few words by way of titles at the top of certain pages, I suppose in a spirit of mystification. On the other hand, I must give credit where credit is due and say that he constantly and vigorously opposed any effort to retouch or correct, however slightly, any passage of this kind which seemed to me unfortunate. In this he was, to be sure, absolutely right.* It is, in fact, difficult to appreciate fairly the various elements present; one may even go so far as to say that it is impossible to appreciate them at a first reading. To you who write, these elements are, on the surface, *as strange to you as they are to anyone else,* and naturally you are wary of them. Poetically speaking, what strikes you about them above all is their *extreme degree of immediate absurdity,* the quality of this absurdity, upon closer scrutiny, being to give way to everything admissible, everything legitimate in the world: the disclosure of a certain number of properties and of facts no less objective, in the final analysis, than the others.

In homage to Guillaume Apollinaire, who had just died and who, on several occasions, seemed to us to have followed a discipline of this kind, without however having sacrificed to it any mediocre literary means, Soupault and I baptized the new mode of pure expression which we had at our disposal and which we wished to pass on to our friends, by the name of SURREALISM. I believe that there is no point today in dwelling any further on this word and that the meaning we gave it initially has generally prevailed over its Apollinarian sense. To be even fairer, we could

*I believe more and more in the infallibility of my thought with respect to myself, and this is too fair. Nonetheless, with this *thought-writing,* where one is at the mercy of the first outside distraction, "ebullitions" can occur. It would be inexcusable for us to pretend otherwise. By definition, thought is strong, and incapable of catching itself in error. The blame for these obvious weaknesses must be placed on suggestions that come to it from without.

probably have taken over the word SUPERNATURALISM employed by Gérard de Nerval in his dedication to the *Filles de feu.** It appears, in fact, that Nerval possessed to a tee the spirit with which we claim a kinship, Apollinaire having possessed, on the contrary, naught but *the letter,* still imperfect, of Surrealism, having shown himself powerless to give a valid theoretical idea of it. Here are two passages by Nerval which seem to me to be extremely significant in this respect:

> I am going to explain to you, my dear Dumas, the phenomenon of which you have spoken a short while ago. There are, as you know, certain storytellers who cannot invent without identifying with the characters their imagination has dreamt up. You may recall how convincingly our old friend Nodier used to tell how it had been his misfortune during the Revolution to be guillotined; one became so completely convinced of what he was saying that one began to wonder how he had managed to have his head glued back on.
>
> . . . And since you have been indiscreet enough to quote one of the sonnets composed in this SUPERNATURALISTIC dream-state, as the Germans would call it, you will have to hear them all. You will find them at the end of the volume. They are hardly any more obscure than Hegel's metaphysics or Swedenborg's MEMORABILIA, and would lose their charm if they were explained, if such were possible; at least admit the worth of the expression. . . .**

Those who might dispute our right to employ the term SURREALISM in the very special sense that we understand it are being extremely dishonest, for there can be no doubt

*And also by Thomas Carlyle in *Sartor Resartus* ([Book III] Chapter VIII, "Natural Supernaturalism"), 1833-34.

**See also *L'Idéoréalisme* by Saint-Pol-Roux.

that this word had no currency before we came along. Therefore, I am defining it once and for all:

SURREALISM, *n*. Psychic automatism in its pure state, by which one proposes to express—verbally, by means of the written word, or in any other manner—the actual functioning of thought. Dictated by thought, in the absence of any control exercised by reason, exempt from any aesthetic or moral concern.

ENCYCLOPEDIA. *Philosophy*. Surrealism is based on the belief in the superior reality of certain forms of previously neglected associations, in the omnipotence of dream, in the disinterested play of thought. It tends to ruin once and for all all other psychic mechanisms and to substitute itself for them in solving all the principal problems of life. The following have performed acts of ABSOLUTE SURREALISM: Messrs. Aragon, Baron, Boiffard, Breton, Carrive, Crevel, Delteil, Desnos, Eluard, Gérard, Limbour, Malkine, Morise, Naville, Noll, Péret, Picon, Soupault, Vitrac.

They seem to be, up to the present time, the only ones, and there would be no ambiguity about it were it not for the case of Isidore Ducasse, about whom I lack information. And, of course, if one is to judge them only superficially by their results, a good number of poets could pass for Surrealists, beginning with Dante and, in his finer moments, Shakespeare. *In the course of the various attempts I have made to reduce what is, by breach of trust, called genius, I have found nothing which in the final analysis can be attributed to any other method than that.*

Young's *Nights* are Surrealist from one end to the other; unfortunately it is a priest who is speaking, a bad priest no doubt, but a priest nonetheless.

Swift is Surrealist in malice,
Sade is Surrealist in sadism.

Chateaubriand is Surrealist in exoticism.
Constant is Surrealist in politics.
Hugo is Surrealist when he isn't stupid.
Desbordes-Valmore is Surrealist in love.
Bertrand is Surrealist in the past.
Rabbe is Surrealist in death.
Poe is Surrealist in adventure.
Baudelaire is Surrealist in morality.
Rimbaud is Surrealist in the way he lived, and elsewhere.
Mallarmé is Surrealist when he is confiding.
Jarry is Surrealist in absinthe.
Nouveau is Surrealist in the kiss.
Saint-Pol-Roux is Surrealist in his use of symbols.
Fargue is Surrealist in the atmosphere.
Vaché is Surrealist in me.
Reverdy is Surrealist at home.
Saint-Jean-Perse is Surrealist at a distance.
Roussel is Surrealist as a storyteller.
Etc.

I would like to stress this point: they are not always Surrealists, in that I discern in each of them a certain number
of preconceived ideas to which—very naively!—they hold.
They hold to them because they had not *heard the Surrealist voice,* the one that continues to preach on the eve of
death and above the storms, because they did not want to
serve simply to orchestrate the marvelous score. They were
instruments too full of pride, and this is why they have
not always produced a harmonious sound.*

But we, who have made no effort whatsoever to filter,
who in our works have made ourselves into simple recep-

*I could say the same of a number of philosophers and painters,
including, among these latter, Uccello, from painters of the past, and,
in the modern era, Seurat, Gustave Moreau, Matisse (in "La Mus-
ique," for example), Derain, Picasso, (by far the most pure), Braque,
Duchamp, Picabia, Chirico (so admirable for so long), Klee, Man Ray,
Max Ernst, and, one so close to us, André Masson.

tacles of so many echoes, modest *recording instruments* who are not mesmerized by the drawings we are making, perhaps we serve an even nobler cause. Thus do we render with integrity the "talent" which has been lent to us. You might as well speak of the talent of this platinum ruler, this mirror, this door, and of the sky, if you like.

We do not have any talent; ask Philippe Soupault:

"Anatomical products of manufacture and low-income dwellings will destroy the tallest cities."

Ask Roger Vitrac:

"No sooner had I called forth the marble-admiral than he turned on his heel like a horse which rears at the sight of the North star and showed me, in the plane of his two-pointed cocked hat, a region where I was to spend my life."

Ask Paul Eluard:

"This is an oft-told tale that I tell, a famous poem that I reread: I am leaning against a wall, with my verdant ears and my lips burned to a crisp."

Ask Max Morise:

"The bear of the caves and his friend the bittern, the vol-au-vent and his valet the wind, the Lord Chancellor with his Lady, the scarecrow for sparrows and his accomplice the sparrow, the test tube and his daughter the needle, this carnivore and his brother the carnival, the sweeper and his monocle, the Mississippi and its little dog, the coral and its jug of milk, the Miracle and its Good Lord, might just as well go and disappear from the surface of the sea."

Ask Joseph Delteil:

"Alas! I believe in the virtue of birds. And a feather is all it takes to make me die laughing."

Ask Louis Aragon:

"During a short break in the party, as the players were

gathering around a bowl of flaming punch, I asked the tree if it still had its red ribbon."

And ask me, who was unable to keep myself from writing the serpentine, distracting lines of this preface.

Ask Robert Desnos, he who, more than any of us, has perhaps got closest to the Surrealist truth, he who, in his still unpublished works* and in the course of the numerous experiments he has been a party to, has fully justified the hope I placed in Surrealism and leads me to believe that a great deal more will still come of it. Desnos *speaks Surrealist* at will. His extraordinary agility in orally following his thought is worth as much to us as any number of splendid speeches which are lost, Desnos having better things to do than record them. He reads himself like an open book, and does nothing to retain the pages, which fly away in the windy wake of his life.

SECRETS OF THE MAGICAL SURREALIST ART

Written Surrealist composition
or
first and last draft

After you have settled yourself in a place as favorable as possible to the concentration of your mind upon itself, have writing materials brought to you. Put yourself in as passive, or receptive, a state of mind as you can. Forget about your genius, your talents, and the talents of everyone else. Keep reminding yourself that literature is one of the saddest roads that leads to everything. Write quickly, without any preconceived subject, fast enough so that you will not re-

*NOUVELLES HÉBRIDES, DÉSORDRE FORMEL, DEUIL POUR DEUIL.

member what you're writing and be tempted to reread what you have written. The first sentence will come spontaneously, so compelling is the truth that with every passing second there is a sentence unknown to our consciousness which is only crying out to be heard. It is somewhat of a problem to form an opinion about the next sentence; it doubtless partakes both of our conscious activity and of the other, if one agrees that the fact of having written the first entails a minimum of perception. This should be of no importance to you, however; to a large extent, this is what is most interesting and intriguing about the Surrealist game. The fact still remains that punctuation no doubt resists the absolute continuity of the flow with which we are concerned, although it may seem as necessary as the arrangement of knots in a vibrating cord. Go on as long as you like. Put your trust in the inexhaustible nature of the murmur. If silence threatens to settle in if you should ever happen to make a mistake—a mistake, perhaps due to carelessness—break off without hesitation with an overly clear line. Following a word the origin of which seems suspicious to you, place any letter whatsoever, the letter "l" for example, always the letter "l," and bring the arbitrary back by making this letter the first of the following word.

How not to be bored any longer when with others

This is very difficult. Don't be at home for anyone, and occasionally, when no one has forced his way in, interrupting you in the midst of your Surrealist activity, and you, crossing your arms, say: "It doesn't matter, there are doubtless better things to do or not do. Interest in life is indefensible. Simplicity, what is going on inside me, is still tiresome to me!" or any other revolting banality.

To make speeches

Just prior to the elections, in the first country which deems it worthwhile to proceed in this kind of public expression of opinion, have yourself put on the ballot. Each of us has within himself the potential of an orator: multicolored loin cloths, glass trinkets of words. Through Surrealism he will take despair unawares in its poverty. One night, on a stage, he will, by himself, carve up the eternal heaven, that *Peau de l'ours*. He will promise so much that any promises he keeps will be a source of wonder and dismay. In answer to the claims of an entire people he will give a partial and ludicrous vote. He will make the bitterest enemies partake of a secret desire which will blow up the countries. And in this he will succeed simply by allowing himself to be moved by the immense word which dissolves into pity and revolves in hate. Incapable of failure, he will play on the velvet of all failures. He will be truly elected, and women will love him with an all-consuming passion.

To write false novels

Whoever you may be, if the spirit moves you burn a few laurel leaves and, without wishing to tend this meager fire, you will begin to write a novel. Surrealism will allow you to: all you have to do is set the needle marked "fair" at "action," and the rest will follow naturally. Here are some characters rather different in appearance; their names in your handwriting are a question of capital letters, and they will conduct themselves with the same ease with respect to active verbs as does the impersonal pronoun "it" with respect to words such as "is raining," "is," "must," etc. They will command them, so to speak, and wherever observation, reflection, and the faculty of generalization prove to be of no help to you, you may rest assured that they will credit you with a thousand intentions you never had. Thus endowed with a tiny number of physical and moral characteristics, these beings who in truth owe you so little will thereafter deviate not one iota from a certain line of conduct about which you need not concern yourself any fur-

ther. Out of this will result a plot more or less clever in
appearance, justifying point by point this moving or comforting denouement about which you couldn't care less.
Your false novel will simulate to a marvelous degree a real
novel; you will be rich, and everyone will agree that
"you've really got a lot of guts," since it's also in this region
that this something is located.

Of course, by an analogous method, and provided you
ignore what you are reviewing, you can successfully devote
yourself to false literary criticism.

*How to catch the eye of a woman
you pass in the street*

. . . .
. . . .
. . . .
. . . .
. . . .

Against death

Surrealism will usher you into death, which is a secret society. It will glove your hand, burying therein the profound M with which the word Memory begins. Do not
forget to make proper arrangements for your last will and
testament: speaking personally, I ask that I be taken to
the cemetery in a moving van. May my friends destroy
every last copy of the printing of the *Speech concerning the
Modicum of Reality.*

Language has been given to man so that he may make
Surrealist use of it. To the extent that he is required to
make himself understood, he manages more or less to express himself, and by so doing to fulfill certain functions

culled from among the most vulgar. Speaking, reading a letter, present no real problem for him, provided that, in so doing, he does not set himself a goal above the mean, that is, provided he confines himself to carrying on a conversation (for the pleasure of conversing) with someone. He is not worried about the words that are going to come, nor about the sentence which will follow after the sentence he is just completing. To a very simple question, he will be capable of making a lightning-like reply. In the absence of minor tics acquired through contact with others, he can without any ado offer an opinion on a limited number of subjects; for that he does not need to "count up to ten" before speaking or to formulate anything whatever ahead of time. Who has been able to convince him that this faculty of the first draft will only do him a disservice when he makes up his mind to establish more delicate relationships? There is no subject about which he should refuse to talk, to write about prolifically. All that results from listening to oneself, from reading what one has written, is the suspension of the occult, that admirable help. I am in no hurry to understand myself (basta! I shall always understand myself). If such and such a sentence of mine turns out to be somewhat disappointing, at least momentarily, I place my trust in the following sentence to redeem its sins: I carefully refrain from starting it over again or polishing it. The only thing that might prove fatal to me would be the slightest loss of impetus. Words, groups of words *which follow one another,* manifest among themselves the greatest solidarity. It is not up to me to favor one group over the other. It is up to a miraculous equivalent to intervene—and intervene it does.

Not only does this unrestricted language, which I am trying to render forever valid, which seems to me to adapt itself to all of life's circumstances, not only does this language not deprive me of any of my means, on the contrary it lends me an extraordinary lucidity, and it does so in an area where I least expected it. I shall even go so far as to maintain that it instructs me and, indeed, I have had occasion to use *surreally* words whose meaning I have forgotten. I was subsequently able to verify that the way in which I had used them corresponded perfectly with their definition. This would lead one to believe that we do not "learn," that all we ever do is "relearn." There are felicitous turns of speech that I have thus familiarized myself with. And I am not talking about the *poetic consciousness of objects* which I have been able to acquire only after a spiritual contact with them repeated a thousand times over.

The forms of Surrealist language adapt themselves best to dialogue. Here, two thoughts confront each other; while one is being delivered, the other is busy with it; but how is it busy with it? To assume that it incorporates it within itself would be tantamount to admitting that there is a time during which it is possible for it to live completely off that other thought, which is highly unlikely. And, in fact, the attention it pays is completely exterior; it has only time enough to approve or reject—generally reject—with all the consideration of which man is capable. This mode of language, moreover, does not allow the heart of the matter to be plumbed. My attention, prey to an entreaty which it cannot in all decency reject, treats the opposing thought as an enemy; in ordinary conversation, it "takes it up" almost always on the words, the figures of speech, it employs; it puts me in a position to turn it to good advantage in my reply by distorting them. This is true to such a degree that in certain pathological states of mind, where the sensorial disorders occupy the patient's complete attention, he limits himself, while continuing to answer the questions, to seizing the last word spoken in his presence or the last portion of the Surrealist sentence some trace of which he finds in his mind.

Q. "How old are you?" A. "You." *(Echolalia.)*
Q. "What is your name?" A. "Forty-five houses." *(Ganser syndrome, or beside-the-point replies.)*

There is no conversation in which some trace of this disorder does not occur. The effort to be social which dictates it and the considerable practice we have at it are the only things which enable us to conceal it temporarily. It is also the great weakness of the book that it is in constant conflict with its best, by which I mean the most demanding, readers. In the very short dialogue that I concocted above between the doctor and the madman, it was in fact the madman who got the better of the exchange. Because, through his replies, he obtrudes upon the attention of the doctor examining him—and because he is not the person asking the questions. Does this mean that his thought at this point is the stronger? Perhaps. He is free not to care any longer about his age or name.

Poetic Surrealism, which is the subject of this study, has focused its efforts up to this point on reestablishing dialogue in its absolute truth, by freeing both interlocutors from any obligations of politeness. Each of them simply pursues his soliloquy without trying to derive any special dialectical pleasure from it and without trying to impose anything whatsoever upon his neighbor. The remarks exchanged are not, as is generally the case, meant to develop some thesis, however unimportant it may be; they are as disaffected as possible. As for the reply that they elicit, it is, in principle, totally indifferent to the personal pride of the person speaking. The words, the images are only so many springboards for the mind of the listener. In *Les Champs magnétiques,* the first purely Surrealist work, this is the way in which the pages grouped together under the title *Barrières* must be conceived of—pages wherein Soupault and I show ourselves to be impartial interlocutors.

Surrealism does not allow those who devote themselves to it to forsake it whenever they like. There is every reason to believe that it acts on the mind very much as drugs do; like drugs, it creates a certain state of need and can push man to frightful revolts. It also is, if you like, an artificial paradise, and the taste one has for it derives from Baudelaire's criticism for the same reason as the others. Thus the analysis of the mysterious effects and special pleasures it can produce—in many respects Surrealism occurs as a *new vice* which does not necessarily seem to be restricted to the happy few; like hashish, it has the ability to satisfy all manner of tastes—such an analysis has to be included in the present study.

1. It is true of Surrealist images as it is of opium images that man does not evoke them; rather they "come to him spontaneously, despotically. He cannot chase them away; for the will is powerless now and no longer controls the faculties."* It remains to be seen whether images have ever been "evoked." If one accepts, as I do, Reverdy's definition it does not seem possible to bring together, voluntarily, what he calls "two distant realities." The juxtaposition is made or not made, and that is the long and the short of it. Personally, I absolutely refuse to believe that, in Reverdy's work, images such as

In the brook, there is a song that flows

or:

Day unfolded like a white tablecloth

or:

The world goes back into a sack

reveal the slightest degree of premeditation. In my opinion, it is erroneous to claim that "the mind has grasped the relationship" of two realities in the presence of each other.

*Baudelaire.

First of all, it has seized nothing consciously. It is, as it were, from the fortuitous juxtaposition of the two terms that a particular light has sprung, *the light of the image,* to which we are infinitely sensitive. The value of the image depends upon the beauty of the spark obtained; it is, consequently, a function of the difference of potential between the two conductors. When the difference exists only slightly, as in a comparison,* the spark is lacking. Now, it is not within man's power, so far as I can tell, to effect the juxtaposition of two realities so far apart. The principle of the association of ideas, such as we conceive of it, militates against it. Or else we would have to revert to an elliptical art, which Reverdy deplores as much as I. We are therefore obliged to admit that the two terms of the image are not deduced one from the other by the mind for the specific purpose of producing the spark, that they are the simultaneous products of the activity I call Surrealist, reason's role being limited to taking note of, and appreciating, the luminous phenomenon.

And just as the length of the spark increases to the extent that it occurs in rarefied gases, the Surrealist atmosphere created by automatic writing, which I have wanted to put within the reach of everyone, is especially conducive to the production of the most beautiful images. One can even go so far as to say that in this dizzying race the images appear like the only guideposts of the mind. By slow degrees the mind becomes convinced of the supreme reality of these images. At first limiting itself to submitting to them, it soon realizes that they flatter its reason, and increase its knowledge accordingly. The mind becomes aware of the limitless expanses wherein its desires are made manifest, where the pros and cons are constantly consumed, where its obscurity does not betray it. It goes forward,

*Compare the image in the work of Jules Renard.

borne by these images which enrapture it, which scarcely leave it any time to blow upon the fire in its fingers. This is the most beautiful night of all, the *lightning-filled night:* day, compared to it, is night.

The countless kinds of Surrealist images would require a classification which I do not intend to make today. To group them according to their particular affinities would lead me far afield; what I basically want to mention is their common virtue. For me, their greatest virtue, I must confess, is the one that is arbitrary to the highest degree, the one that takes the longest time to translate into practical language, either because it contains an immense amount of seeming contradiction or because one of its terms is strangely concealed; or because, presenting itself as something sensational, it seems to end weakly (because it suddenly closes the angle of its compass), or because it derives from itself a ridiculous *formal* justification, or because it is of a hallucinatory kind, or because it very naturally gives to the abstract the mask of the concrete, or the opposite, or because it implies the negation of some elementary physical property, or because it provokes laughter. Here, in order, are a few examples of it:

The ruby of champagne.   (LAUTRÉAMONT)

Beautiful as the law of arrested development of the breast in adults, whose propensity to growth is not in proportion to the quantity of molecules that their organism assimilates.   (LAUTRÉAMONT)

A church stood dazzling as a bell. (PHILIPPE SOUPAULT)

In Rrose Sélavy's sleep there is a dwarf issued from a well who comes to eat her bread at night. (ROBERT DESNOS)

On the bridge the dew with the head of a tabby cat lulls itself to sleep.   (ANDRÉ BRETON)

A little to the left, in my firmament foretold, I see—

but it's doubtless but a mist of blood and murder—the gleaming glass of liberty's disturbances.   (LOUIS ARAGON)

In the forest aflame
The lions were fresh.   (ROBERT VITRAC)

The color of a woman's stockings is not necessarily in the likeness of her eyes, which led a philosopher who it is pointless to mention, to say: "Cephalopods have more reasons to hate progress than do quadrupeds."

(MAX MORISE)

1st. Whether we like it or not, there is enough there to satisfy several demands of the mind. All these images seem to attest to the fact that the mind is ripe for something more than the benign joys it allows itself in general. This is the only way it has of turning to its own advantage the ideal quantity of events with which it is entrusted.* These images show it the extent of its ordinary dissipation and the drawbacks that it offers for it. In the final analysis, it's not such a bad thing for these images to upset the mind, for to upset the mind is to put it in the wrong. The sentences I quote make ample provision for this. But the mind which relishes them draws therefrom the conviction that it is on the *right track;* on its own, the mind is incapable of finding itself guilty of cavil; it has nothing to fear, since, moreover, it attempts to embrace everything.

2nd. The mind which plunges into Surrealism relives with glowing excitement the best part of its childhood. For such a mind, it is similar to the certainty with which a person who is drowning reviews once more, in the space of less than a second, all the insurmountable moments of

---

*Let us not forget that, according to Novalis' formula, "there are series of events which run parallel to real events. Men and circumstances generally modify the ideal train of circumstances, so that it seems imperfect; and their consequences are also equally imperfect. Thus it was with the Reformation; instead of Protestantism, we got Lutheranism."

his life. Some may say to me that the parallel is not very encouraging. But I have no intention of encouraging those who tell me that. From childhood memories, and from a few others, there emanates a sentiment of being unin.te-grated, and then later of *having gone astray,* which I hold to be the most fertile that exists. It is perhaps childhood that comes closest to one's "real life"; childhood beyond which man has at his disposal, aside from his laissez-passer, only a few complimentary tickets; childhood where every-thing nevertheless conspires to bring about the effective, risk-free possession of oneself. Thanks to Surrealism, it seems that opportunity knocks a second time. It is as though we were still running toward our salvation, or our perdi-tion. In the shadow we again see a precious terror. Thank God, it's still only Purgatory. With a shudder, we cross what the occultists call *dangerous territory.* In my wake I raise up monsters that are lying in wait; they are not yet too ill-disposed toward me, and I am not lost, since I fear them. Here are "the elephants with the heads of women and the flying lions" which used to make Soupault and me tremble in our boots to meet, here is the "soluble fish" which still frightens me slightly. SOLUBLE FISH, am I not the soluble fish, I was born under the sign of Pisces, and man is soluble in his thought! The flora and fauna of Sur-realism are inadmissible.

3rd. I do not believe in the establishment of a conven-tional Surrealist pattern any time in the near future. The characteristics common to all the texts of this kind, includ-ing those I have just cited and many others which alone could offer us a logical analysis and a careful grammatical analysis, do not preclude a certain evolution of Surrealist prose in time. Coming on the heels of a large number of essays I have written in this vein over the past five years, most of which I am indulgent enough to think are ex-tremely disordered, the short anecdotes which comprise the balance of this volume offer me a glaring proof of what I am saying. I do not judge them to be any more worthless, because of that, in portraying for the reader the benefits which the Surrealist contribution is liable to make to his consciousness.

Surrealist methods would, moreover, demand to be heard. Everything is valid when it comes to obtaining the desired suddenness from certain associations. The pieces of paper that Picasso and Braque insert into their work have the same value as the introduction of a platitude into a literary analysis of the most rigorous sort. It is even permissible to entitle POEM what we get from the most random assemblage possible (observe, if you will, the syntax) of headlines and scraps of headlines cut out of the newspapers:

POEM

A burst of laughter
of sapphire in the island of Ceylon

The most beautiful straws
HAVE A FADED COLOR
UNDER THE LOCKS

on an isolated farm

FROM DAY TO DAY

the pleasant

grows worse

A carriage road

takes you to the edge of the unknown

coffee

preaches for its saint

THE DAILY ARTISAN OF YOUR BEAUTY

M ADAM,

a pair

# of silk stockings

is not

A leap into space

A STAG

Love above all

Everything could be worked out so well

PARIS IS A BIG VILLAGE

Watch out for
the fire that covers
THE PRAYER
of fair weather

Know that
The ultraviolet rays
have finished their task
short and sweet

THE FIRST WHITE PAPER
OF CHANCE
Red will be

The wandering singer
WHERE IS HE?
in memory
in his house
AT THE SUITORS' BALL

I do
as I dance
What people did, what they're going to do

And we could offer many many more examples. The theater, philosophy, science, criticism would all succeed in finding their bearings there. I hasten to add that future Surrealist techniques do not interest me.

Far more serious, in my opinion*—I have intimated it often enough—are the applications of Surrealism to action. To be sure, I do not believe in the prophetic nature of the Surrealist word. "It is the oracle, the things I

---

*Whatever reservations I may be allowed to make concerning responsibility in general and the medico-legal considerations which determine an individual's degree of responsibility—complete responsibility, irresponsibility, limited responsibility (sic)—however difficult it may be for me to accept the principle of any kind of responsibility, I would like to know how the first punishable offenses, the Surrealist character of which will be clearly apparent, will be *judged*. Will the accused be acquitted, or will he merely be given the benefit of the doubt because of extenuating circumstances? It's a shame that the violation of the laws governing the Press is today scarcely repressed, for if it were not we would soon see a trial of this sort: the accused has published a book which is an outrage to public decency. Several of his "most respected and honorable" fellow citizens have lodged a complaint against him, and he is also charged with slander and libel. There are also all sorts of other charges against him, such as insulting and defaming the army, inciting to murder, rape, etc. The accused, moreover, wastes no time in agreeing with the accusers in "stigmatiz-ing" most of the ideas expressed. His only defense is claiming that he does not consider himself to be the author of his book, said book being no more and no less than a Surrealist concoction which pre-cludes any question of merit or lack of merit on the part of the person who signs it; further, that all he has done is copy a document without offering any opinion thereon, and that he is at least as for-eign to the accused text as is the presiding judge himself.

What is true for the publication of a book will also hold true for a whole host of other acts as soon as Surrealist methods begin to enjoy widespread favor. When that happens, a new morality must be substituted for the prevailing morality, the source of all our trials and tribulations.

say."* Yes, *as much as I like,* but what of the oracle it-self?** Men's piety does not fool me. The Surrealist voice that shook Cumae, Dodona, and Delphi is nothing more than the voice which dictates my less irascible speeches to me. My *time* must not be its time, why should this voice help me resolve the childish problem of my destiny? I pretend, unfortunately, to act in a world where, in order to take into account its suggestions, I would be obliged to resort to two kinds of interpreters, one to translate its judgments for me, the other, impossible to find, to trans-mit to my fellow men whatever sense I could make out of them. This world, in which I endure what I endure (don't go see) this modern world, I mean, what the devil do you want me to do with it? Perhaps the Surrealist voice will be stilled, I have given up trying to keep track of those who have disappeared. I shall no longer enter into, however briefly, the marvelous detailed description of my years and my days. I shall be like Nijinski who was taken last year to the Russian ballet and did not realize what spec-

*Rimbaud.

**Still, STILL. . . . We must absolutely get to the bottom of this. Today, June 8, 1924, about one o'clock, the voice whispered to me: "Béthune, Béthune." What did it mean? I have never been to Béthune, and have only the vaguest notion as to where it is located on the map of France. Béthune evokes nothing for me, not even a scene from *The Three Musketeers.* I should have left for Béthune, where perhaps there was something awaiting me; that would have been too simple, really. Someone told me they had read in a book by Chesterton about a detective who, in order to find someone he is looking for in a certain city, simply scoured from roof to cellar the houses which, from the outside, seemed somehow abnormal to him, were it only in some slight detail. This system is as good as any other. Similarly, in 1919, Soupault went into any number of impossible buildings to ask the concierge whether Philippe Soupault did in fact live there. He would not have been surprised, I suspect, by an affirmative reply. He would have gone and knocked on his door.

tacle it was he was seeing. I shall be alone, very alone within myself, indifferent to all the world's ballets. What I have done, what I have left undone, I give it to you.

And ever since I have had a great desire to show forbearance to scientific musing, however unbecoming, in the final analysis, from every point of view. Radios? Fine. Syphilis? If you like. Photography? I don't see any reason why not. The cinema? Three cheers for darkened rooms. War? Gave us a good laugh. The telephone? Hello. Youth? Charming white hair. Try to make me say thank you: "Thank you." Thank you. If the common man has a high opinion of things which properly speaking belong to the realm of the laboratory, it is because such research has resulted in the manufacture of a machine or the discovery of some serum which the man in the street views as affecting him directly. He is quite sure that they have been trying to improve his lot. I am not quite sure to what extent scholars are motivated by humanitarian aims, but it does not seem to me that this factor constitutes a very marked degree of goodness. I am, of course, referring to true scholars and not to the vulgarizers and popularizers of all sorts who take out patents. In this realm as in any other, I believe in the pure Surrealist joy of the man who, forewarned that all others before him have failed, refuses to admit defeat, sets off from whatever point he chooses, along any other path save a reasonable one, and arrives wherever he can. Such and such an image, by which he deems it opportune to indicate his progress and which may result, perhaps, in his receiving public acclaim, is to me, I must confess, a matter of complete indifference. Nor is the material with which he must perforce encumber himself; his glass tubes or my metallic feathers . . . As for his method, I am willing to give it as much credit as I do mine. I have seen the inventor of the cutaneous plantar reflex at work; he manipulated his subjects without respite, it was much more than an "examination" he was employing; *it was obvious that he was following no set plan.* Here and there he formulated a remark, distantly, without nonetheless setting down his needle, while his hammer was never still. He left to others the futile task of curing patients. He was wholly consumed by and devoted to that sacred fever.

Surrealism, such as I conceive of it, asserts our complete *nonconformism* clearly enough so that there can be no question of translating it, at the trial of the real world, as evidence for the defense. It could, on the contrary, only serve to justify the complete state of distraction which we hope to achieve here below. Kant's absentmindedness regarding women, Pasteur's absentmindedness about "grapes," Curie's absentmindedness with respect to vehicles, are in this regard profoundly symptomatic. This world is only very relatively in tune with thought, and incidents of this kind are only the most obvious episodes of a war in which I am proud to be participating. Surrealism is the "invisible ray" which will one day enable us to win out over our opponents. "You are no longer trembling, carcass." This summer the roses are blue; the wood is of glass. The earth, draped in its verdant cloak, makes as little impression upon me as a ghost. It is living and ceasing to live that are imaginary solutions. Existence is elsewhere.

SOLUBLE FISH
(1924)

1

The park, at this time of day, stretched its blond hands over the magic fountain. A meaningless castle rolled along the surface of the earth. Close to God the register of this château was open at a drawing of shadows, feathers, irises. The Young Widow's Kiss was the name of the country inn caressed by the speed of the automobile and the drapings of horizontal grasses. Thus the branches dated the year before never stirred at the approach of the window blinds, when the light sends the women hurrying to the balcony. The young girl from Ireland, troubled by the jeremiads of the east wind, listened in her breast to the seabirds laughing.

"Daughters of the blue sepulcher, feast days, forms of the angelus of my eyes and my head that ring when I awaken, customs of provinces set aflame, you bring me the sun of white carpentry shops, of mechanical sawmills and wine. My hands, so reassured, are my pale angel. Seagulls of the lost paradise!"

The phantom enters on tiptoe. He quickly inspects the tower and descends the triangular staircase. His red silk stockings throw a whirling light on the slopes of rushes. The phantom is around two hundred years old; he still speaks a bit of French. But in his transparent flesh the dew of evening and the sweat of stars are paired. He is lost to himself in this countryside moved to pity. The dead elm and the bright green catalpa alone sigh in the avalanche of milk from the fierce stars. A fruit stone bursts into a fruit. Then the nacelle-fish passes, its hands over its eyes, asking for pearls or gowns.

A woman is singing at the window of this four-teenth-century château. In her dreams are black walnut trees. I do not know her yet because the phantom too often brings on nice weather around him. Night has suddenly fallen like a great rose window of flowers turned inside out over our heads.

A building is the steeple bell of our flights: flight at five o'clock in the morning, when paleness assails beautiful lady travelers on the express in their bed of ferns, flight at one o'clock in the afternoon as one passes through the olive of murder. A building is the steeple bell of our flight into a church resembling the shadow of Madame de Pompadour. But I was ringing the bell at the gate of the château.

Several maidservants came to meet me clad in satin tights the color of daylight. In the mad night, their com-passionate faces were proof of the fear of being compro-mised. "What may I do for you?"

"Tell your mistress that the edge of her bed is a river of flowers. Take her back into the theater vault where three years ago the heart of a capital that I have forgotten beat longingly. Tell her that her time is precious to me and that all her reveries are aflame in the chandelier of my head. Do not forget to inform her of my desires incubating under the stones that you are. And you who are more beautiful than a grain of sunshine in the beak of the dazzling parakeet in this doorway, tell me immediately how she is, whether it is true that the drawbridge of the ivy vines of speech is lowered here simply by knocking with the stirrup."

"You are right," she says to me. "The shadow here present went out on horseback a while ago. The reins were made of words of love, I believe, but since the nostrils of fog and the sachets of azure have brought you to this eternally swinging door, enter and caress me all the way up these stairs seeded with thought."

Great isosceles wasps flew up from below. The pretty dawn of evening preceded me, its eyes on the heaven of my eyes, without turning round. Thus do ships lie down in the silver storm.

Several echos answer one another on land: the echo of rains like a cork on a line, the echo of the sun like solder mixed with sand. The present echo is that of tears, and of the beauty appropriate to unreadable adventures, to mutilated dreams. We were arriving at the destination. The phantom who took a notion along the way to assume the body of Saint Denis claimed he saw his severed head in each rose. A stammering glued to the windowpanes and the railing, a cold stammering, mingled with our unrestrained kisses.

On the edge of the clouds a woman stands, on the edge of the islands a woman stands as grape clusters ripen on high walls decorated with sparkling grapevines, with beautiful black and gold grapes. There is also the American grapevine, and this woman was an American grapevine, of the sort most recently acclimated to France that produces seeds of that purple foxglove whose full flavor has not yet been savored. She was walking back and forth in a corridor apartment like the corridor pullmans of the great European express trains, the one difference being that the light shed by the lamps did not clearly pick out the lava flows, the minarets, and the great indolence of the beasts of the air and the water. I coughed several times and the train in question glided through tunnels, put suspension bridges to sleep. The divinity of the place staggered. Having caught her in my arms, all rustling, I placed my lips on her throat

without a word. What happens next escapes me almost
entirely. It is only later that I find us again, her in a terribly bright-colored outfit that makes her look like a gear
in a brand-new machine, me buried as deeply as possible
inside this impeccable black suit that I have not taken
off since.

Meanwhile, I must have passed through a cabaret
run by very elderly Leaguers whom my civil status threw
into a bird's perplexity. I also remember a crane raising
packages heavenward that must have been hair, and, my
God, how frighteningly light they were. Then it was the
future, the very future itself. The Flame-Child, the marvelous Wave of just a while before, guided my footsteps
like garlands. The small cracks in the sky finally awoke
me: there was no more park, no more night or day, no
more white burials conducted by glass hoops. The woman
who was standing near me caught sight of her feet in a
puddle of winter water.

Looking back I no longer see clearly, it is as if a
waterfall stood between the theater of my life and me,
who am not the principal actor in it. A much-cherished
buzzing accompanies me, along which grasses yellow and
even break. When I say to her: "Take this smoked glass
which is my hand in your hands, an eclipse is here," she
smiles and dives into the seas to bring back the branch of
blood coral. We are not far from the meadow of death
and yet we take refuge from the wind and from hope in
this faded salon. I have dreamed of loving her the way one
loves in reality. But I have not been able to rid myself
completely of half a green lemon, her scull-like hair, the
inadvertence of traps for catching animals alive. She
is sleeping now, facing the boundlessness of my loves, in
front of this mirror that earthly breaths cloud. It is when
she is asleep that she really belongs to me; I enter her
dream like a thief and I truly lose her as one loses a
crown. I am stripped, surely, of golden roots, but I hold
the strings of the storm and I keep the wax seals of
crime.

The least hem of the breezes, there where the pheasant of the moon flees and dies, there where the dazzling comb of dungeons wanders, there where the hyacinth of evil steeps, I have described in my rarer and rarer moments of lucidity, lifting this distant fog too tenderly. Now it is tenderness that takes hold once again, the boulevard like a swamp seasoning the luminous signboards with salt. I bring back wild fruits, sunny bays that I give her and that in her hands are immense jewels. Shivers must still be awakened in the underbrush of the bedroom, brooks must be laced into the window of day. This task is the amusing apotheosis of everything which keeps us, a man and a woman, awake, though we are rather tired, in accordance with the itineraries of light when it has been possible to slow it down. Maidservants of frailty, maidservants of happiness, the women take unfair advantage of the light in a burst of laughter.

2

Less time than it takes to tell, fewer tears than it takes to die: I have counted everything, and there you are. I have made an inventory of the stones; they number as many as my fingers and a few more besides; I have distributed prospectuses to the plants, but all of them refused to accept them. I have played along with the music just for a second, and now I don't know what to think of suicide, for if I want to separate myself from myself the exit is on this side and, I spitefully add, the entry, the reentry is on this other side. You see what else you still have to do. I don't keep reasonable track of the hours, of sorrow; I am alone, I am looking through the window; there isn't anybody going by, or rather nobody *goes by* (I underline *goes by*). Don't you know this gentleman? It's Monsieur Likewise. Allow me to introduce Madame Madame. And their children. Then I retrace my footsteps, my footsteps go back too, but I don't know exactly what they're going back on. I consult a timetable; the names of the cities have been replaced by names of persons who have been rather closely related to me. Shall I go to A, shall I return to B, shall I change at X? Yes, naturally, I'll change at X. If only I don't miss the connection with boredom! Here we are: boredom, neat parallels, oh how neat parallels are beneath God's perpendicular!

3

In those days the one thing people were all talking about around the place de la Bastille was an enormous wasp that went down the boulevard Richard-Lenoir in the morning singing at the top of its lungs and asking the children riddles. The little modern sphinx had already made quite a few victims when, as I left the café whose façade some thought would look good with a cannon, although the Prison in the neighborhood may pass today for a legendary building, I met the wasp with the waist of a pretty woman and it asked me the way.

"Good heavens, my pretty one, it is not up to me to put a point on your lipstick. The sky-slate has just been wiped clean and you know that miracles no longer happen except between seasons. Go back home; you live on the fourth floor of a nice-looking building and even though your windows look out on the court, you will perhaps find some way not to bother me any more."

The insect's buzzing, as unbearable as a lung congestion, at this moment drowned out the noise of the tramways, whose trolley was a dragonfly. The wasp, after having looked at me for a long time, no doubt for the purpose of conveying to me its ironical surprise, now approached me and said in my ear: "I'll be back." It did disappear, as a matter of fact, and I was already delighted to be rid of it so easily when I noticed that the Genius of the place, ordinarily very alert, seemed to be having an attack of vertigo and be on the verge of falling on people passing by. This could only be a hallucination on my part,

due to the great heat: the sun, moreover, kept me from
concluding that there had been a sudden transmission of
natural powers, for it was like a long aspen leaf, and I
had only to close my eyes to hear the motes of dust sing.

The wasp, whose approach had nonetheless made me
feel most uncomfortable (people for several days now
had been talking about the exploits of mysterious stingers
that respected neither the coolness of subways nor the
solitude of the woods), had not completely ceased having
her say.

Not far from there, the Seine was inexplicably carrying along an adorably polished woman's torso, although
it had no head or members, and a few hooligans who had
pointed it out not long before maintained that this torso
was an intact body, but a new body, a body such as had
never been seen before, never been caressed before. The
police, who were worn out, were deeply moved, but since
the boat that had been launched to pursue the new Eve
had never come back, they had given up a second more
costly expedition, and there had been an unconfirmed
report that the beautiful palpitating white breasts had
never belonged to a living creature of the sort that still
haunts our desires. She was beyond our desires, like
flames, and she was, as it were, the first day of the femi-
nine season of flame, just one March 21st of snow and
pearls.

4

Birds lose their form after they lose their colors. They
are reduced to a spider-like existence so deceptive that
I throw the gauntlet down far away. My yellow gauntlets
with the black stitching fall on a plain with a fragile
tower looking down on it. I then cross my arms and
watch. I watch for laughs that come out of the ground
and immediately flower, umbels. Night has come, like a
carp jumping on the surface of violet water, and strange

laurels are interlaced in the sky that descends from the sea. Someone ties together a bundle of burning faggots in the woods and the woman or the fairy who loads it on her back seems to be flying now, while stars the color of champagne become motionless. Rain begins to fall; it is an eternal grace and it has the most delicate reflections. In a single drop there is the passage of a yellow bridge through lilac gypsy caravans; in another that outdistances it are a carefree life and crimes in country inns. In the south, in a cove, love shakes its hair full of shadow and is a propitious boat that circles on the roofs. But the rings of water break one by one and the dawn of a finger is placed ôn the towering packet of nocturnal landscapes. The prostitute begins her song that is more roundabout than a cool brook in the country of Cloven Garlic, but despite everything it is only an absence. A real lily elevated to the glory of stars undoes the thighs of combustion that is awakening and the group that they form goes off to find the shore. But the soul of the other woman is covered with white feathers that gently fan her. Truth rests on the mathematical reeds of the infinite and everything moves forward by order of the eagle riding pillion, while the genius of vegetable flotillas claps and the oracle is pronounced by fluid electric fish.

5

Leo the cameo had just taken the floor. He waved his feather duster back and forth in front of me as he addressed me in the fourth person as befits a valet of his hazy sort. With all the playfulness of which I am capable I one by one raised objections concerning the noise, the perfect idiocy of the upper floors and the elevator cage which presented newcomers with a great tidal wave of light. The last to enter, a man and woman in the business of amorous navigation, wished to speak to Madame de Rosen. That is what Leo the cameo came to tell me when the bell rang and the *brilliantine* began to slide. From my bed all I could see was the enormous night light of the hotel beating in the street like a heart; on one of the arteries was written the word *central,* on another the word *cold*—lion's cold, duck's cold, or baby's cold? But Leo the cameo knocked at my door again. The sun was just finishing emptying its billets from his waistcoat with the vibrations that were well defined up as far as the roots of his moustache. He uttered imprudent words, wanting absolutely to annoy me. At that point I was terrified by tenderness and the contract to stand watch that the dears at the foot of the table had tried to make me sign. The great shoulderer of lights asked me to point out the road to immortality to him. I reminded him of the famous seance in the printing plant, when, as I descended the stairway of shellfish, I took ignorance by the sleeve like an ordinary little typist. If I had listened to him, Leo the cameo would have gone to wake up Madame de Rosen. It was probably about four o'clock in the morning, the hour when the fog kisses dining rooms with an orange-colored brise-bise; the storm was raging inside the houses. The end had come with the milkman's trucks, tintinnabulating in the laurel corridors of the peevish day. At the first alert, I had taken refuge in the stone cuirassier, where no one could find me. Using my last resources, as when one abandons an agricultural machine to bindweed, I closed my eyes to spy or purify myself. Madame de Rosen was still sleeping and her lilac curls on the pillow, in the direction of Romainville, were nothing but distant plumes of smoke from the railway. I needed only to fascinate Leo the cameo for him to take the gaping windows by the ears and go off to sell them at auction. The light of day barely filtered through in the shape of a little girl who knocks at the door of your bedroom: you go to open it, and looking in front of you, you are surprised at first not to see anybody. Madame de Rosen and I would soon be the prisoners of the most pleasant murmurs. Leo was changing the magnolias' water. This pupil that slowly dilates at the surface of murder, the pupil of a unicorn or a griffon, made me promise to get along without its services. For I was not to see Madame de Rosen again, and that very day, taking advantage of a suspension of the seance to refresh myself—a great debate in the house of lords that night—I broke on a step the head of the cameo that came to me from the empress Julie and delighted the lovely one-legged lady of the boulevards with the sunshade of crows.

6

The ground beneath my feet is nothing but an enormous unfolded newspaper. Sometimes a photograph comes by; it is a nondescript curiosity, and from the flowers there uniformly rises the smell, the good smell, of printers' ink. I heard it said in my youth that the smell of hot bread is intolerable to sick people, but I repeat that the flowers smell of printers' ink. The trees themselves are only more or less interesting minor news items: a fire here, a derailment there. As for the animals, they have long since withdrawn from the commerce of men; with these latter, women now have only episodic relations, that are like shop windows early in the morning when the head window dresser goes out onto the street to see the effect of the waves of ribbon, the slots, the wheedling winks of mannequins.

The majority of this newspaper I am looking through is devoted, properly speaking, to ship movements and places to vacation in the country, a column that occupies a fine place at the top of the first page. It says there, in particular, that tomorrow I shall go to Cyprus.

At the bottom of the fourth page the newspaper has an unusual fold that I can describe as follows: it looks as if it has been wrapped around a metallic object, judging by a rusty spot that might be a forest, and this metallic object might be a weapon of an unfamiliar shape, akin to the dawn and a large Empire bed. The writer signing the fashion column, near the aforementioned forest, speaks a most obscure language in which I nonetheless believe that I can make out that the negligee of the young bride will be ordered this season at the Partridge Company, a new department store that has just opened in the Glacière district. The author, who seems to be particularly interested in the trousseaus of young women, emphasizes that these latter are free to change their body linen for soul linen in the event of divorce.

I go on to read a few advertisements, well-written ones, in which contradiction plays a lively role: it really served as a hand-blotter in this advertising agency. The light—which, moreover is very poor—that falls on the fattest letters, this very same light is celebrated by great poets with an abundance of detail that does not allow it to be judged other than by analogy with white hair, for example.

There is also a remarkable view of the sky, in the very same style as business letterheads showing a factory with all its chimneys smoking.

Politics, finally, which it seems to me has been given scant space, tends above all to govern good relations between men of different metal, the first rank of which is occupied by calcium men. In the minutes of the seances in the chamber, as simple as a chemistry report, they have been more than partial: thus the movements of wings have not been recorded.

It doesn't matter, since the steps that led me to this desolate shore will take me farther another time, even more desperately farther! I have only to close my eyes if I do not wish to bestow my attention, which is mechanical and therefore most unfavorable, on the Great Awakening of the Universe.

7

If the resplendent posters betrayed their secret, we would be forever lost to ourselves, knights that we are of this white marble table at which we take our places each eve-

ning. The echoing apartment! The floor is an immense
pedal. Bolts of lightning from time to time scatter the
splendid silver service, from the time of the Incas. We
have at our disposal a great variety of crimes of passion,
endlessly capable of moving the Friends of the Variant.
This is the name we call ourselves by on occasion, eye to
eye, at the end of one of those afternoons when we can no
longer find anything to divide us. The number of secret
doors within us keeps us most favorably disposed, but the
alert is very seldom given. We also play games of strength
and skill, as the case may be. While we sleep, the queen
of caprices, with the collar of dead stars, takes a hand in
choosing the color of time. Thus the rare intermediate
states of life take on unparalleled importance. Just look
at these marvelous knights. From very far away, from a
vast height, from the place that one is not sure of coming
back from, they throw the marvelous lasso made of the
two arms of a woman. Then the planks floating on the
river tip over and the lights of the salon tip along with
them (for the whole central salon rests on a river) ; the
furniture is suspended from the ceiling; when one raises
one's head one discovers great grassplots which no longer
exist and birds fulfilling their usual role between earth
and sky. The *sky-plots* are just barely reflected in the
river where the birds are drinking.

We seldom enter this room unless we are wearing
glass diving suits that permit us, as we go where the tip-
ping planks take us, to meet when necessary at the bottom
of the sea. This is where we spend our best moments. The
number of women sliding into these depths—our ever-
changing guests—is difficult to imagine. They too are
dressed, naturally, in glass; some of them add to this
monotonous accoutrement one or two gayer accessories:
hat trimmings made of wood shavings, spider-web veils,
gloves, and a sunflower parasol. Vertigo takes possession
of them, they hardly pay any attention to us but we rap
on the bottom with the shoe of our horse every time we
want to signal to one or the other of them that we would
be very happy to take her back to the surface. A cloud of

flying fish then escapes from the prints of the shoes and shows the imprudent beauties the way. There is an underwater bedroom built on the model of a bank basement, with armored beds, and novel dressing tables where one's head is seen right side up, upside down, and lying horizontally to the right or left. There is an underwater smoking room, constructed in a particularly clever way, which is bounded in the water by a shadow theater that we have found a way to project without any apparent screen, the shadow of hands picking hideous flowers and getting pricked, the shadow of charming and fearful beasts, the shadow of ideas too, not to mention the shadow of the marvelous that no one has ever seen.

We are the prisoners of the mechanical orgy pursued inside the earth, for we have dug mines, underground galleries through which we sneak in a band beneath the cities that we want to blow up. We already have Sicily, and Sardinia. It is we who provoke at will the tremors that those delightfully sensitive instruments record. I needn't add that a year ago certain of us approached the Korea Strait. The great mountain chains on the border are the only thing that forces us to make detours, but the delay will not be so great, in spite of everything. It is all a question of living where life is still capable of provoking upheaval or general conversion without resorting to anything other than the reproduction of natural phenomena. The aurora borealis in one's bedroom, that's one thing accomplished; that is not all. Love shall be. We shall reduce art to its simplest expression, which is love; we shall also reduce work, to what, in heaven's name? To the music of slow corrections that are paid for with death. We shall greet births, as an experiment, with that air appropriate to the occasion that we assume when funeral processions pass by. All births. Light will follow; the day will make honorable amends, barefoot, a string of stars around its neck, in a green shirt. I swear to you that we, the last kings, will know how to render injustice beneath an invisible reed. For the moment we are taking the machines that have ceased to be useful, and also a few others that were beginning to be useful, to the bottom of the water, at great expense, and it is a pleasure to see the mud voluptuously paralyze things that worked so well. We are the creators of wrecks; there is nothing in our minds that anyone will manage to set afloat again. We take our places at the underwater command post of these balloons, these bad vessels built on the principle of the lever, the winch, and the inclined plane. We start up this or that, in order to assure ourselves that all is lost, that this compass is finally constrained to pronounce the word *South*, and we laugh up our sleeves at the great immaterial destruction under way.

One day, however, we brought back from our expeditions a ring that jumped from finger to finger; the danger of the ring did not become apparent to us until much later. The ring did us a great deal of harm before the day that we hurriedly threw it away. Before sinking into the water it described a blinding spiral of fire in the air, so white it burned us. But the state of ignorance we have remained in as regards its precise intentions allows us to take no further notice of it, or so it seems to me at least. Furthermore, we have never seen it again. Let us keep on looking for it, if you like.

Here I am in the corridors of the palace with everyone asleep. Are verdigris and rust really the song of sirens?

8

On the Montagne Sainte-Geneviève is a large watering trough where at nightfall all the disturbing animals and surprise-plants still left in Paris come to refresh themselves. You would think it was dried up if, on examining things more closely, you did not see a little red stream that nothing can dry up gliding capriciously over the stone. What precious blood, then, continues to flow in this place, that the feathers, the down, the white hairs, the dechlorophylled leaves that it runs past turn away from its apparent goal? What princess of royal blood thus devotes herself after her disappearance to the upkeep of what is most sovereignly tender in the flora and fauna of this country? What saint with an apron of roses has caused this divine extract to flow in veins of stone? Each evening the marvelous casting, more beautiful than a breast, opens itself to new lips, and the thirst-quenching virtue of the rose-blood is communicated to all the sky round about, while on a milestone a young child counting the stars shivers; in a short while he will take his flock with age-old hair back from the archer or arrow of water that has three hands, one for extracting, another for caressing, the other for shading or guiding, from the archer of my days to the Alsatian that has one blue eye and one yellow eye, the dog of the anaglyphs of my dreams, the faithful companion of the tides.

9

Foul night, night of flowers, night of death rattles, heady night, deaf night whose hand is a contemptible kite held back by threads on all sides, black threads, shameful threads! Countryside of red and white bones, what have you done with your unspeakably filthy trees, your arborescent candor, your fidelity that was a purse with dense rows of pearls, flowers, so-so inscriptions, and when all is said and done, meanings? And you, you bandit, you bandit, ah, you are killing me, water bandit that sharpens your knives in my eyes, you have no pity then, radiant water, lustral water that I cherish! My imprecations will long follow you like a frighteningly pretty child who shakes her gorse broom in your direction. At the end of each branch there is a star and this is not enough, no, chicory of the Virgin. I don't want to see you any more, I want to riddle your birds that aren't even leaves any more with little lead pellets, I want to chase you from my doorway, hearts with seeds, brains of love. Enough crocodiles over there, enough crocodile teeth on the cuirasses of samurais, enough spurts of ink anyway, and renegades everywhere, renegades with purple sleeves, renegades with currant eyes, with hen's hair! It is over and done with, I shall no longer hide my shame, I shall now be calmed by nothing, by less than nothing. And if the shuttlecocks are big as houses, how do you expect us to play, to keep our vermin, to place our hands on the lips of shells that speak endlessly (who will finally silence these shells?). No more breaths, no more blood, no more soul but hands to knead the air, to toast but once the bread of the air, to slam the great eraser of sleeping flags, of solar hands, finally, frozen hands!

10

A man is passing one arm, then the other, but never the two of them at once, through the sides of a solidly nailed crate. Then the crate slides down the hillsides, the arm is no more, and where is the man? Where is the man, the great silk neckerchiefs of brooks ask, where is the man, the evening ankle-boots ask too. And the crate bumps against each of the trees, one by one, that cast bright blue sunlight on it for a few hours, when a bull more courageous than the others, or a rock, makes no attempt to stave it in. A curious remark: on the side of the box Top and Bottom do not exist, and I have been told that a shepherd read Paul and Virginia where one would have expected to read Fragile. Yes, Paul and Virginia, semicolon. At first I did not want to believe my ears as a fine caterpillar crossed the road looking to the right and to the left. It was on the second floor of a miserable hotel that I once again found the box that I left one day in search of, having nothing to guide me but the inimitable seals that boldness impresses on events that the marvelous has something to do with.

The crate was standing upright on its base in a dark corner of the landing, among iron hoops and heads of herring. It appeared to have suffered somewhat, which is quite natural, but not enough for me to desire to haul it back into the light. Phosphorescent as it was, I couldn't dream of bringing it aboard; the other pieces of baggage would have called the cabin boys to help them and perhaps even those squill-fish whose path beneath the water is exactly the same as their path through the air, and whose wings crackle when one takes them in one's hand. I put Paul and Virginia on my shoulders. A terrible storm broke immediately. The inside of shelves remained the only thing visible in the houses: in some of them were dead girls, in others a white form like a sack two times too tall was rolled up in a ball, in others still a lamp of flesh, real flesh, was lighted. Far from protecting my eyes with my forearm I was busily using my lips to tie up a bouquet of oaths that two days later I wanted to betray.

The crate had nothing in it but starch. Paul and Virginia were two crystallized forms of this substance that I was never to see again, love having taken me back at this time and driven me to other outbursts that I shall be pleased to tell you about.

11

The place du Porte-Manteau, with all the windows open this morning, is furrowed by taxis with green flags and the cars of masters. Beautiful inscriptions in letters of silver spell out the names of bankers, of celebrated runners, on every floor. In the center of the square, the Portmanteau itself, with a roll of paper in its hand, seems to be showing its horse the road where once the birds of paradise that appeared one evening over Paris swooped down. The horse, whose white mane is dragging on the ground, rears up with all the majesty desirable, and little lights whirling round despite the broad daylight ricochet in its shadow. Casks are smashed open on the left side of the square; the boughs of the trees dip down into them now and again and then spring back covered with crystal buds and inordinately long wasps. The windows of the square resemble slices of lemon, both because of their circular form, called an oeil-de-boeuf, and because of their perpetual vaporizations of women in a state of undress. One of them leans down over the visibility of the shells on the bottom, the ruins of a stairway that plunges into the ground, the stairway that miracle one day took. For a long time she palpates the walls of dreams like a bouquet of fireworks rising above a garden. In a show window the hull of a superb white ocean liner whose seriously damaged prow is a prey to ants of an unknown species. All the men are in black but are wearing the uniform of a bank messenger, the one difference being that the traditional briefcase with a chain is replaced by a screen or by a black mirror. Rapes take place on the place du Porte-Manteau and disappearance has had a latticework summer shelter built there.

12

A certain journal made a specialty of publishing the results of psychic operations that up to that time were unheard of and gave rise to completely different opinions as to their advisability. The journal thus decided to send one of its best reporters to the grand master of deadly speculation, for the sole purpose of getting the opinion of the illustrious expert on the long-envisaged reform of the death rites, particularly as regards the procession for violent death, that it is not very moral not to be able to distinguish from the procession of compulsory death.

The journalist got into the scientist's laboratory—not without some difficulty—thanks to his acquaintance with a woman of easy virtue who was a reader for the scientist.

He spent almost a whole day hidden in a stack of oats which concealed the latest model of torture machine from all eyes, and when night had fallen he managed to visit the lodgings of the master without disturbing any of the patients stretched out mercilessly on sheets of glass that followed the contour of their bodies. One of them that caught his attention was a woman who was the victim of shared love, on whom Professor T was trying out a progressive depersonalization from which he expected marvelous results. Thus each morning a letter said to be from the woman's beloved was delivered to her, the most beautiful sample imaginable of all the figures of thought, particularly poisonous new varieties of which had just been acclimatized. From a clever mixture of little lies and these rare flowers, the experimenter was expecting an effect so toxic that the subject was as good as dead.

Another patient, around fifteen years old, was submitted to the treatment by images, which was decomposed as follows: each time he awoke, there was so-called compensation treatment, in the course of which the boy was given permission to exercise his night rights, insofar as this was possible, naturally, but this domain was extended by all possible means, including the crudest hoaxes. Thus an extremely emotional state was reached, conducive to the sudden discouragement that allowed the next stage to be reached, from the moment, for example, that the patient asked for a glass of water he said he needed and was brought leeches instead. In the second stage cosmography, as well as chemistry and music, was taught directly through images. In order to inculcate some few notions of these sciences it was necessary, obviously, to keep to generalities. Thus, for example, the blackboard which was to serve for the demonstrations was represented by a very elegant young priest who I suppose celebrated the law of falling bodies as a mass is celebrated. Another time theories of almost-naked girls developed ethics rhythmically. The very talented boy who served for the magnificent proof sought by Professor T, being thus deprived of all possibility of abstraction but not of the wish to abstract, was incapable of experiencing the most elementary desires: he was perpetually led back to the sources of his ideas by the images themselves, each of them pledged to possess him mortally.

Professor T was to lecture on his system the next day, in a completely empty hall with a ceiling made up of a single flat mirror, but during the night the reporter took it into his head to divide the mirror into two equal parts that he set up as a roof above the lecture hall, after which he made himself up so as to look exactly like the scientist and entered the hall at the same time that he did. He slowly sat down next to him, and favored by a ray of sunshine, he succeeded, without saying a word, in persuading the formidable inquisitor that the tumblers of solar fire, so familiar to the young boy in the amphitheater, were having fun dividing him into his active person and his passive person, which caused him to find this latter very likable and allowed him to take a few liberties with the reporter. Unfortunately this was not all he did; as the reporter made a feeble gesture, in deference to the unacceptable privacy that he had just been the object of, the scientist suddenly threw himself upon him and shoved him into a plaster bath, in which he immersed him, trying to get him to harden in the masterful pose of the dead Marat, but a Marat stabbed by Scientific Curiosity, whose allegorical and threatening statue he caused to be erected near him. The inquiry was not pursued and the journal that had conducted it later had its share in lighting the fire of progress.

13

Out of fear that men who follow her in the street may get a wrong idea of her feelings, this young girl employed a charming trick. Instead of making herself up as for the theater (aren't the footlights sleep itself and isn't it advisable to signal stage entrances right on women's legs?)

she used chalk, red-hot coal, and an extremely rare green diamond that her first lover had left her in exchange for several drums of flowers. In the bed, after having carefully thrown back the eggshell sheets, she bent her right leg so as to place her right heel on her left knee, and with her head turned to the right, she prepared to touch the red-hot coal with the tip of her breasts, round about which the following things happened: a sort of green halo the color of the diamond formed and came to be studded with entrancing stars; blades of straw gave birth to ears whose grains were like the spangles on dancers' dresses. She then thought the moment had come to moiré the air as she passed, and to do this she again called on the diamond and threw it against the window pane. The diamond, which hasn't fallen yet, dug a little hole in the glass of the same shape and exactly the same size as itself, and in the sunlight, as the precious stone continued its flight, it took on the appearance of an egret of the ditches. Then she delightedly bit into the astonishing white stratifications that remained at her disposal, that is to say the sticks of chalk, and these wrote the word *love* on the slate of her mouth. She thus ate a veritable little château of chalk, built in a patient and insane style, after which she threw a mouse-colored mantle over her shoulders, and with two mouse skins as shoes she descended the stairway of freedom which led to the illusion of the *jamais-vu*. The guards let her pass; they were green plants kept at the edge of the water by a feverish card game. She thus reached the Stock Exchange, which gave not the slightest sign of life after butterflies took a notion to proceed with a capital execution there: I still see them all lined up when I close my eyes. The young girl sat down on the fifth step and there called upon the horny powers to appear to her and subject her to the savage roots of the place. Since that day she goes below the famous stairway every afternoon, an underground rumor putting the trumpet of ruin to her lips at certain fixed hours.

14

After the closing of the cemetery my tomb takes on the form of a seaworthy boat. There is no one in this boat except one woman, now and then, through the venetian blinds of the night, a sort of figurehead for my skyworthy dream. Elsewhere, in a farmyard probably, a woman is juggling with several balls of bluing, which burn in the air like fingernails. The anchors of women's eyebrows, that's what you're getting at. The day has been one long party on the sea. Whether the barn ascends or descends, it's just a hop, skip, and a jump into the countryside. At worst, if it rains, the wait will be bearable in this roofless house made of multiform birds and winged seeds that we are heading toward. The fence that surrounds it, far from distracting me from my reverie, does not shut very well on the sea side, on the side of the sentimental spectacle of the sea withdrawing like two sisters of charity.

This is the story of the second sister, of the blue ball and of a supernumerary who will make his appearance soon enough. Flowers, stars, open slowly on the soft boat of the cemetery. A voice says: "Are you ready?" and the boat rises noiselessly. It glides at a low altitude over plowed fields, whose song no longer matters to you, but which is very old and winds itself around fortified châteaux. The boat scatters the evening fogs whose white hairs go back all by themselves to the stable on the farm draped with night which is all the attention that one is incapable of. A red plant runs down one side of the boat, like an immense mane of fire. The invisible crew badly mistreats the butterflies that lag behind, and when the ascent of lights to the ring of branches, as hangings take place in the woods, comes to break the pebbles on the road, only a highway worker who is thought to be mad remembers having picked up a diamond necklace, heavier than the heaviest chains, by raising his hand. This boat where the satisfactions of the day are running low, as can be seen by anyone who keeps an eye open, is now like an all-white train of a lady's dress because it passes above a bridge twisted by the wind. A train of dust and sand, the birds bite you and you sometimes break away to discover a painfully beautiful face, as unforgettable as the muddy bottoms. Is it true that on stormy days you grow tense in the elegant gale of leaves, to the point of robbing me of the best of myself? The boat, as silent and long as forgetfulness, uses up the air by shamming its breaths and we do not notice it.

Fire has never departed this equivocal shore to cast a spell on colored rings. The search for the sea is pursued among waves of incense. If the will of men is then done, it is through surprise, I assure you, and the highest rocks have nothing to do with it. The race to the stars grows uneven. The blue ball has been replaced by a ring of the same nature that encircles all women around the waist and unfortunately causes them to pale. The boat tacks into the current beyond suspicion that results from the convergent glances of the night. Fantasy passes over the bell towers, with handcuffs on its wrists, nonetheless fleeing sanity and insanity. And the man that I am erases even the most humble memory of his stops on the braids of the earth. In order to keep on living in intimacy, in rhythm with the music of the tables, with a very beautiful companion who holds out the cord of pardon.

15

In the school's chalk there is a sewing machine; the little children shake their curls of silver paper. The sky is a blackboard ominously erased from moment to moment by the wind. "You know what happened to the lilies that wouldn't go to sleep," the teacher begins, and the birds begin to let their voices be heard a short while before the last train goes by. The class is on the topmost branches of the corner, between green linnets and burns. It's rusticating in every sense of the word. The prince of stagnant pools, who bears the name of Hugues, is at the oars of sunset. He is spying on the wheel with a thousand spokes that is cutting glass in the country and that the little children, those at least who have colchicum eyes, will warmly welcome. The Catholic pastime is abandoned. If ever the bell tower turns back into grains of corn, it will be the end of factories, and the bottom of the sea will no longer light up except under certain conditions. The children break the windows of the sea at this time of day and assume heraldic emblems so as to approach the château. They let their turn on night patrol go by and count on their fingers the signs that they will not have to rid themselves of. The day is defective and applies itself more to rekindling slumbers than to reviving acts of courage. An oncoming day that has grown no higher than a woman's dress of the sort that are on the watch for the great violins of nature. A proud and fierce day that has no need to count on the indulgence of the earth and that will surely end up tying its bouquet of stars up like the others when the little children come back, their eyes slung over their shoulders, along the roads of chance. We will speak of this day again, from top to bottom, in the royal courts, in the printing plants. We will speak of it again so as to be silent about it.

16

Plain rain is divine; that is why when storms shake their great ornaments over us, and throw us their purse, we make a vague gesture of revolt which is comparable only to a rustle of leaves in a forest. I saw great lords with jabots of rain pass by on horseback one day, and I am the one who welcomed them at the Good Inn. There is yellow rain, whose raindrops as large as our heads of hair fall straight down on the fire and put it out, and black rain that streams down our window panes with terrifying courtesy, but let us not forget that plain rain is divine.

On this rainy day, a day like so many others when I am the only one guarding the flock of my windows on the edge of a precipice spanned by a bridge of tears, I look at my hands which are masks on faces, dominoes that adapt themselves so well to the lace of my sensations. Sad hands, you perhaps hide all beauty from me; I don't like your conspiratorial look. I will cut off your heads, it is not from you that I am waiting for a signal; I am waiting for rain like a lamp raised three times in the night, like a crystal column ascending and descending between the sudden arborescences of my desires. My hands are Virgins in the little work-niche with a blue background: what are they holding? I don't want to know; I don't want to know anything but the rain like a harp at two o'clock in the afternoon in a salon of Malmaison, the divine rain, the orange-colored rain with fern leaves on its underside, the rain like entirely transparent eggs of hummingbirds and like snatches of voices sent back by the thousandth echo.

My eyes are no more expressive than these raindrops that I like to catch in the hollow of my hand; inside my thought there falls a rain that pulls the stars along as a clear river carries gold that will make blind men kill each other. A dazzling pact has been drawn up between the rain and me, and it is in memory of this pact that it sometimes rains even when the sun is shining. Greenery is also rain, o lawns, lawns. The underground cave at the entrance of which there is a gravestone engraved with my name is the cave where it rains the best. Rain is the shadow beneath the immense straw hat of the young girl of my dreams, the ribbon of which is a rill of rain. How beautiful she is and how much her song, in which the names of famous roofers are heard again and again, how much this song touches me! What could be done with diamonds, except make rivers of them? The rain, the white rain that women dress themselves in for their wedding, and that smells of apple blossoms, swells these rivers.

Even though people keep ringing my bell continually, I only open my door to rain, and I am on the verge of fainting as their ring becomes insistent, but I am counting on the jealousy of rain to finally deliver me, and when I set out my nets to catch the birds of sleep, I hope above all to capture the marvelous paradise of total rain; there is a rain-bird as there is a lyre-bird. So don't ask me if I will soon force my way into the consciousness of love as certain people would have it; I repeat that if you see me heading toward a glass château where nickeled measures of volume are preparing to welcome me, it is to surprise the Sleeping Rain Beauty who is to become my beloved.

17

On a magnificent September afternoon two men were chatting in a park, talking, naturally, of love since it was September, at the end of one of those dusty days that provide women with minuscule jewels which their maids quite wrongly throw out the window the next day, using to loosen them one of those musical instruments whose sound has always been a particular favorite of mine and whose name is *brushes*.

There are several sorts of brushes, among which I shall cite, so as to be incomplete, the hairbrush and the shoe-polishing brush. There are also the sun and the horsehair massage glove, but properly speaking these are not brushes.

The two men, then, were walking in the park smoking long cigars which, even though partially consumed, nonetheless measured one yard five inches and one yard thirty-five inches respectively. Explain that as best you can after I have told you that they had lighted both of them at the same time. The younger man, the one whose cigar ash was a young blonde that he could make out very well by lowering his eyes and who gave signs of unparalleled excitement, gave his arm to the second man, whose cigar ash, a brunette, had already fallen.

18

The lamppost imperceptibly creeping toward the post office that night stopped at each moment to listen. Does this mean that it was afraid?

In the Turkish bath, two very beautiful, severely made-up women had rented the most luxurious stall an hour before, and as they were expecting not to be alone there, it had been arranged that on the first signal (in this particular case an unusually large Japanese flower that would open in a glass of water) a saddled chestnut horse would stand behind the door. This animal pranced proudly and the fire from his nostrils threw white spiders on the walls, as when one is within earshot of distant naval gunnery practice.

The crowd came and went on the boulevard without being familiar with anything. From time to time it cut bridges, or took as witnesses great pearl geometrical locuses. It trampled underfoot a space that might be judged to be equal to that of coolness around fountains or that covered by illusions brought on by the mantle of youth, that mantle that the sword of dreams riddles with holes. The lamppost avoided being caught in the shuffle. Up at the porte Saint-Denis a dead song was still befuddling a child and two representatives of law and order: the newspaper *Le Matin* entranced by the thickets of its linotypes, and the Globe Café occupied by lancers or else by music-hall performers brought there by disdain.

The view of Paris, the nightingale of the world, varied from one minute to the next, and its pretty spring trees, equal to the angle of inclination of the soul on the horizon, shot up among the waxes of its hairdressers.

It was then that the lamppost, which had gone down the rue Etienne Marcel, thought it wise to stop, so I was able to overhear a part of its monologue as I happened to pass by like an artist's portfolio under my own arm, as meanwhile it played a trick in order not to stop the bus that was charmed by its green hands which were like a network of mosquitoes dogging my footsteps.

The lamppost: "Sonia and Michelle really ought to be suspicious of the branch of fever guarding the gates of Paris; there is evidence that the wood of love will not be split before tonight. So that . . . so that I won't see them looking white in this nocturnal spring, even if their horse is momentarily frightened. It would be better for them to avoid the curiosity of lips, if they succumb to the temptation of bridges spanning glances. (I am going to trace them.)"

These words didn't worry me at all, even as day was breaking in the form of a little acrobat whose head was bandaged and who appeared to be on the verge of fainting. After carelessly leaning against the lamppost, the boy shot off toward the "Special Pickup" mailbox, and before I could stop him he slid his arm far down inside the opening. I had begun tying my shoelace on the stairs when he came down, thinner than ever, worn out from his effort, covered with dust and feathers like someone who has fallen into a hedge, a simple car accident that one doesn't always die from.

The chronology of these facts, of the first of them at least, a chronology in which I appeared to take an inexplicable part at the beginning of this tale, leads me to add that the timbre of the absent instruments, Sonia and Michelle, was much more muted after the letter had gone. Moreover, this chronology was to catch up with them shortly. In fact, barely ten minutes had gone by when I again heard a shirt, which was probably green, slide slowly from the back of the chair of the stall onto the floor, where for a time it led the life of a thistle in sand at the edge of the sea. The lamppost had moved to a boulevard in Dieppe where it was trying to beam for a man of forty or so who was busy looking for something in the sand. I could have shown him this lost object, for it was a carnation. But he walked back and forth without managing to find it and I couldn't help smiling when he decided that this little game had lasted long enough, and when, making a wild decision, he began to follow the road to the left, which is the continuation of the avenue of the casino. Michelle next undid her bracelet, put it on the window sill, and then closed the window again, after having admired the charming mark that the bracelet left on her skin. This woman, a blonde, seemed rather cold-hearted to me, and for a long time I chased her as she ran before me like a gazelle. Sonia, a creature of splendid mahogany, had long since got undressed, and her body was modeled by the light of the most marvelous house of pleasure that I have ever seen. Her glances were green and blue serpentines, in the midst of which, though it was continually broken, there even spiraled a white serpentine, like a special favor saved for me. Between the bars of water she sang these words that I have not learned:

"Death of azure and delicate storm, untie these boats, wear out these knots. Give divinities calm, and humans wrath. I know you, death of powder and acacia, death of glass. I too am dead, beneath kisses."

The lure of dreams is now stimulating the music of my head. These two women belonged to me for the whole of a day when I was gloomily ceasing to be young. And here I am, a prophet with a temple purer than mirrors, enchained by the lights of my story, covered with chilling loves, a prey to the phantasmagorias of the broken wand and asking that, out of pity, I be brought back to life, in one brilliant finale.

19

Enter the spring. The spring has gone through the city looking for a bit of shade. She has not found what she needed, she complains as she tells what she has seen: she has seen the sunlight of lamps, that is more touching than the other sunlight, to be sure; she has sung one or two tunes on the terrace of a café and people have thrown heavy yellow and white flowers at her; she has pulled her hair over her face but its perfume was strong. She is only too inclined to fall asleep; is it necessary for her to sleep under the stars among her necklaces of insects, her glass bracelets? The spring laughs softly, she has not felt my hand on her; she bends imperceptibly beneath my hand, thinking of the birds which want nothing of her but her coolness. Let her be on her guard; I am capable of taking her to quite different places, where there are no longer either cities or countryside. A beautiful mannequin will model the Mirage dress for elegant women this winter, and do you know who will make this adorable creation a great success? Why, the spring, of course, the spring that I have no trouble taking into those latitudes where my ideas withdraw beyond the possible, and even beyond the inorganic sand where the Tuaregs, with origins less obscure than mine, are content to live a nomad life with their overdressed women. The spring is all of me that passes into the whirl of leaves standing watch up there beyond my shifting ideas that the slightest draft displaces; she is the tree that the woodsman's axe endlessly attacks; she bleeds in the sun and she is the mirror of my words.

20

Someone took it into his head one day to gather the fuzz of fruits in a white earthenware bowl; he coated several mirrors with this vapor and came back long after: the mirrors had disappeared. The mirrors had got up one after the other and left, trembling. Much later still, someone confessed that as he was coming home from work he found one of these mirrors that had drawn imperceptibly closer and had taken it home with him. He was a young apprentice who was very handsome in his overalls that made him look like a basin full of water that a wound has been washed in. The head of this water had smiled like a thousand birds in a tree with submerged roots. He had got the mirror up the stairs of his house with no trouble, and all he remembered was that two doors had slammed as he went past them, two doors that each had a narrow glass plate around the handle. He held his two arms away from his sides so as to support his load and put it very carefully down in a corner of the single room on the eighth floor that he lived in, and then he went to bed. He didn't close his eyes all night long: the mirror reflected itself, to an unprecedented depth, an incredible distance. Cities only had time enough to make their appearance between two of its thicknesses: fever-cities traversed in every direction by women alone, abandoned cities, cities of genius too, whose buildings had animated statues on top, whose freight elevators were built to resemble human beings, cities of sorry storms, this one more beautiful and more fleeting than the others, all of whose palaces and factories were in the form of flowers: a violet was the mooring for boats. On the back side of the cities the only open fields were heavens, mechanical heavens, chemical heavens, mathematical heavens where the signs of the zodiac went round and round, each in its own element, but the Twins came round more often than the others. The young man hurriedly got up about one in the morning, convinced that the mirror was leaning forward and about to fall. He straightened it up with great difficulty and, suddenly worried, he decided it was dangerous to go back to bed and remained sitting in a rickety chair just one step away from the mirror and exactly opposite it. He then thought he heard someone else breathing in the room, but no, it was nothing. He now saw a young man in a great doorway. This young man was almost naked; behind him there was nothing but a black landscape that might have been made of burnt paper. Only the forms of objects remained and it was possible to make out the substances these objects were molded out of.

There is nothing more tragic, really. Some of these things had belonged to him: jewels, gifts of love, relics of his childhood, and even a little bottle of perfume whose cork was nowhere to be found. Others were unknown to him, and he doubtless could not make out what they would be used for in the future. The apprentice looked farther and farther into the ashes. He felt a guilty sense of satisfaction when he saw this smiling man, whose face was like a globe inside which two hummingbirds were flying, draw closer to hand. He took him by the waist, which was the mirror's waist, you see, and after the birds had flown away music rose along their line of flight. What ever happened in this room? The fact remains that since that day the mirror has not been found again, and I never put my lips closer to one of its possible shatterings without feeling strong emotion, even though I thus chance never seeing those rings of down, swans on the verge of bursting into song.

21

The characters in the comedy are assembling beneath a porch, the ingénue with the spitcurl of honeysuckle, the duenna, the wax knight, and the child villain. Skirts fly up above the brooks that are gallant prints, unless arms like those of Achilles are offered to the beauties to help them cross the alleys. The signal for the departure of the corvettes bearing gold and printed cloth is sounded over and over in the little port. The charming currant bush in bloom which is a farmer-general slowly holds out its arms on its couch. Its sword at its side is a blue dragonfly. When it walks, a prisoner of the graces, the winged horses that paw the ground in its stable seem about to take off in the maddest of directions.

Meanwhile the mountebanks taunt each other for their pink shadows; they raise their favorite monkey with butterfly cuffs to the sun. In the distance can be

seen a fire in which great iron gates are swallowed up:
this is because the forests stretching as far as the eye
can see are on fire and the laughter of women looks like
mistletoe on the trees of the canal. The stalactites of
night, in every color, make the flames still brighter toward Cythera and the dew, that slowly fastens its necklace around the shoulders of the plants, is a marvelous
prism for the end of the century of centuries. The thieves
are musicians who have been standing motionless against
the wall of the church since the instruments of their profession were found intermingled with violas, guitars, and
flutes. A golden greyhound is playing dead in each of the
rooms of the château. Nothing can stop time in its flight
since the same clouds as the evening before are making
their way to the boiling sea.

On the ramparts of the city a company of light cav-
alry caressed by gray shadows, corsets, and coats of mail,
goes off to take cover at the bottom of the water.

22

I met this woman in an immense grapevine, a few days
before the harvest, and one night I followed her around
the wall of a convent. She was in full mourning, and I
felt that I could not resist this crow's nest that the brilliance of her face had looked like to me a short while
before, when I tried to levitate the garments of red leaves
inside which sleigh bells were dangling. Where did she
come from and what did this grapevine in the center of
a city where there was a theater remind me of? I won-
dered. She had not turned around to me again, and without the sudden glitter of her calf that the road gave me
glimpses of now and then, I would have despaired of ever
touching her. I was getting set, however, to catch up with
her when she suddenly turned about, half-opened her
coat, and showed me her nakedness, more bewitching
than birds. She had stopped and was holding me away

with one hand, as if it were a question of my climbing to unknown heights, or to snows that were too high. I could find no way, moreover, to profit from the dazzling radiance of this moment and managed only to pronounce words heard by marvels when one makes an attempt on one's own life or when one decides that it is time not to wait for oneself any longer. This woman, who was the very image of the bird called the widow-bird, then described a splendid curve in the air, her veil dragging on the ground as she rose.

Seeing how fatal patience would be for me, I changed my mind in time to grab one corner of the veil that I had put my foot on, and this brought into my hands the whole of her coat, that was like the look of an ermine when it feels itself trapped. This veil was extremely light and the material it was made of was unusual in that even though it was transparent and had no lining whatsoever the outer meshes of it were black, while the meshes that had been turned toward her flesh had kept their color. I brought the inside of the cloth, which was warm and perfumed, to my lips, and as if I had expected long-lasting pleasures from this mysterious tunic, I took it home so as to enjoy its disturbing properties. The laugh of the most desirable woman sang within me—was it in the veil, or was it in my memory? The fact remains that once she had freed herself of her outer garment, she had disappeared immediately, and I resolved not to pay any more attention to the disappointing miracle of the grapevine so as to devote my entire attention to the admirable real coat.

I had thrown this impalpable shadow, which only the very pleasant sensations that I was feeling conferred any semblance of life on, over my shoulders. Delightful! It was as if a woman had given me a glance full of promises and I had been shut up inside this look, as if the pressure of a hand had concealed all the strange complicities of forest plants whose leaves are impatient to turn yellow. I put the veil on my bed and there rose from it a music a thousand times more beautiful than that of love.

I was at a concert given by instruments shaped like many others but whose strings were black, as if spun out of glass for looking at eclipses. The veil stirred a little with undulating movements like those of a river in the dark, but a river that one surmises is terribly clear without seeing it. A fold that it formed on the edge of the bed opened sudden sluices of milk or flowers; I was both before a fan of roots and a waterfall. The walls of the room were covered with tears which, as they detached themselves, evaporated before they touched the floor, and were strung up again by a rainbow so small that one could easily have taken hold of it. When I touched it, the veil gave a distinct sigh, and each time that I threw it back on the bed I noticed that it had a tendency always to present me its light side, though it was made of all possible stars. I made love to it several times, and when I awoke after barely an hour of sleep at daybreak, the only thing I could put my hands on was the laggard shadow of a lamp with a green shade that I had forgotten to turn out.

Since the oil happened to be running out, I had time to hear the last gasps of the flame, that came at greater and greater intervals until it went out completely, the end of them being marked by a noise that I shall never forget, the laughter of the veil when it left me, as the woman whose shadow it was had left me.

23

You will know later, when I will no longer be worth the rain to hang me, when the cold, pressing its hands on the window panes there where a blue star has not yet played its role, at the edge of a forest, will come to say to all those women who remain faithful to me without having known me: "He was a handsome captain, with stripes of grass and black cuffs, a mechanic perhaps who gave his life for life. He had no orders to carry out in that regard, that would have been too soft, but the end of his dreams was the meaning that had to be given to the movements of the celestial Balance that made him tireless when night fell and miserable when day broke. He was far from sharing your joys and your sorrows; he didn't split hairs. He was a fine captain. In his rays of sunshine there was more shadow than in shadow, but he really never tanned except in the midnight sun. Deer made his head swim in the clearings, especially white deer whose horns are strange musical instruments. He would dance then, and see to the free growth of the ferns whose blond scrolls later loosen in your hair. Comb your hair for him; never stop combing it, that's the only thing he asks. He isn't here any more but he's going to come back; perhaps he's already back. Don't let another woman draw water at the fountain: if he came back, that is doubtless the way he'd come. Comb your hair at the fountain and let them flood the plain with it." And you will see into the bowels of the earth, you will see me more alive than I am now when the boarding saber of the sky threatens me. You will take me farther than I have been able to go, and your arms will be roaring grottoes full of pretty animals and ermines. You will make only a sigh of me, that will go on and on through all the Robinsons of earth. I am not lost to you: I am only apart from what resembles you, on the high seas, where the bird called Heartbreak gives its cry that raises the pommels of ice of which the stars of day are the broken guard.

24

"A kiss is so soon forgotten"; I was listening to this refrain pass by in the grand promenades of my head, in the province of my head, and I no longer knew anything about my life that was unfolding on its blond track. What madness to want to hear past oneself, past this wheel, one of the spokes of which there ahead of me barely brushes

the ruts. I had spent the night in the company of a frail
and experienced woman, squatting in the high grass of a
public square in the direction of the Pont-Neuf. We
laughed for an hour over the vows that the late evening
strollers who came to sit down one by one on the closest
bench suddenly exchanged. We stretched our hands out
toward the capuchin nuns leaning out of a balcony of the
City Hotel, with the intention of abolishing everything in
the air that has the ring of hard cash, like the antique
coins that were circulating that night contrary to the
usual order of things.

My lady friend spoke in such aphorisms as "He who
beds me often forgets himself better," but it was only a
game of paradise, and as we threw flags down around us
that ended up being placed at windows, we gave up little
by little all insouciance, so that in the morning all that
was left of us was that song—"A Kiss Is So Soon Forgotten"—that lapped a bit of night water in the center of
the square. The milkmen noisily drove their gold-bearing
trucks about instead of fleeing forever. We separated,
yelling at the top of our hearts. I was alone and along the
Seine I discovered benches full of birds, benches full of
fish; I cautiously dove into the thickets of nettles of a
white village. This village was cluttered with those reels
of telegraph wires that one sees hanging at equal dis-
tances apart on both sides of poles along major highways.
It looked like one of those pages of a romance that can be
bought for a few pennies in suburban population centers.
"A Kiss Is So Soon Forgotten." On the cover of the village
that was turned toward the ground and was the only
thing that remained of the countryside, one could barely
make out a sort of woman of easy virtue jumping rope
at the edge of a forest of gray laurel.

I plunged into this wood, where the hazelnuts were
red. Rusty hazelnuts, were you the lovers of the kiss that
pursued me so that I might forget it? I was afraid so; I
quickly drew away from each bush. My eyes were the
flowers of a hazel tree, my right eye the male flower, my
left the female flower. But I had long since ceased to

please myself. Paths whistled on all sides ahead of me. Near a spring the beauty of the night joined me again, panting. A kiss is so soon forgotten. Her hair was nothing but a patch of pink mushrooms, among pine needles and very fine glassware of dry leaves.

We thus reached the city of Squirrel-by-the-Sea. There fishermen were unloading baskets full of earthshells, with a great many ears among them, that stars circulating through the city were painfully cupping over their hearts to hear the sound of the earth. In this way they were able to reconstruct, to their pleasure, the noise of streetcars and great pipe organs, just as in our loneliness we seek out the sounds of levels under water, the purr of underwater elevators. We passed by unnoticed by the curves down there, sinusoids, parabolas, geysers, rains. We now belonged only to the despair of our song, to the sempiternal evidence of those words about the kiss. Very close to that spot we vanished, what's more, into a window display where the only thing the men and women showed was what is most generally visibly naked, that is to say, roughly, the face and the hands. One girl, however, was barefoot. We in turn put on the garments of the pure air.

25

Who is he? Where is he going? What has become of him? What has become of the silence around him, and what about this pair of socks, this pair of silk socks, that were his most chaste thoughts? What did he do with his long stains, his eyes of mad gasoline, his noises of a human crossroads, and what happened between his triangles and his circles? The circles wasted the noise that reached his ears; the triangles were the stirrups that he put on to go where wise men don't go when someone comes to say that it is time to sleep, when a messenger with a white shadow comes to say that it is time to sleep. What wind pushes him, him whose way up the stairway of the occasion is lighted by the candle of his tongue? And in what style do you picture the buffoons of his eyes at the world scrap-iron fair? What have you done with his courtesy to you when he wished you a good cellar and the sun dressed the red brick chimneys that were his flesh, that smoked with the music of his flesh? Aren't his intakes of current from you, along the canal of the Ourcq, of such a sort as to move away the little ice cream and nougat truck parked under the subway overpass? And did he himself not reject the agreement? Did he not follow the path that disappears into the burial vaults of the idea, was he not part of the gurgling of the bottle of death? What did this man of eternal reproaches, cold as a wolf, expect us to do with his mistress when he abandoned her to the pistol grip of summer? What did he listen to on the cutting edge of the air, like the Indian, on those moonstone evenings when he moved a half-empty glass about on a table of wind? I am not stronger than he is, I have no buttons on my vest, I don't know what the order is, I shall not be the first to enter the city with wooden billows. But may I be given the blood of a white squirrel if I am lying and may the clouds pile up in my hand when I peel an apple: these linen cloths form a lamp, these words drying on the meadow form a lamp that I will not allow to go out for lack of the glass of my arms raised heavenward.

26

The woman with breasts of ermine was standing at the entrance of the passage Jouffroy in the light of songs. She readily consented to follow me. I flung the chauffeur the address of Rendezvous, Rendezvous in person, who was an early acquaintance. Neither young nor old, Rendezvous ran a little broken-glass shop near the porte de Neuilly.

"Who are you?"

"One of the stabbing pains of the mortal lyre that vibrates at the edge of capitals. Forgive me the pain that I shall cause you."

She also told me that she had broken her hand on a mirror on which the usual inscriptions were gilded and silvered and blued. I took this hand in mine; raising it to my lips I suddenly noticed that it was transparent and that through it one could see the great garden where the most experienced divine creatures go to live.

The spell ended when we stepped out of the car. Guided by a rain of nettles, we crossed the threshold of Rendezvous's residence, not without pushing the great rabbit skins of the sun aside with horror.

Rendezvous was on his guard, busily repairing a long light-colored latticework. Capuchin nuns had long ago found a way to undo it and hang their indiscreet wrists on the sky. Rendezvous was busy repairing the damage by means of a white vine that may have come from my youth. He was whistling gaily as he did this, and seemed not to attach any more importance to our approach than to the song of a lark. He did little more than fling a vague good evening of blue wine our way, which was reflected by the hour and became lost in the tragic furrows of fears running crosswise.

The form of my thoughts and I took shelter beneath this tarred roof before leaving again. Earthmoving was going on at this late hour, on the fortifications. It was as if someone had tried to bottle us up with glass roses. In the terrible din the fortifications made when they fell now and again, being pushed over by tall cranes made of hair, the only thing there was room for was our extreme discontent.

But hadn't we come there to use our sovereign power to bathe in glass to rid ourselves of all the rocky dreams, the persistent hopes that water could not wash away? That is why Rendezvous looked so haggard; this man fulfilled such a painful function that no leisure-time pursuit could distract him. We took our leave of him in the morning, with a simple look that meant both that we no longer belonged to life and that if we ever came back from our new state it would be in the guise of sorcerers to touch heaven with our lightning-wand.

From that moment on a profound metamorphosis of the sensible world took place. In New York harbor it was no longer the Statue of Liberty that lighted the world, but Love, which is different. In Alaska the eternal dogs, their ears to the wind, flew away with their sleds. India was shaken by a mercuryquake and right in Paris, along the Seine, passports for that very city were delivered, yes, for Paris *once it had been left.*

It is in the sweet escape called the future, an escape that is always possible, that the stars that until now have bent down over our distress are resorbed.

Thus a man and a woman, all by themselves on a great white highway, drain to the dregs their gradual conviction that they are no more now than a grafted tree.

But the genius that watches over the predicaments of which this story furnishes us more than one example is waiting for me to suddenly become impatient. What does the reader's assent to these things matter, does the reader believe that the leaps of the antelope are calculated on the basis of the desire to escape the sudden sweep of lawns that this animal demonstrates? We woke up side by side that morning. Our bed, of normal dimensions, was the very image of the architecture of a bridge; I mean that a long time had passed. A limpid river rolled its cages of noise above us. A frozen skyscraper, covered with gigantic starfish staggering badly, was heading toward us. An eagle as white as the philosophers' stone soared above New Guinea. She whom I no longer call anything but The-Blind-Woman-of-All-Light or Albinos Gate sighed at this point and called me over to her. We made love for a long time, as cracks are produced in furniture. We made love as the sun beats, as coffins close, as silence calls, and night shines. And at the same time in our eyes that had never opened nothing but our purest fortunes floundered.

Up by the ephemera nothing was produced but very brief sparks that caused us to clench our fists in surprise and pain.

With infinite caution we then prepared to disappear. Having rented a very luxurious furnished apartment, we gave marvelous entertainments there every evening. The entry of Albinos Gate in her gown with an immense train was always sensational. The famous Agates appeared at our illusory receptions; an immense quartz cannon was trained on the garden. Then at a word spoken in a lower tone than the other Albinos Gate was illuminated again, and I spent hours watching the scalares that I was very fond of pass through her head. It became one of my most frequent weaknesses to kiss her so as to see the charming little blue arrows that these fish are flit to the other side of her head.

The day came when I no longer saw her who was my defense and my loss here below.

I have since met a man who had a mirror for flesh; his hair was of the purest Louis XV style and mad refuse shone in his eyes. I saw the splendid bird of sabotage perch on a railway switch and saw the cold obstinacy of blood that is an irresistible look pass into the fixity of wounds that are still eyes.

I am not on earth willingly.

As you take the child by the hand to lead him to the villa, or the woman by the waist to charm her, or the old man by the beard to greet him, quick as lightning I for my part spin my web of false seduction, that strange polygon that attracts approaches. Later, when the bottle of vintage dew explodes and you enter the leaves silently, and the absolute springtime that is readying itself opens its sluice-gates, you will dream of the lover of Albinos Gate who will lie on the wattles of pleasure, asking only to take back from God what God has taken from him.

Albinos Gate is there in the shadow. Step by step she effaces everything that still terrifies me and makes me weep in the splendor of her gongs of fire. I stand watch near Albinos Gate with the determination to allow only cadavers to come by in both directions. I am not dead yet and sometimes I enjoy the spectacle of love affairs. Men's love affairs have followed me everywhere; whatever I may say about them, I know that they are full of traps like the vases that wolves place on the snow. The loves of men are great peasant mirrors edged in red velvet or, more rarely, in blue velvet. I stay behind these mirrors, near Albinos Gate who opens up inside, always.

27

Once there was a turkey on a dike. This turkey had only a few days to bask in the bright sun and he looked at himself with mystery in a Venetian mirror placed on the dike for this purpose. At this point the hand of man, that flower of the fields that you have certainly heard of, intervenes. The turkey who answered to the name of Threestars, as a joke, didn't know which way his head was screwed on. Everyone knows that the head of a turkey is a prism with seven or eight faces, just as a top hat is a prism with seven or eight reflections.

The top hat swung back and forth on the dike like an enormous mussel singing on a rock. The dike had no reason for existing since the sea had forcefully drawn back that morning. The whole of the port, furthermore, was lighted by an arc light the size of a schoolchild.

The turkey felt he would be lost if he couldn't touch the heart of this passerby. The child saw the top hat, and since he was hungry, he went about emptying it of its contents, which in this particular case was a beautiful jellyfish with a butterfly beak. Can butterflies be said to be similar to lights? Obviously; that is why the funeral procession stopped on the dike. The priest sang in the mussel, the mussel sang in the rock, the rock sang in the sea and the sea sang in the sea.

So the turkey stayed on the dike and since this day has frightened the schoolchild.

28

I had just received my thousandth ticket for exceeding the speed limit. No one has forgotten this news item: the car hurtling along at top speed on the road to Saint-Cloud one evening, the car whose passengers were wearing armor. Now I was one of this anachronistic crew that caused the shadow of the trees, the whirling shadow of dust, to come to grips with our shadow of deadly white carrier pigeons. There were leaps over rivers, I remember, whose daring has been equaled only by the solemn entry of cage-men into the lobby of the Hotel Claridge, one beautiful February afternoon. Disaster ensued as promptly as it had the day that the *ray,* since discovered, began to sweep over the frozen plains of Russia, at a time when Napoleon was expecting nothing but infrared light. Leaps over rivers and soaring flight right in the middle of Paris, in a car whose occupants are all clad in the armor of dreams! We went much farther than Saint-Cloud, in the shadow of that equestrian statue that it took certain people all their life to get out of. What centuries-old chestnut tree was it that we tried to drive around? Here a chestnut comes down, pretends to fall, and, stopping a few yards above the ground, remains suspended like a spider.

When they raised their visors, I discovered that two of my companions were ladies with chestnut eyes. Forms had long since been revealed, the form of the umbrella especially, which covers itself with sky, and the form of a boot, which crowds flowers together on a traffic island as they cross one of the streets. Although we were certain not to land, the inhabitants had been given orders to stay at home. The car now passed its hands with rubber gloves over the furniture of bedroom-Paris. (It is a well-known fact that in palaces no one, certainly, would number the rooms, the apartments; this sort of designation, thus, is pure luxury.) But I for my part had gone far beyond the stage of luxury: I did not want to stop until we reached city 34. It was no use for my companions to object that we risked running out of air before reaching this figure; I listened only to my remorse, that remorse at being alive that I have never missed the opportunity of telling people about in confidence, even women with their visors lowered. It was on the outskirts of city 26 that the miracle happened: a car coming in the opposite direction, which began to write my name backwards in a marvelous flaming signature, had a slight collision with us; the devil knows whether it was going faster than we were. It is at this point, I know, that my explanation will be of a sort to satisfy only the most towering sporting minds of this era: *In time there is neither right nor left,* this is the moral of this journey. The two speeding cars—green and white and red and black— wiped each other out, and since that time, dead or alive, I get my bearings only temporarily, putting a price on myself on big signboards like this one that I nail up on all the trees with the dagger of my heart.

29

That year a hunter witnessed a strange phenomenon, previous accounts of which are lost in time and which kept tongues wagging for many months. The day the season opened this man in yellow boots walking out on the plains of Sologne with two large dogs saw above his head a sort of gas-propelled lyre that shed only a dim light, and one of its wings alone was as long as an iris while the other one, which was atrophied but much brighter, looked like a woman's little finger with a marvelous ring on it. A flower then detached itself and came back and fastened itself by the end of its aerial stem to the rhizome of the sky, which was the hunter's eye. Then the finger, approaching him, offered to take him to a place where no other man had ever been. He consented, and was

guided by the left wing of the bird for a long, long time.
Its fingernail was made of a light so fine that no eye could
quite endure it; it left behind it a spiraling trail of blood
like the shell of an adorable murex. The hunter thus got
as far as the border of France without turning around
and started down a gorge. There was shadow on all sides
and the absentmindedness of the finger made him fear
for his life. They had gotten past the precipices, since
from time to time a flower fell beside him that he did
not bother to pick up. The finger then turned around, and
it was a terribly attractive pink star. The hunter was a
man about twenty years old. His dogs crawled mournfully
along beside him.

The gorge kept getting narrower and narrower,
when suddenly the star began to speak in a low voice that
was more and more audible and finally shouted "Prometheus" or "Promise."* The echoes took up the word, so
that the hunter could not make out whether he was the
object of a summons or of an order. He couldn't make
himself heard, so to speak, and he was deaf as a post as
he tried to question the star: "Unimaginable finger and
branch that is greener that the others, answer, what do
you want of me, what must I promise you, outside of
fire, which you already have?" And as he said these words
he aimed his rifle at it and hit it. He could then see the
astonishing treasure detach itself from the flaming
aigrettes, while a dreadful jangling of bells was heard. But
the dogs that had tried to rush forward fell dead, while
bushes on each side of the road advanced and retreated.
The star then reappeared above his head, whiter than
ever, and around it there opened a veritable flower bed
of irises, but these were as yellow as those that grow on
the water's edge. The man was staggering now because
of the threat of the graceful sparrow hawk. He threw his
rifle away and, as if he were supposed to make honorable
amends, he got rid of his cartridge belt and his game

*The phonetic pun is lost in translation: in French "Prométhée"
(Prometheus) and "Promettez" (Promise) sound almost identical.
—*Tr.*

bags. He started on his way, with his hands free. It was then that the star, or the finger, saw fit to chain him to a telegraph pole with a transparent net of algae. He waited. At nightfall, the impassible lover of the ring finger was nothing but a little human foliage seen through the blinds of a bedroom readied for love. The plants around him went on about their business, some manufacturing silk, others in the stables milking the goats of shadow. The rocks whistled. There was no way of keeping one's eyes off the filth in the sky.

The corpse of the lucky man was discovered a few days later by a lodestone of men and women exploring the region. It was almost intact except for its frightfully brilliant head. This head was resting on a pillow which was made up of a multitude of little sky-blue butterflies and which disappeared when someone picked it up. Right next to the body an iris-colored flag was planted, and the fringes of this worn flag batted like great eyelashes.

30

The central furnace with blue eyes told me as she glanced up at me with the look of white coordinates on the blackboard, crossing her great hands OX and OY:

"Dancer, you will henceforth dance only for me, and for me only will your white sandals knotted around the instep of your foot with a false weed be undone. It is time to sleep and dance more naked than you are. Drop those veils that still enfold you and give your hand to the pure seasons that you rouse in your dreams, those seasons when the echo is nothing but a great chandelier of fish advancing in the sea, those seasons when love has only one head, which is covered with hoops of the moon, and animals in flames: love, that cubic yard of butterflies."

The door said to me:

"Close me forever on the outside, that needle that the loveliest of your illusions cannot manage to thread because it is so dark; condemn me, yes, condemn me as one condemns women to sing of their marvelous malady: red-headed women, since by firelight all women are red-headed."

The ceiling said to me:

"Turn turtle, turn turtle and sing, and weep too when the rose window of cathedrals, that rose window that is not as beautiful as mine, asks you to, and I will capture your yellow rays, your extravagantly yellow rays in the plaster. See the pleasure-mill turning in the salon and this piercing bird that flies up at each turn of the wheel, at each turn of the cards. And promise me."

I was about to give the floor to the hollow air that speaks in its hands as one looks when one doesn't want to pretend to be seeing (the air speaks in its hands so as not to pretend to be speaking) but the candle laughed just then and my eyes were only a shadow-theater.

31

The stage shows a system of pedals such that the up-and-down motion is combined with a lateral left-to-right motion, one character corresponding in the beginning to each dead-center point or knot of the machine (two men in the vertical system, two women in the horizontal system).

Cast of characters: LUCIE, HELEN, MARC, SATAN. *Black curtains, the two women dressed in white, Marc in a black suit, Satan the color of fire.*

All the action takes place in a perfect cream-colored cube so as immediately to suggest the idea of a giant gyroscope in its case, revolving around its vertical axis with one of its points resting on the edge of a footed glass. Inside the foot is a soldier presenting arms.

HELEN: The window is open. The flowers smell sweet. Today's champagne, a glass of which is bubbling in my ear, makes my head swim. The cruelty of the day molds my perfect forms.

SATAN: Can you see the Ile Saint-Louis above these Ladies and Gentlemen? That's where the poet's little room is.

HELEN: Really?

SATAN: Every day he was visited by waterfalls, the purple waterfall that would have liked to sleep and the white waterfall that came through the roof like a sleepwalker.

LUCIE: It was I who was the white waterfall.

MARC: I recognize you in the strength of the pleasures here, although you are only the lace of yourself. You are the ultimate uselessness, the laundress of fish.

HELEN: She is the laundress of fish.

SATAN: Now the hostage of seasons whose name is man is leaning on the reed table, the gaming table. He is the guilty one with gloved hands.

HELEN: Begging your pardon, Sire, the hands were beautiful. If the mirror had been able to speak, if kisses had fallen silent . . .

LUCIE: The rocks are in the living room, the beautiful rocks in which water sleeps, beneath which men and women bed. The rocks are enormously high: white eagles leave their plumes there and in each plume there is a forest.

MARC: Where am I? Worlds, the possible! How fast the locomotives went: one day the false, one day the true!

SATAN: Was it worth the trouble to leave the place, the trouble of losing one's footing running after corpses and spitting out lamp-bracket lightning? The poet was poor and slow in his dwelling; the poet did not even have a right to the punch that he was very fond of. The purple waterfall carried with it revolvers whose grips were made of little birds.

LUCIE: I can resign myself to the perpetual thaw, Sire; Marc was blond as gypsum.

SILENCE

LUCIE: It is time to go downstairs, my friends; this was only a gymnastics show, and down below, behind the fifth row of spectators, I see a very pale woman who is giving herself over to prostitution. The strange thing is that this creature has wings.

Marc lifts himself by his hand; the apparatus runs faster and faster. Because of the speed picked up, Lucie is standing erect inside Marc's extended arm. The motion comes to a stop when Marc and his motionless horsewoman reach the top of the circuit. Night. The curtain comes down. Satan appears in front of the curtain and makes a prolonged bow.

SATAN: Ladies and Gentlemen, I am the author of the play that we have just had the honor of performing for you. The clockwork is of little importance, the symbols in this new form of theater being no more than a promise. And its transparency is not entirely a question of time. Hell has just been completely restored; during these last few centuries it had value only in a few cases: intellectually it was perfect, but from the viewpoint of moral suffering it left something to be desired. I went to the Opera one day, and there, profiting from the general lack of attention, I first caused several reddish lights to appear on the façade of the building, lights which looked most unpleasant and which, in the opinion of people of taste, still dishonor this monument. Then I made a superb dive into the human conscience, that I have infested with strange chances, formless flowers, and cries of marvels. From this day forward the father was no longer alone with his son; between them the rent in the air allowed a fan with a glowworm resting on it to pass through. In factories I strove to encourage division of labor by every possible means, so that today, in order to manufacture a *fingernail file,* for example, several teams of workers working night and day are needed, some flat on their bellies, others on a ladder. During this time women workers go out to gather bouquets in the fields and others busy themselves writing letters where the same verb in the same tense and the same formula of tenderness are used over and over again. The play you have just seen is one of these new-model fingernail files, to the manufacture of which everything contributes today, from the ivory of your teeth to the color of the sky, a periwinkle black if I am not mistaken. But I shall soon have the honor of inviting you to less rational spectacles, for I do not despair of making eternity the only ephemeral poetry, do you hear, the only ephemeral poetry! Ha ha ha ha! *(He exits snickering.)*

32

I was tan when I met Solange. Everyone sang the praises of the perfect oval of the look in my eye, and my words were the only fan that I could put between faces and myself to hide how disturbing they were to me. The ball was coming to an end at five o'clock in the morning, not without the most fragile gowns being scratched by invisible brambles. O badly fenced properties of Montfermeil where people go looking for lilies of the valley and a princely crown. In the grounds, where there was no longer a single couple who had drawn apart, the icy rays of the false sun of that hour, veritable paths of pearl, had only thieves who had been attracted by the luxury of this life to daze, thieves who began to sing, in voices exactly on pitch, on different steps of the flight of stairs. Snakes, reputed to be impossible to acclimate, sliding in the grass like mandolins, impossible low-cut necklines and geometrical figures of flame-colored paper lighting up among them, that made people afraid when they saw them through the window, for a long time made the velvet and cork scamps display a sort of miraculous respect.

Overwhelmed with presents and weary of these fine instruments of idleness that I did exercises on one by one in a dreadfully voluptuous room, I then made up my mind to dismiss my maidservants and consult an agency to procure what I needed : an awakening at twilight and a bird from diamond mines that would keep its promise to extract the roots of a minor suffering whose existence I had surmised. I was no sooner in possession of this double treasure than I fainted away.

The next day was a day that I knew was to be devoted to the performing of a very obscure rite in the religion of a tribe on the banks of the Ohio. With the protection of the storm that I intended placing myself under, nothing could touch me except a very bright light that only I could distinguish from a flash of lightning. With my head thrown back and my temples protected by two very thin sheets of sapphire, I still bore within me this void pierced with arrows as I went down the coast that runs along the edge of the drill field. Morning roll call had just been sounded, and the blond young men were counting off. The admirable rain with the smell of gorse that was beginning to fall so upset the day that I felt like applauding. From the shadow of a little grove of trees, a hundred yards or so away, a few of those lace panties that are so marvelous in the theater were still flying up toward the sun, but I had something else in mind beside the release of carrier pigeons.

I know a rainbow that augurs nothing good. When the wind curls up in a corner of the earth like a top and your eyelashes bat until they almost break because you feel an imaginary arm around your waist, try to break into a run. I was under a viaduct, pale at the idea of those hoodlums that are hired to whistle with their fingers on locomotives. Nothing, obviously, was going to happen. I reached the little path that the railroad track leaves only when it enters Paris. Was I one of those poor children that can be seen in winter hanging on to the coal

cars and, if need be, making holes in the sacks? Perhaps.
A railroad man, one of those who always have a little
red worm set in a lump of dirt in their hand, said hello
to me.

No one knows the human heart as I do. A convict
who had taken part in the launching of the battleship
Devastation assured me one day that in the immense cone
of light that no one else but him had managed to get out
of, one had the privilege of being present at the creation
of the world. Similarly, as far back as I can remember,
nothing of the love game was hidden from me. I approached the gare d'Est-Ceinture just when the factories
were letting out. The nacelles tied down in the yards took
off one by one, and all the lady passengers seemed to have
lost their minds over a branch of lilac. A marvelous chandelier of semiquavers shone here and there in front of
the wall of red and white bricks. The work put off to another day left the night free: hands were going to be able
to fill the blue salad bowls. Beneath the twill smock that
is yet another mold, the Parisian working woman with
the high chignon watches the rain of pleasure falling.

Everyone ought to have the experience of walking
about with a scepter in the alleys of the capital as night
is falling. The rue Lafayette swings its windows from
left to right. It is the hour of political meetings, and
above the doors one can make out the inscription in capital letters: "No more bets." For a quarter of an hour I
had been at the mercy of those dismal seers who extort a
cigarette from you with their violet eyes. I have always
been taught that the most important sign of seriousness
was talking to yourself. I was, however, less weary than
ever. One of the magnetic poles of my route would probably be, I had long known, the neon sign that says *Lon-
gines* on the corner of the rue de la Paix and the place de
l'Opéra. From that point, for example, I would no longer
have any idea of where to go.

Task for task, obligation for obligation, I have the
definite feeling that I will not do what I wanted to do.
The little lanterns with the coat of arms of Paris that

make cars turn around after a certain hour have always made me regret the absence of pavers. You should have seen them, at least once, their eye on their level of alcohol, keeping otters gloved in chalk from getting the least little bump. The wooden paving blocks whose edges the sun slowly wears down are lighter than prayers. If one of them is lighter than another, in your wallet is a telegram that you haven't read yet. However, was the orange-colored clearing at one of the prettiest bends of the boulevards, surmounted by a lightning rod and covered with a Liberty-print ground swell, there for the circulation of animals more graceful than others? It was child's play for me to climb over the vials of perfume meant to keep me out, without being seen. A police directive, apparently dating from the last century, partly hid the handle of a bow-shaped instrument that I recognized because I had already seen it, incrusted with precious stones, in the window of a gunsmith's shop along one of the covered walkways. This time it was resting on a clump of dried leaves, so that I suspected a trap. In the time it took me to get rid of this idea, I brought to light the two top rungs of a rope ladder. I immediately decided to use the apparatus that thus offered itself, and when nothing was left to emerge from the earth but my head, I took time out to kiss madly from afar two high black boots laced around cream-colored stockings. This was the last memory I was to carry away from a life that had been short, for I don't quite remember if I was on the shady side of twenty.

To understand the movement that drove this dismal elevator, one must call upon some of one's knowledge of astronomy. The two planets farthest from the sun combine their movement around it with this strange back-and-forth movement. The light was that of mineral-water shops. For what audience of haggard children did I perform such perilous exercises? I perceived discontinuous moldings passing through all the colors of the spectrum, mantelpieces of white marble, accordions, and, alternately, hail, ciliate plants, and the lyrebird. Hold off, shipwrecks; sigh, ear trumpets to the sound of which I shall one day be received by my brother, that charming mollusk who has the property of being able to fly under water.

Little by little the slowness of the oscillations made me have a presentiment of the approach of the goal. This was the mystery, for I will have said nothing when I say that being subject to such swaying back and forth in the upper air, I might just as well have stopped at Naples or in Borneo. The torrid, glacial, luminous, or dark-and-light zones were ranged in tiers, in squares. When a girl on a farm allows the water of a nearby spring to flow through her bedroom, and her fiancé comes to lean on the curved sill of her window, they too leave, never to meet each other again. Let others believe if they like that they are at the mercy of a convalescence: I whom the whitest equestriennes have feted for my skill at launching their blind chariots on dusty roads shall save no one, and I do not ask anyone to save me. I once laughed at fortune-telling, and on my right shoulder I have a five-leaf clover. As I go on my way I may happen to fall from a precipice or be pursued by stones, but each time, I beg you to believe, it is only a reality.

It is, rather, each step that I take that is a dream, and don't talk to me of those benign-looking tramways in which the conductor hands out raffle tickets. He takes advantage of each of the stops to go have a drink. Then the vehicle, which tends to retire from its rounds after the street sprinkler, sees itself surrounded by the most photogenic of stags. For my part, my convictions have never permitted me to ride in it except at a reduced fare, early in the morning, with workers wearing a knapsack full of partridges slung across their shoulders.

Still, I had come to Paris, and a great flame escorted me, as I have said, with its forty blond feet.

Underground boulevards did not exist yet.

At this moment the female enemy of society went into the building situated at number 1, boulevard des Capucines. But all she did was go in and come out. I had never seen her and yet my eyes filled with tears. She was discreet as crime and her black dress with little pleats looked by turn brilliant and dull because of the breeze. This was all that was provocative in her pose: as she went off I noticed that her foot kept coming down quite lightly. To her left, to her right, names of perfumes, of pharmaceutical specialties, were endlessly inscribed on the sidewalk in letters of every color. In all cases it's nice to follow women like that who one is sure are not coming to you and are not going anywhere. Just as this woman crossed the threshold of a house on the rue de Hanovre, again for nothing, I went briskly over to meet her, and before she had a chance to recognize me, I imprisoned with my hand the hand of hers that was clutching a revolver so small that the end of the barrel didn't reach as far as the first knuckle of her bent index finger. The unknown woman then had a look of supplication and triumph in her eye. Then, with her eyes closed, she silently took my arm.

Nothing, certainly, is simpler than saying to a woman, to a taxi: "Take care of me." Sensibility is nothing but this vehicle glassed all around in which you have seated yourself; a vulgar cotton lace thrown over the seat does its best to make you forget the ruts in the road. Sometimes the luggage rack is full of trunks and oblong hat boxes like pendants. The whole ends up hurtling into a little lake at the foot of the shrub with its hands joined. Did I not once wait, by force of circumstances, for a reason to live to come to me from these pain-parties? The most wrathful of women are divorcées, who manage so well with their pearl-gray crepe veils. At the seashore I found it the right time to fondle their knees. The whip of the victorias that had disappeared now described only a rain of stars in time, and it must be confessed that these two coldly distinct images were the only ones to be superimposed at the point where I found myself seated. Thus in the light of the footlights a mouth appears to be exactly like an eye, and who does not know that, if only one tilts the prism of love, the bow runs across the legs of the dancers?

When it's Solange . . . For a week we lived in a region
more delicate than the impossibility of alighting for certain swallows. On pain of separation we had forbidden
each other to speak of the past. The window overlooked a
ship lying on the prairie, breathing regularly. In the distance could be seen an immense tiara made of the wealth
of ancient cities. The sun lassoed the finest adventures.
We lived exquisitely forgettable hours there, in the company of the harlequin from Cayenne. I must add that
Solange took off her hat and lighted the straw fire right
in the middle of the stairway that led to our bedroom.
There was a call button for the realization of each of our
desires and there was time for everything. The bedspread
was made of news items close at hand :

"The golden ball rolling over the azure bottom of
this cage is not connected to any apparent stem, yet it is
the ball of a marvelous condenser. We are in a bar on the
rue Cujas and it is here that Cécilas Charrier, following
the assault on train 5, came to try on the elegantly gloved
hand thanks to which he managed to make himself recognized."

"Rosa-Josepha, the Siamese twin sisters, eight days
ago got up from the table when a butterfly displaying
my colors described a figure eight around their heads. Up
to that time the monster, mated with a blusterer, seemed
not to have much of an idea of the great destiny that
awaited him."

It would soon be September. On a blackboard in the
office of the hotel, an equation traced in a child's hand
showed only the variables. The ceiling, the mirrored
wardrobe, the lamp, the body of my mistress, and the air
itself had taken on the resonance of a drum. Sometimes
Solange took off between midnight and one o'clock. But
I was sure to find her again next morning in her spangled
chemise. I still don't know what to think about her sleeping and perhaps all she ever did was wake up at my side.
Year-round strawberries flowered once more in the fire-

place beneath the roof of trembling greenery divided among the echoes of the night. Solange always looked as if she had come out of a redoubt. The terrible impersonality of our relationship excluded jealousy to such a point that the great tinted glasses of water of disappearances never grew tepid. It was only later that I understood the extraordinary feebleness of these famous white magic tricks.

Our best times were spent in the bathroom. It was on the same floor as our bedroom. A thick cloud of steam, "thick enough to cut with a knife," spread out over certain parts of it, especially around the toilet, to the point that it was impossible to put one's hands on anything. A great number of cosmetics came, incomprehensibly, to be there. One day about eight o'clock in the morning when I was the first to enter this room that was full of some vague superior malaise, in the hope, I believe, of experiencing the mysterious fate that was beginning to hover above our heads, to my great surprise I heard a great noise of wings followed almost immediately by that of a square of window-glass falling, a square that had the peculiarity of being the color that is called "dawn," while the windowpane, which had remained intact, was, on the contrary, faintly blue. Lying on the massage table was a woman of great beauty whose last convulsion I was happy to witness by chance and who, by the time I had reached her, had ceased to breathe. A burning metamorphosis was taking place around this lifeless body: if the sheet pulled taut at the four corners was growing perceptibly longer and was becoming perfectly transparent, the silver paper that ordinarily covered the walls of the room, on the other hand, was shriveling. It was no longer good for anything but powdering the wigs of two lackeys out of some operetta who were strangely disappearing into the mirror. An ivory file that I picked up on the floor instantly caused a certain number of wax hands to open up around me, remaining suspended in the air until alighting on green cushions. As has been seen, I lacked the means to question the breath of the dead woman. Solange had not appeared all night, and yet this woman did not look like her, except for the little white shoes whose sole, where the toes went in, had imperceptible scratches like those of dancers. I lacked the slightest sign. It was odd that the young woman had come into the room completely undressed. As I was running my fingers through her freshly cut hair, I suddenly got the impression that the beauty had just shifted her body from left to right, which, along with the position of her right arm behind her back and the hyper-extension of her left hand, could not help but suggest the idea that she was doing the splits.

Having limited myself to noting these few scanty facts, I left without useless precautions. The only decorations, certainly, that I respect in any way are those gold stars sewed to the lining of men's jackets just below the inside pocket. I nonetheless readjusted the red ribbon I was wearing in my buttonhole.

Only one mediocre book has been written about celebrated escapes. What you must know is that beneath all the windows that you may take a notion to jump out of, amiable imps hold out the sad sheet of love by the four cardinal points. My inspection had lasted only a few seconds, and I knew what I wanted to know. The walls of Paris, what is more, had been covered with posters showing a man masked with a black domino, holding in his left hand the key of the fields: this man was myself.

PREFACE
FOR THE NEW EDITION
OF THE SECOND MANIFESTO
(1946)

In allowing the SECOND SURREALIST MANIFESTO *to be re-published today, I have talked myself into believing that time has accomplished for me the task of blunting its po-lemical angles. I only hope that it has corrected on its own —even though it were to a certain extent at my expense— the sometimes hasty judgments I made about various peo-ple's behavior such as I tended to see it in those days. This aspect of the text will in fact be justifiable only to those who take the time and trouble to situate the* SECOND MANI-FESTO *in the intellectual climate of the year it appeared. It was in fact around 1930 that a few unfettered souls be-gan to perceive the imminent, ineluctable return of world catastrophe. To the vague dismay and confusion which resulted from this realization was added, for me, another concern: how were we to save, from this ever more com-pelling current, the bark which a few of us had constructed with our own hands in order to move against this very current? I am fully aware that the following pages bear unfortunate traces of nervousness. They bear witness to grievances of varying degrees of importance: it is obvious*

*that certain defections were deeply resented and, immedi-
ately, in itself the attitude—however episodic it may have
been—taken with regard to Baudelaire, to Rimbaud, will
lead one to believe that the worst offenders might well be
those in whom one had placed one's greatest confidence
initially, those from whom one expected the most. Viewed
in retrospect, most of them have in fact realized this as
well as I, and as a result certain reconciliations have been
possible, whereas agreements which proved to be of a more
lasting nature were in turn denounced. A human association such as the one which enabled Surrealism to be
built—an association such as had not been seen, as far as
its goals and its enthusiasm were concerned, at least since
Saint-Simonism—cannot help but obey certain laws of fluc-
tuation about which it is probably all too human not to
be able to know how, from within, to make up one's mind.
Recent events, which have found all those whom the*
SECOND MANIFESTO *discusses allied on the same side, show
that their common background was healthy and, objectively, set reasonable limitations on their disputes. To the
extent that certain of them were the victims of these events
or, more generally, victims of life itself—I am thinking of
Desnos, of Artaud—I hasten to say that the wrongs I have
upon occasion ascribed to them fall by the wayside, as
they do for Politzer, whose activity has constantly been determined outside the framework of Surrealism and who,
therefore, had no accounting to make to Surrealism for
that activity; I have no compunction whatsoever about
admitting that I completely misjudged his* character.

*Those things which, fifteen years after the fact, accen-
tuate the* fallible *aspect of some of my judgments about
this or that person or group of persons does not prevent
me from protesting against the allegation made recently**
that within the inner sanctum of Surrealism "political

*See Jules Monnerot, *La Poésie moderne et le sacré,* p. 189.

*differences" were predetermined by "personal differences."
Matters relating to various individuals were discussed by
us only a posteriori, and were made public only in those
cases when it seemed that the basic principles on which
our agreement had been founded had been breached in
the most flagrant manner, thus affecting the history of our
movement. It was then, and still is today, a question of
trying to maintain a platform flexible enough to cope with
the changing aspects of the problems of life and at the
same time remain stable enough to attest to the* nonrup-
*ture of a certain number of mutual—and public—com-
mitments made at the time of our youth. The broadsides
which the Surrealists "unleashed with fire and brimstone,"
as people have been known to describe it, against one
another on many occasions reveal, more than anything
else, how impossible it was for them to carry on the debate
on any lesser level. If the violence of expression in these
pamphlets sometimes seems out of all proportion to the
deviation, the error, or the "sin" they are claiming to cas-
tigate, I believe that, aside from the ambivalence of feelings to which I have already alluded, the blame for it must
be placed squarely upon the period itself and also upon
the formal influence of a good portion of revolutionary
literature which allowed, side by side with the expression
of far-reaching and well-disciplined ideas, a profusion of
aggressive offshoots of mediocre importance, aimed at this
or that specific group of our contemporaries.**

---

*See, for example, *Misère de la philosophie, anti-Dühring ma-
terialisme, et empiriocriticisme*, etc.

SECOND MANIFESTO
OF SURREALISM
(1930)

ANNALES MEDICO-PSYCHOLOGIQUES
JOURNAL
DE
L'ALIÉNATION MENTALE
ET DE
LA MÉDECINE LÉGALE DES ALIÉNÉS

Report
Legitimate Defense

In the last issue of the Annales médico-psychologiques *Dr. A. Rodiet discussed, in the course of an interesting article, the professional risks run by a doctor working in a mental institution. He cited the recent attacks that had been made upon several of our colleagues, and he sought the means of protecting us effectively against the danger which the constant contact between the psychiatrist on the one hand and the insane person and his family on the other represents.*

But the insane person and his family constitute a danger which I shall describe as "endogenous," it is part and parcel of our mission; it is the necessary corollary of it. We simply accept it. The same does not hold true for a danger I shall this time describe as "exogenous," which deserves our closest attention. It seems that it should give rise to more extraordinary reactions on our part.

Here is a particularly significant example: one of our patients, an especially dangerous and demanding madman with a persecution complex, suggested to me with gentle irony that I read a book that is being freely passed from hand to hand among the inmates. This book, recently published by the Nouvelle Revue Française, commends itself to our attention by its origin and its proper and inoffensive presentation. The work in question was Nadja, by André Breton. Surrealism flourished within its covers, with its deliberate incoherence, its cleverly disjointed chapters, that delicate art which consists of pulling the reader's leg. In the midst of strangely symbolic drawings, one could make out the photograph of Professor Claude. In fact, one chapter was devoted especially to us. The poor maligned psychiatrists were generously reviled and insulted, and one passage (underlined in blue pencil by the patient who had so kindly lent us this book) especially caught our attention. It contained the following sentences: "I know that if I were mad and confined for several days, I would take advantage of any momentary period of lucidity to murder in cold blood one of those, preferably the doctor, who happened to come my way. At least I would be put into a cell by myself, the way the violent patients are. Perhaps they would leave me alone."

If this is not tantamount to inciting to murder, then nothing is. We can only react to it with complete disdain, or with utter indifference.

In such cases, to pass the problem on to higher authorities strikes us as revealing a state of anxiety which is so unwarranted that we prefer not even to consider it. And yet every day brings new evidence of this kind of thing, in ever-increasing numbers.

In my opinion what we are most guilty of is lethargy. Our silence puts our sincerity in question and encourages any and every audacity.

Why do our professional societies, our medical association, not react to such incidents, be they collective or individual? Why don't we send a letter of protest to a publisher who publishes a work like Nadja, and institute proceedings against an author who, as far as we and our profession are concerned, has exceeded the bounds of propriety?

I believe it would be in our best interest (and it would be our only means of defense) to consider—within the framework of our medical association, for instance—forming a committee whose special function it would be to deal with these matters.

Dr. Rodiet concluded his article by saying: "The doctor

working in an insane asylum can in all fairness demand the right to be protected without restriction by the society that he himself is defending. . . . "

But this society sometimes seems to forget the reciprocal nature of its duties. It is up to us to remind it of these duties.

Paul Abély.

SOCIÉTÉ MÉDICO-PSYCHOLOGIQUE

M. Abély having presented a paper concerning the tendencies of authors who call themselves Surrealists and concerning the attacks they are making upon mental specialists, this communication gave rise to the following discussion:

DISCUSSION

DR. DE CLÉRAMBAULT: *I would like to ask Professor Janet what links he finds between the mental state of the subjects and the nature of their output.*

PROFESSOR JANET: *The Surrealists' manifesto contains an interesting philosophical introduction. The Surrealists maintain that reality is by definition ugly; beauty exists only in that which is not real. It is man who has introduced beauty into the world. In order to produce beauty, one must remove oneself as far as possible from reality.*

The works by the Surrealists are above all confessions of men obsessed, and men who doubt.

DR. DE CLÉRAMBAULT: *Extremist writers and artists who initiate impertinent fashions, sometimes with the help of manifestoes condemning all tradition, seem to me, from the technical point of view, to fall without exception into the category I might call "methodists"—no matter what names they might give themselves or what art or period is being dealt with. Methodism consists of saving oneself the trouble of thinking, and even more of observing, so as to rely upon a method or predetermined formula in order to produce an effect of itself unique, schematic, and conventional: thus one produces rap-*

idly, with some semblance of style, and avoiding the criticisms that a similarity to life would facilitate. This degradation of work is especially easy to detect in the plastic arts, but in the verbal realm it can be demonstrated just as clearly.

The kind of prideful sloth which engenders or encourages Methodism is not confined to our own age. In the sixteenth century the Concettists, *the* Gongorists *and* Euphuists; *in the seventeenth century, the Precieuses were all Methodists. Vadius and Trissotin were Methodists—they were simply much more moderate and hardworking than those of today, perhaps because they were writing for a more select and erudite public.*

In the plastic arts, the emergence of Methodism seems to date only from the last century.

PROFESSOR JANET: *In support of Dr. de Clérambault's opinion, I am reminded of some of the Surrealists'* methods. *For example, they take five words absolutely at random out of a hat and make various series of associations with these five words. In the Introduction to Surrealism they tell a whole story with these two words: turkey and top hat.*

DR. DE CLÉRAMBAULT: *At a certain point in his paper, M. Abély described to you a campaign of slander. This point deserves further comment.*

Slander and libel are an essential part of the professional risks a mental specialist has to take; we are, upon occasion, subjected to unjust accusations, both because of our administrative functions or the mission with which we have been entrusted as medical experts: it would only be fair that the powers which invest us with our authority also protect us.

.   .   .   .

Against any and all professional risks, of whatever kind they may be, *the medical practitioner must be protected by very clearly stated rules and regulations which will assure him immediate and permanent guarantees. These risks are not only of a material kind, but also moral. Protection against these risks should include physical assistance, subsidies, juridical and judicial support, indemnities, and, last but not least, retirement benefits of a permanent nature. In urgent situations, costs can be defrayed out of a Common Insurance Fund. But in the final analysis these costs must be borne by the same area of responsibility in whose service the injury has been sustained.*

.   .   .   .

The meeting was adjourned at 6:00 P.M.

One of the secretaries,
Guiraud

In spite of the various efforts peculiar to each of those who used to claim kinship with Surrealism, or who still do, one must ultimately admit that, more than anything else, Surrealism attempted to provoke, from the intellectual and moral point of view, *an attack of conscience,* of the most general and serious kind, and that the extent to which this was or was not accomplished alone can determine its historical success or failure.

From the intellectual point of view, it was then, and still is today, a question of testing by any and all means, and of demonstrating at any price, the meretricious nature of the old antinomies hypocritically intended to prevent any unusual ferment on the part of man, were it only by giving him a vague idea of the means at his disposal, by challenging him to escape to some meaningful degree from the universal fetters. The bugaboo of death, the simplistic theatrical portrayal of the beyond, the shipwreck of the most beautiful reason in sleep, the overwhelming curtain of the future, the tower of Babel, the mirrors of inconstancy, the impassable silver wall bespattered with brains— these all too gripping images of the human catastrophe are, perhaps, no more than images. Everything tends to make us believe that there exists a certain point of the mind at which life and death, the real and the imagined, past and future, the communicable and the incommunicable, high and low, cease to be perceived as contradictions. Now, search as one may one will never find any other motivating force in the activities of the Surrealists than the hope of finding and fixing this point. From this it becomes obvious how absurd it would be to define Surrealism solely as constructive or destructive: the point to which we are referring is a fortiori that point where construction and destruction can no longer be brandished one against the other. It is also clear that Surrealism is not interested in giving very serious consideration to anything that happens outside of itself, under the guise of art, or even anti-art, of philosophy or anti-philosophy—in short, of anything not aimed at the annihilation of the being into a diamond, all blind and interior, which is no more the soul of ice than that of fire. What could those people who are still concerned about the position they occupy *in the world* expect from the Surrealist experiment? In this mental site, from which one can no longer set forth except for oneself on a dangerous but, we think, supreme feat of reconnaissance, it is likewise out of the question that the slightest heed be paid to the footsteps of those who arrive or to the footsteps of those who leave, since these footsteps occur in a region where by definition Surrealism has no ear to hear. We would not want Surrealism to be at the mercy of the whims of this or that group of persons; if it declares that it is able, by its own means, to uproot thought from an increasingly cruel state of thralldom, to steer it back onto the path of total comprehension, return it to its original purity—that is enough for it to be judged only on what it has done and what it still has to do in order to keep its promises.

Before proceeding, however, to verify the balance sheet, it is worthwhile to know just what kind of moral virtues Surrealism lays claim to, since, moreover, it plunges its roots into life and, no doubt not by chance, into *the life of this period,* seeing that I laden this life with anecdotes like the sky, the sound of a watch, the cold, a malaise, that is, I begin to speak about it in a vulgar manner. To think these things, to hold any rung whatever of this weather-beaten ladder—none of us is beyond such things until he has passed through the last stage of asceticism. It is in fact from the disgusting cauldron of these meaningless mental images that the desire to proceed beyond the insufficient, the absurd, distinction between the beautiful and the ugly, true and false, good and evil, is born and sustained. And, as it is the degree of resistance that this choice idea meets with which determines the more or less certain flight of the mind toward a world at last inhabitable, one can understand why Surrealism was not afraid to make for itself a tenet of total revolt, complete insubordination, of sabotage according to rule, and why it still expects nothing save from violence. The simplest Surrealist act consists of dashing down into the street, pistol in hand, and firing blindly, as fast as you can pull the trigger, into the crowd. Anyone who, at least once in his life, has not dreamed of thus putting an end to the petty system of debasement and cretinization in effect has a well-defined place in that crowd, with his belly at barrel level.* The justification

*I know that these last two sentences are going to delight a certain number of simpletons who have been trying for a long time to catch me up in a contradiction with myself. Thus, am I really saying that "the simplest Surrealist act . . . ?" So what if I am! And while some, with an obvious axe to grind, seize the opportunity to ask me "what I'm waiting for," others raise a hue and cry about anarchy and try to pretend that they have caught me in *flagrante delicto* committing an act of revolutionary indiscipline. Nothing is easier for me than to deprive these people of the cheap effect they might have. Yes, I am concerned to learn whether a person is blessed with violence before asking myself whether, in that person, violence *compromises* or *does not compromise*. I believe in the absolute virtue of anything that takes place, spontaneously or not, in the sense of non-acceptance, and no reasons of general efficacity, from which long, pre-revolutionary patience draws its inspiration—reasons to which I defer —will make me deaf to the cry which can be wrenched from us at every moment by the frightful disproportion between what is gained and what is lost, between what is granted and what is suffered. As for

of such an act is, to my mind, in no way incompatible with
the belief in that gleam of light that Surrealism seeks to
detect deep within us. I simply wanted to bring in here the
element of human despair, on this side of which nothing
would be able to justify that belief. It is impossible to give
one's assent to one and not to the other. Anyone who
should pretend to embrace this belief without truly sharing this despair would soon be revealed as an enemy.
This frame of mind which we call Surrealist and which
we see thus occupied with itself, seems less and less to
require any historical antecedents and, so far as I am personally concerned, I have no objection if reporters, judicial experts, and others hold it to be specifically modern.
I have more confidence in this moment, this present moment, of my thought than in the sum total of everything
people may try to read into a finished work, into a human
life that has reached the end of its road. There is nothing
more sterile, in the final analysis, than that perpetual
interrogation of the dead: did Rimbaud become converted
on the eve of his death? can one find in Lenin's last will
and testament sufficient evidence to condemn the present
policy of the Third International? was an unbearable,
and completely personal, disgrace the mainspring of Alphonse Rabbe's pessimism? did Sade, in plenary session
of the National Convention, commit a counterrevolutionary act? It is enough to allow these questions to be asked to
appreciate the fragility of the evidence of those who are

---

that act that I term the simplest: it is clear that my intention is not
to recommend it above every other because it is simple, and to try and
pick a quarrel with me on this point is tantamount to asking, in
bourgeois fashion, any nonconformist why he doesn't commit suicide,
or any revolutionary why he doesn't pack up and go live in the u.s.s.r.
Don't come to me with such stories! The haste with which certain
people would be only too happy to see me disappear, coupled with
my own natural tendency to agitation, are in themselves sufficient reason for me not to clear out of here for no good reason.

no longer among us. Too many rogues and rascals are interested in the success of this undertaking of spiritual highway robbery for me to follow them over this terrain. When it comes to revolt, none of us must have any need of ancestors. I would like to make it very clear that in my opinion it is necessary to hold the cult of men in deep distrust, however great they may seemingly be. With one exception—Lautréamont—I do not see a single one of them who has not left some questionable trace in his wake. Useless to cite the example of Rimbaud again: Rimbaud was mistaken, Rimbaud wanted to fool us. He is guilty in our eyes for having allowed, for not having made completely impossible, certain disparaging interpretations of his thought, such as those made by Paul Claudel. So much the worse for Baudelaire too ("O Satan . . .") and that "eternal rule" of his life: "to say a prayer every morning to God, *source of all strength and all justice, to my father, to Mariette, and to Poe,* as intercessors." The right to contradict himself, I know, but really! To God, to Poe? Poe who, in the police magazines, is today so properly presented as the *master of scientific policemen* (from Sherlock Holmes, in fact, to Paul Valéry . . .). Is it not a shame to present in an intellectually attractive light a type of policeman, *always a policeman,* to bestow upon the world a police *method?* Let us, in passing, spit on Edgar Poe.* If, through Surrealism,

*At the time of the original publication of *Marie Roget,* footnotes at the bottom of the pages were considered superfluous. But several years have passed since the event on which this story is based occurred, and it seemed worthwhile to us to restore them here, together with a few words of explanation relative to the general scheme of things. A girl, Mary Cecilia Rogers, was murdered in the vicinity of New York; and although her death aroused a strong and continuing interest, the mystery surrounding her death was still not solved at the time this piece was written and published (November 1842). Here, under the pretext of relating the fate of a Parisian girl of easy virtue, the author scrupulously traced the essential facts, and at the same time gave the nonessential and simply parallel facts of

we reject unhesitatingly the notion of the sole possibility
of the things which "are," and if we ourselves declare that
by a path which "is," a path which we can show and help
people to follow, one can arrive at what people claimed
"was not," if we cannot find words enough to stigmatize
the baseness of Western thought, if we are not afraid to
take up arms against logic, if we refuse to swear that something we do in dreams is less meaningful than something
we do in a state of waking, if we are not even sure that we
will not do away *with time,* that sinister old farce, that
train constantly jumping off the track, mad pulsation, in-
extricable conglomeration of breaking and broken beasts,
how do you expect us to show any tenderness, even to be
tolerant, toward an apparatus of social conservation, of
whatever sort it may be? That would be the only madness
truly unacceptable on our part. Everything remains to be
done, every means must be worth trying, in order to lay
waste to the ideas of *family, country, religion.* No matter
how well known the Surrealist position may be with respect to this matter, still it must be stressed that on this
point there is no room for compromise. Those who make
it their duty to maintain this position persist in advancing
this negation, in belittling any other criterion of value.

---

the actual murder of Mary Rogers. Thus any argument founded on
fiction is applicable to the truth; and the search for the truth is the
goal.

   "The Mystery of Marie Roget was composed far from the theater
of the crime, and without any other means of investigation save the
newspapers the author was able to procure for himself. Thus he had
to do without a great number of documents he could have used to
good advantage if he had been in the country and if he had inspected
the localities. It is worthwhile pointing out, nonetheless, that the
confessions of two persons (one of whom is the Madame Deluc of
the novel), made at different times and long after the publication of
this work, fully confirmed not only the general conclusion but also
all the principal hypothetical details on which this conclusion had
been based." (Introductory note to *The Mystery of Marie Roget.*)

They intend to savor fully the profound grief, so well played, with which the bourgeois public—inevitably prepared in their base way to forgive them a few "youthful" errors—greets the steadfast and unyielding need they display to laugh like savages in the presence of the French flag, to vomit their disgust in the face of *every* priest, and to level at the breed of "basic duties" the long-range weapon of sexual cynicism. We combat, in whatever form they may appear, poetic indifference, the distraction of art, scholarly research, pure speculation; we want nothing whatever to do with those, either large or small, who use their minds as they would a savings bank. All the forsaken acquaintances, all the abdications, all the betrayals in the book will not prevent us from putting an end to this damn nonsense. It is noteworthy, moreover, that when they are left to their own devices, and to nothing else, the people who one day made it necessary for us to do without them have straightway lost their footing, have been immediately forced to resort to the most miserable expedients in order to reingratiate themselves with the defenders of *law and order,* all proud partisans of leveling via the head. This is because unflagging fidelity to the commitments of Surrealism presupposes a disinterestedness, a contempt for risk, a refusal to compromise, of which very few men prove, in the long run, to be capable. Were there to remain not a single one, from among all those who were the first to measure by its standards their chance for significance and their desire for truth, yet would Surrealism continue to live. In any event, it is too late for the seed not to sprout and grow in infinite abundance in the human field, with fear and the other varieties of weeds that must prevail over all. This is in fact why I had promised myself, as the preface for the new edition of the *Manifesto of Surrealism* (1929) indicates, to abandon silently to their sad fate a certain number of individuals who, in my opinion, had given themselves enough credit: this was the case for Messrs. Artaud, Carrive, Delteil, Gérard, Limbour, Masson, Soupault, and Vitrac, cited in the *Manifesto* (1924), and for several others since. The first of these gentlemen having been so brazen as to complain about it, I have decided to reconsider my intentions on this subject:

"There is," writes M. Artaud to the *Intransigeant,* on September 10, 1929, "there is in the article about the *Manifesto of Surrealism* which appeared in l'*Intran* last August 24, a sentence which awakens too many things: 'M. Breton has not judged it necessary to make any corrections —especially of names—in this new edition of his work, and this is all to his credit, but the rectifications are made by themselves.' " That M. Breton calls upon honor to judge a certain number of people to whom the above-named rectifications apply is a matter involving a sectarian morality with which only a literary minority was hitherto infected. But we must leave to the Surrealists these games of little papers. Moreover, anyone who was involved in the affair of *The Dream* a year ago is hardly in a position to talk about honor.

Far be it from me to debate with the signatory of this letter the very precise meaning I understand by the term "honor." That an actor, looking for lucre and notoriety, undertakes to stage a sumptuous production of a play by one Strindberg to which he himself attaches not the slightest importance, would of course be neither here nor there to me were it not for the fact that this actor had upon occasion claimed to be a man of thought, of anger, of blood, were he not the same person who, in certain pages of *La Révolution surréaliste,* burned, if we can believe his words, to burn everything, who claimed that he expected nothing save from "this cry of the mind which turns back toward itself fully determined desperately to break its restraining bonds." Alas! that was for him a role, like any other; he was "staging" Strindberg's *The Dream,* having heard that the Swedish ambassador *would pay* (M. Artaud knows that I can prove what I say), and it cannot escape him that that is a judgment of the moral value of his undertaking; but never mind. It is M. Artaud, whom I will always see in my mind's eye flanked by two cops, at the door of the Alfred Jarry Theatre, sicking twenty others on the only friends he admitted having as lately as the night before, having previously negotiated their arrests at the commissariat, it is M. Artaud, naturally, who finds me out of place speaking of honor.

Aragon and I were able to note, by the reception given our critical collaboration in the special number of *Varietés,* "Le Surréalisme en 1929," that the lack of inhibition that we feel in appraising, from day to day, the degree of moral qualification of various people, the ease with which Surrealism, at the first sign of compromise, prides itself in bidding a fond farewell to this person or that, is less than ever to the liking of a few journalistic jerks, for whom the dignity of man is at the very most a subject for derisive laughter. Has it really ever occurred to anyone to ask as much of people in the domain—aside from a few romantic exceptions, suicides and others—heretofore the least closely watched! Why should we go on playing the role of those who are fed up and disgusted? A policeman, a few gay dogs, two or three pen pimps, several mentally unbalanced persons, a cretin, to whose number no one would mind our adding a few sensible, stable, and upright souls who could be termed energumens: is this not the making of an amusing, innocuous team, a faithful replica of life, a team of men paid piecework, winning on points?

SHIT.

Surrealism's confidence cannot be well or ill placed for the simple reason that it is not placed. Neither in the palpable world, nor palpably outside of this world, nor in the perpetuity of mental associations which favor our existence with a natural demand or a superior whim, nor in the interest which the "mind" may have in sparing itself our transient clientele. And it is placed even less, it goes without saying, in the shifting fortunes of those who started out by putting their trust in Surrealism. It is not the man whose revolt becomes channeled and runs dry who can keep this revolt from rumbling, it is not any number of men you care to name—and history is hardly comprised of their ascent on their knees—who can keep this revolt from taming, in the great mysterious moments, the constantly renascent beast of "this is better." There are still today, in the lycées, even in the workshops,* in the

---

*Even? people will say. It is up to us, in fact—without thereby taking the edge off the specifically intellectual flavor of curiosity with which Surrealism irritates, on their own ground, the poetry specialists, the art critics, and the narrow-minded psychologists—it is up to us to move, as slowly as necessary, without any sudden fits or starts, toward the worker's way of thinking, by definition little inclined to follow us in a series of undertakings which the revolutionary concern for the class struggle does not, ultimately, imply. We are the first to deplore the fact that the only interesting segment of society is systematically kept in ignorance of what the head of the other is doing, that it only has time to devote to those ideas relating directly to its emancipation, which leads it to confuse, with summary mistrust, anything which is undertaken, willingly or not, outside its own sphere, because of the mere fact that the social problem is not absolutely the only one that has been posed. It is therefore not surprising that Surrealism refrains from deflecting, however slightly, from the course of its own admirably effective reflections, that part of the youth which *drudges* while the other, more or less cynical, part watches it drudge. In return, what should it try if not, as a start, to stop, on the edge of the definitive concession, a small number of men armed only with scruples but about whom there is no certainty—the silver spoon with which they were born is no proof—that they too will opt for wealth against poverty? Our fondest desire is to keep within the reach of these people a nucleus of ideas which we ourselves found astounding, meanwhile being careful to keep the communication of these ideas from becoming an end rather than remaining the means that it should be, since the end must be the total elimination of the claims of a class to which we belong in spite of ourselves and which we cannot help abolish outside ourselves as long as we have not succeeded in abolishing them within ourselves.

street, the seminaries and military barracks, pure young people who refuse to knuckle down. It is to them and them alone that I address myself, it is for them alone that I am trying to defend Surrealism against the accusation that it is, after all, no more than an intellectual pastime like any other. Let them in all objectivity try to ascertain what it is we have tried to do, let them lend us a hand, let them take our places one by one if need be. It is hardly worthwhile for us to refute the allegation that we ever were interested in constituting a closed circle, and the only persons who may derive any benefit from the propagation of such rumors are those who saw eye-to-eye with us for a brief moment and who were denounced *by us* for redhibitory defect. Such a one was M. Artaud, as we have seen, and as he also might have been seen being slapped in a hotel corridor by Pierre Unik, calling out for help *to his mother!* Another was M. Carrive, a man incapable of considering the political or sexual problem other than from the viewpoint of Gascony terrorism, a poor apologist, in the final analysis, for M. Malraux's Garine. Another was M. Delteil: see his disgusting article on love in issue number 2 of *La Révolution surréaliste* (edited by Naville) and, since his expulsion from Surrealism, in "Les Poilus," "Jeanne d'Arc": let me not belabor the point. Still another is M. Gérard, of whom there is only one of a kind, a man actually thrown out for congenital imbecility: a different evolution from the preceding person; innocuous tasks now at *La Lutte des classes,* at *La Verité,* nothing serious. There is M. Limbour, who has also virtually dropped out of sight: skepticism, literary coquetry in the worst sense of the word. There is M. Masson, whose Surrealist convictions, however loudly proclaimed, were unable to resist the reading of a book entitled *Le Surrealisme et la peinture,* in which the author, more than a trifle careless when it came to hierarchy, found himself unable, or unwilling, to rank Masson above Picasso, whom the former judges to be a scoundrel, or above Max Ernst, whom he accuses merely of

painting less well than he: I have these explanations from
his own lips. And then there is M. Soupault, and with him
we reach a new low of dishonor—let us not even concern
ourselves with the articles he signs, let us rather say a few
words about those pieces he fails to sign, those little items
of gossip that he lets "slip," while, like a rat running in
circles around his rat cage, he claims he never did any such
thing—items which appear in scandal sheets such as *Aux
ecoutes:* "M. André Breton, the leader of the Surrealist
group, has disappeared from the group's old haunts on the
rue Jacques-Callot [he is referring to the former Galerie
Surréaliste]. A Surrealist friend informs us that with him
have vanished several of the account books of the strange
Latin Quarter society for the suppression of everything.
However, we learn that M. Breton's exile is rendered less
harsh by the company of a delectable Surrealist blonde."
René Crevel and Tristan Tzara also know to whom they
are indebted for such astounding revelations about their
lives, such slanderous insinuations. Speaking personally,
I admit to feeling a certain pleasure knowing that M.
Artaud is, without the least provocation, trying to pass me
off as a dishonest man, and that M. Soupault has the gall
to accuse me of theft. Last but not least, there is M. Vitrac,
a veritable slut of ideas—let us turn "pure poetry" over to
him and that other cockroach, l'abbé Bremond—a poor
luckless wight who in his faultless ingenuousness has gone
so far as to confess that his ideal, as a man of the theater—
an ideal which, naturally, is shared by M. Artaud—was to
organize spectacles which could rival police roundups
when it came to beauty (statement of the Alfred Jarry Theater, published in the *Nouvelle revue française**). It is, as
one can see, enough to warm the cockles of one's heart.
Others, still others, moreover, who have not been included

---

*"And anyway, the hell with the Revolution!" his historical
word while a member of the Surrealist group.—No doubt.

in this line-up—either because their public activity is too unimportant or because their chicanery was exercised in a less conspicuous area, or because they tried to wiggle out of it by resorting to humor—took it upon themselves to prove to us that very few men, among those who appear, are of a caliber to meet with the Surrealists' exacting standards, and also to convince us that what, at the first sign of weakness, condemns them and sends them irrevocably to their doom—even though those who remain may be fewer in number than those who fall—is fully in favor of these standards.

It would be asking too much of me to request that I abstain any longer from commenting on all this. To the extent that it is within my powers, I judge that I am not authorized to let cads, shammers, opportunists, false witnesses, and informers run around loose. The time lost in waiting to be able to confront them can still be made up, and can only work to their disadvantage. I believe that this very precise discrimination is of itself full worthy of the goal we are pursuing, that it would be tantamount to mystical blindness were we to underestimate the dissolvent nature of these traitors' presence among us, as it would be a most unfortunate illusion of a positivist kind to presume that these traitors, who are still rank beginners, can remain unaffected by such a punitive action.*

*I could not have been more accurate: since these lines first appeared in *La Révolution surréaliste*, I have been the target of such a chorus of imprecations that, if there is in all this one thing to my credit, it is that I put off this mass slaughter for some time. If there is one accusation I have long known I was open to, it is that I am without doubt far too indulgent: outside the circle of my real friends there have been in fact clear-sighted people who have noted this. I have, it is true, occasionally been extremely tolerant when it concerns personal excuses for a specific activity and, even more, personal excuses for a specific inactivity. Provided that a small number of generally assumed ideas are not called into question, I have overlooked—I can honestly say it: overlooked—this person's insults, that

And heaven help, once again, the Surrealist idea, or any other idea which tends to assume a concrete shape, or tends to submit, as wholeheartedly as can possibly be imagined in the order of *fact,* in the same sense in which the idea of love tends to create a being, or the notion of Revolution tends to bring about the day of that Revolution, failing which these ideas would lose all meaning whatsoever—let us not lose sight of the fact that the idea of Surrealism aims quite simply at the total recovery of our

---

person's idiosyncrasies, and a third's virtual absence of talent. Let there be no mistake about it: I am trying to remedy this defect.

It did not displease me to have provided, all by myself, the twelve signers of the *Cadavre* (such was the name they gave, to no real purpose, to the pamphlet they devoted to me) with the opportuity to display a zest and animation which, for some, had ceased to exist and, for others, had never been, properly speaking, exactly overwhelming. I was able to note that the subject which they had on this occasion undertaken to deal with had at least succeeded in keeping them in a state of high excitement, which no other subject had managed to do, or come close to doing; one would presume that the most breathless among them had needed, in order to rekindle the flame of their own lives, to await my dying breath. And yet, thank you very much, I am in fine fettle: it is gratifying for me to see that the profound knowledge that certain souls have of me, from having carefully cultivated me over the years, leaves them perplexed as to the kind of "mortal" grievance they might hold against me, and only suggests to them impossible insults such as those which, as items of curiosity and to indicate the tone, I reproduce on pages 191–93 of this manifesto. To have bought a few paintings, and then refused to enslave myself to them—you can judge the seriousness of the crime—this is the sum total of which, if one is to believe these gentlemen, I am guilty . . . no: I am guilty, too, of having written this manifesto.

That the newspapers, without any prompting, and though they are more or less ill-disposed toward me, have conceded that in this instance they are scarcely able to figure out what moral blame I can be saddled with, suffices to exempt me from dwelling at any greater length on the subject and shows all too clearly the limits of the harm they can do me for me to try and convince my enemies once again of the good they can do me when they persist in trying to hurt me:

"I have just read *Un Cadavre,*" M.A.R. writes to me. "Your

psychic force by a means which is nothing other than the dizzying descent into ourselves, the systematic illumination of hidden places and the progressive darkening of other places, the perpetual excursion into the midst of forbidden territory, and that there is no real danger of its activities coming to an end so long as man still manages to distinguish an animal from a flame or a stone—heaven help, I say, the Surrealist idea from beginning to progress without its ups and downs. It is absolutely essential for us to act as though

---

friends could have done you no greater service or rendered you any greater honor.

"Their generosity, their solidarity, are striking. Twelve against one.

"You do not know me, but I am not a stranger to you. I hope you will allow me to express my esteem for you, and send you my greeting.

"If and when you decide to issue a call for others to rally behind you, this rally would be enormous and would provide you with the testimony of those who follow you, many of whom are different from you but, like you, are generous and sincere, and alone. As for me, I have over the past several years been greatly involved in what you have done, and in the thoughts you have expressed."

I am in fact awaiting, not my day, but, if I may use the term, *our* day, the day when all of us will recognize one another by this sign, that we do not swing our arms when we walk the way the others do—have you noticed, even those of us most in a hurry? My thought is not for sale. I am thirty-four years old, and more than ever I am of the opinion that my thought is capable of lashing like a burst of laughter those who never had a thought in the first place and those who, having once had one, have sold it.

I insist on appearing to be a fanatic. Anyone who deplores the establishment on the intellectual plane of customs as barbarous as those that tend to become established and who may call upon foul courtesy, must of necessity consider me as one of the men who, in the battle underway, has been the least willing to emerge from it with but a few decorative cuts and scratches. The deep, nostalgic yearning of the professors of literary history notwithstanding. For the past hundred years summonses of a most serious nature have been issued. We are at a great remove from the sweet, the charming "battle" of *Hernani*.

we were really "part of the world," in order thereafter to
dare formulate certain reservations. With all due respect
therefore to those who despair at seeing us frequently de-
scend from the heights to which they confine us, I shall try
to speak here of the political, "artistic," and polemical attitudes which can, at the tag end of 1929, be ours, and to
show, apart from this stance, what exactly certain individual behavior taken today from among the most typical and
characteristic proposes in opposition to it.

I have no idea whether there is any point in my reply-
ing here to the puerile objections of those who, calculating
the possible conquests of Surrealism in the realm of poetry,
where its initial efforts occurred, became worried when
they saw it getting involved in the social struggle and maintain that it has everything to lose therein. This is unquestionably sheer laziness on their part, or a round-about way
of expressing their desire to circumscribe us. "In the
sphere of morality," we believe that Hegel has expressed
the thought once and for all, "in the sphere of morality,
insofar as it can be distinguished from the social sphere,
one has only a formal conviction, and if we mention true
conviction it is in order to indicate the difference and to
avoid the confusion into which one can slip by considering
conviction such as it is here, that is formal conviction, as
though it were true conviction, whereas this latter occurs
initially only in social life." *(Philosophy of Law.)*

No one needs any longer to be convinced of the adequacy of this formal conviction, and to desire to have us
hold to it at all costs does no credit to the honor, to
the intelligence, or to the sincerity of our contemporaries.
Since Hegel, there is no ideological system that can, without risk of immediate collapse, fail to compensate for the
void which would be created, in thought itself, by the principle of a will acting only for its own sake and fully disposed to reflect upon itself. Once I have reminded the

reader that "loyalty" in the Hegelian sense of the term, can only be a function of the penetrability of subjective life by "substantial" life, and that, whatever their differences may be in other respects, this notion has not met with any serious objection on the part of persons with as widely differing viewpoints as Feuerbach, who ultimately denies consciousness as a specific faculty; as Marx, entirely preoccupied with the need to modify the external conditions of social life from top to bottom; as Hartmann, who managed to derive from a basically pessimistic theory of the unconscious a new and optimistic affirmation of our will to live; as Freud, with his ever-increasing emphasis on the primacy of the superego—considering all this, I doubt that anyone will be surprised to see Surrealism turn its attention, in passing, to something other than the solution of a psychological problem, however interesting that problem may be. It is in the name of the overwhelming awareness of this necessity that I believe it impossible for us to avoid most urgently posing the question of the social regime under which we live, I mean of the acceptance or the non-acceptance of this regime. It is also in the name of this awareness that I take a certain degree of pleasure in condemning, by way of digression, those refugees from Surrealism for whom what I maintain is too difficult or too much beyond their reach. No matter what they do, no matter what false cry of joy accompanies their withdrawal, no matter what vulgar disappointment they may have in store for us—and with them all those who say that one regime is as good as another, since in any event man will be vanquished—they will not make me lose sight of the fact that it is not they, but, I trust, I who will enjoy the "supreme" irony which applies to everything, *and to regimes as well,* an irony which will be denied them because it is beyond, but presupposes a priori, the entire voluntary act which consists in describing the cycle of *hypocrisy, probabilism,*

the will which desires the good, and conviction. (Hegel,
Phenomenology of the Mind.)

Surrealism, although a special part of its function is to ex-
amine with a critical eye the notions of reality and unre-
ality, reason and irrationality, reflection and impulse,
knowledge and "fatal" ignorance, usefulness and uselessness, is analogous at least in one respect with historical materialism in that it too tends to take as its point of departure
the "colossal abortion" of the Hegelian system. It seems
impossible to me to assign any limitations—economic limitations, for instance—to the exercise of a thought finally
made tractable to negation, and to the negation of negation.
How can one accept the fact that the dialectical method
can only be validly applied to the solution of social problems? The entire aim of Surrealism is to supply it with
practical possibilities in no way competitive in the most
immediate realm of consciousness. I really fail to see—some
narrow-minded revolutionaries notwithstanding—why we
should refrain from supporting the Revolution, provided
we view the problems of love, dreams, madness, art, and
religion from the same angle they do.* Now, I have no
hesitation in saying that, prior to Surrealism, nothing systematic has been done in this direction, and at the point

*Quoting me incorrectly is one of the recent means most fre-
quently employed against me. As an example, let me cite the way
in which *Monde* tried to make use of this sentence: "Claiming to
consider the problems of love, dreams, madness, art, and religion
from the same viewpoint as that of the revolutionaries, Breton has
the gall to write . . ." etc. It is true that, as anyone can read in the
next issue of the same paper: *"La Révolution surréaliste* takes us to
task in its last issue. It is common knowledge that the stupidity of
these people knows absolutely no bounds." (Especially since they
have refused your offer, without so much as taking the trouble to
answer it, to contribute to *Monde,* right? But so be it.) In the same
vein, a contributor to *Cadavre* sharply reprimands me for purportedly
having written: "I swear that I'll never wear the French uniform
again." *I'm sorry, but it isn't me.*

where we found it *the dialectical method, in its Hegelian
form, was inapplicable for us too.* There was, for us too, the
necessity to put an end to idealism properly speaking, the
creation of the word "Surrealism" would testify to this,
and, to quote Engels' classic example once again, the necessity not to limit ourselves to the childish: "The rose is a
rose. The rose is not a rose. And yet the rose is a rose," but,
if one will forgive me the parenthesis, to lure "the rose"
into a movement pregnant with less benign contradictions,
where it is, successively, the rose that comes from the garden, the one that has an unusual place in a dream, the one
impossible to remove from the "optical bouquet," the one
that can completely change its properties by passing into
automatic writing, the one that retains only those qualities
that the painter has deigned to keep in a Surrealist painting, and, finally, the one, completely different from itself,
which returns to the garden. That is a far cry from an ideal-
istic view of any kind, and we would not even bother to refute the allegation if we could cease to be the object of
attacks of simplistic materialism, attacks which stem both
from those who by base conservatism have no desire to
clarify the relations between thought and matter and from
those who, because of a revolutionary sectarianism only
partly understood, confuse, in defiance of what is required,
this materialism with the materialism that Engels basically
distinguishes from it and which he defines above all as an
"intuition of the world" called upon to prove itself and
assume concrete form:

"In the course of the evolution of philosophy, idealism
became untenable and was repudiated by modern materialism. The latter, which is the negation of negation, is not
the simple restoration of the former materialism: to the
durable substructure of the latter it adds all the thought
that philosophy and science has amassed in the course of
two thousand years, and the product of that long history
itself."

We also intend to place ourselves at a point of departure such that for us philosophy is "outclassed." It is, I think, the fate of all those for whom reality is not only important theoretically but for whom it is also a matter of life or death to make an impassioned appeal, as Feuerbach desired, to that reality: our fate to give as we do, *completely,* without any reservations, our allegiance to the principle of historical materialism, his to thrust into the face of the shocked and astounded intellectual world the idea that "man is what he eats" and that a future revolution would have a better chance of success if the people were better nourished, in this specific case with peas instead of potatoes.

Our allegiance to the principle of historical materialism . . . there is no way to play on these words. So long as that depends solely on us—I mean provided that communism does not look upon us merely as so many strange animals intended to be exhibited strolling about and gaping suspiciously in its ranks—we shall prove ourselves fully capable of doing our duty as revolutionaries. This, unfortunately, is a commitment that is of no interest to anyone but ourselves: two years ago, for instance, I was personally unable to cross the threshold of the French Communist Party headquarters, freely and unnoticed as I desired, that same threshold where so many undesirable characters, policemen and others, have the right to gambol and frolic at will. In the course of three interrogations, each of which lasted for several hours, I had to defend Surrealism from the puerile accusation that it was essentially a political movement with a strong anticommunist and counterrevolutionary orientation. It goes without saying that I hardly expected from those who had set themselves up as my judges that the basic premises of my thought would be gone through with a fine tooth comb. "If you're a Marxist," Michel Marty bawled at one of us at about that same time, "you have no need to be a Surrealist." And needless to say it was not we who

were making a point of being Surrealists in such a circumstance: this epithet had gone before us in spite of ourselves
just as the title of "relativists" might have preceded the
followers of Einstein or "psychoanalysts" those of Freud.
How is it possible not to be extremely concerned about
such a noticeable decline in the ideological level of a party
which not long ago had sprung so brilliantly armed from
two of the greatest minds of the nineteenth century! It is
an all too familiar story: the little that I can glean on this
point from my own personal experience is similar to the
rest. I was asked to make a report on the Italian situation
to this special committee of the "gas cell," which made it
clear to me that I was to stick strictly to the statistical facts
(steel production, etc.) *and above all not get involved with
ideology.* I couldn't do it.

I am, however, willing to accept that as the result of an
error I was considered in the Communist Party to be one
of the most undesirable intellectuals. My sympathies are
in fact too wholeheartedly with those who will bring about
the social Revolution for me to be any the worse for wear
in that misadventure, even temporarily. What I refuse to
accept is that, using the specific possibilities offered by the
movement, certain intellectuals I know whose moral qualities are at best subject to close scrutiny, having tried their
hand at poetry or philosophy, fall back on revolutionary
agitation and, thanks to the general confusion rampant
within the revolutionary movement, manage to convey
some vague impression that they are doing something, and
then, for convenience' sake, turn right around and disown
as loudly as they can something such as Surrealism which
has forced them to formulate most clearly whatever
thoughts they have and, what is more, obliges them to give
an accounting for what they do and justify their position
on a human level. The mind is not a weathervane; at least
it is not merely a weathervane. It is not enough to suddenly

decide that one must devote oneself to a specific activity, and it is not unusual that, when someone takes such a step, he feels himself incapable of demonstrating objectively how he arrived at that point and where precisely he had been prior to reaching it. And please don't come to me with any stories about a religious kind of conversion that some people limit themselves to claiming they have had, adding that they cannot consciously explain it. When one takes this tack there cannot even be any question of rupture, nor any solution of continuity of thought. Or else one would have to go through once more the old non-sense of grace to get there . . . I'm only joking. But it is apparent that I am extremely dubious. Let's presume I know a man: I mean, I can picture where he comes from, I have a fairly good idea which way he is going, and suddenly I'm supposed to believe that this system of references is all wrong, that this man arrived at some place other than where he was heading! And if that were possible, it would have been necessary for this man, whom we had seen only in the pleasant chrysalis stage, to have emerged from the cocoon of his thought in order to fly with his own wings. Once again I find it hard to believe. I am of the opinion that it should have been absolutely essential, not only on a practical but also on a moral plane, for each of those who thus broke away from Surrealism to subject it to an ideo-logical examination and let us know, from his viewpoint, what its worst failings were: no one even bothered to do so. The fact of the matter is that sentiments of the most mediocre sort seem, almost without exception, to have dictated these sudden shifts of attitude, and I believe that the key to the secret must be sought, as it must to explain the great lack of stability in most men, rather in a progres-sive loss of awareness than in a sudden explosion of reason, as different from the preceding explosion as skepticism is from faith. To the great satisfaction of those who balk at the control of ideas, such as it is practiced in Surrealism, this control cannot be exercised in political circles, which straightway leaves them free to give full rein to their ambition, which already existed and—this is the crucial point—to the discovery of their so-called revolutionary vocation. You should see them preaching, as though they knew it all, to the old militants; you should see them skipping, faster than their own pens could skip a line or two, the various stages of critical thought, which are here more rigorous than anywhere else: you should see them, one using a cheap little statue of Lenin to support what he is saying, another poking a finger in Trotsky's belly. What I also refuse to accept is that various people with whom we have had personal contact and whose insincerity, opportunistic tendencies, and counterrevolutionary objectives we have denounced at every possible opportunity over the past three years—having had occasion to test them at our own expense—the Morhanges, the Politzers, and the Lefèvres—should discover the means of gaining the confidence of the Party leaders to such an extent that they were able to publish, at least with their apparent approval, two issues of a *Revue de psychologie concrète* and seven issues of the *Revue marxiste* in which they take it upon themselves to enlighten us once and for all as to their baseness, the second of these three by deciding, *after one full year* of "working" and scheming together, to go and denounce the first to the Party because there is talk of doing away with concrete psychology, which does not "sell," claiming that he, Morhange, was guilty of having squandered in a single day at Monte Carlo the sum of 200,000 francs he had been entrusted with for the purpose of furthering revolutionary propaganda, and the accused, infuriated merely by the method employed, suddenly comes to cry on my shoulder, although fully admitting the truth of the accusation. It is therefore permissible today, with the help of M. Rappoport, to misuse Marx's name in France without anyone so much as raising an eyebrow.

Under these circumstances, I would be grateful if some-one would kindly tell me what has become of revolutionary morality.

One can see that the ease with which these gentle-men took such complete advantage of those who welcomed them—yesterday into the Communist Party, tomorrow into the parties opposed to Communism—was, and still is, such as to sorely tempt certain unscrupulous intellectuals, *who had also been taken into Surrealism* and who subse-quently became its most outspoken detractors.* Some, such as M. Baron, the author of poems clearly plagiarized from Apollinaire, but also a pleasure-seeker in a harum-scarum sort of way and completely lacking in any original ideas of his own, in the immense forest of Surrealism a poor little sunset over a stagnant sea—some, I say, bring to the "revolutionary" world their contribution in the form of a kind of collegiate exaltation, a "crass" ignorance embel-lished with visions of July 14. Writing in a priceless style, M. Baron informed me a few months ago of his complete

---

*However galling this realization may be in certain respects, I am of the opinion that Surrealism, *this tiny foot bridge over the abyss,* could not under any circumstances be flanked by hand rails. We have good reason for trusting in the sincerity of those whose good or evil spirit will impel them to join us. At present, it would be ask-ing too much of them to demand an unequivocal and unending allegiance, and it would amount to an inhuman prejudgment of the impossibility of any ultimate development in them of any base appe-tite. How does one test the solidity of thought of a twenty-year-old man who himself is thinking of commending himself to you solely on the basis of the purely artistic qualities of the few pages he is sub-mitting, a man whose manifest horror of constraints, if what he sub-mits proves that he has been subjected to them, does not prove that he will be incapable of inflicting them? And yet the quickening of an ageless idea infinitely depends on this very young man and the momentum that he brings to it. But what blighted hopes! Scarcely does one have the time to think of it than there is already another man who is twenty. Intellectually, true beauty is very difficult to dis-tinguish a priori from the bloom of youth.

conversion to Leninism. I have his letter, in which the most comical propositions vie with the most frightful clichés lifted straight out of *L'Humanité* and with touching professions of friendship, a letter which is available for any interested party to read. I shall not bring it up again (unless he forces me to). Others, such as M. Naville, whose insatiable penchant for notoriety we are patiently waiting to devour him—in less time than it takes to tell he has been the director of *L'Oeuf dur,* director of *La Révolution Surréaliste,* has had his hand in the student paper, *L'Etudiant d'avant-garde,* he has been the director of *Clarté,* of *La Lutte des classes,* he has come within an ace of being the director of *Camarade,* and now we see that he has become one of the leading lights of *La Verité*—others are angry with themselves for having to pay even the slightest lip service to any cause, in much the same manner as those ladies given to charitable works who, when dealing with the poor and unfortunate, dismiss them with a word or two of cheap advice. Simply by seeing M. Naville pass by, the French Communist Party, the Russian Party, most of the members of the opposition parties in every country, foremost among them the men to whom he was somehow indebted—Boris Souvarine, Marcel Fourrier, as well as Surrealism and myself—cut a sorry figure. M. Baron, who wrote *L'Allure poétique,* is to that allure what M. Naville is to the revolutionary allure. A three-month trial period in the Communist Party, M. Naville said to himself, is quite enough, since for me what matters is to make capital out of the fact that I have *left* the Party. M. Naville, or at least M. Naville's father, is very rich. (For those of my readers who do not mind a touch of the picturesque, let me add that the office of *La Lutte des classes* is located at 15, rue de Grenelle, in a building owned by M. Naville's family, which is none other than the former private mansion of the ducs de la Rochefoucauld.) Such considerations strike me as less unimportant than ever. I note, in fact, that at

the time M. Morhange decided to found *La Revue marxiste,* he was subsidized to the tune of 5,000,000 francs in
that venture by M. Friedmann. It matters not that poor
luck at the roulette table forced him to pay back, not long
thereafter, the greater part of that sum, the fact still remains that it was thanks to that exorbitant financial assistance that he succeeded in usurping the position he holds
and in having the incompetence for which he is notorious
overlooked. It was also by subscribing to a certain number
of shares for the venture "Les Revues" upon which *La
Revue marxiste* was dependent that M. Baron, who had
just come into an inheritance, was able to believe that
broader horizons were opening up before him. Now, when
M. Naville informed us, some months ago, of his intention
to publish *Le Camarade,* a newspaper which, in his opinion, filled the need of giving new vigor to criticism on the
part of the opposition, but which in reality was first and
foremost meant to enable him to take one of those quiet
leaves, for which he is famous, from Fourrier, who was too
perspicacious for M. Naville's own good, I was curious to
learn from his own lips who was underwriting that publication, a publication of which, as I have said, he was to be
the director—and the only director, I might add. Was it
those mysterious "friends" with whom long and very amusing conversations are engaged on the last page of every
paper and whom they try to interest so deeply in the price
of paper? No. It was, purely and simply, M. Pierre Naville
and his brother, who contributed 15,000 out of a total of
20,000 francs. The balance was furnished by the so-called
"friends" of Souvarine, whose names, M. Naville was
forced to confess, he did not even know. You can see that,
in order to impose one's point of view in circles which,
on this point, ought to be extremely careful, it is less important that this viewpoint be of a nature to be imposed
than that one be the son of a banker. M. Naville, who art-
fully employs the method of playing one person off against

the other, with classically predictable results in mind, will not shrink from any means whatsoever, that is obvious, in order to attain his goal, which is to dictate revolutionary opinion. But, as in that same allegorical forest where not long ago I saw M. Baron displaying his tadpole-like charm, there have already been a few off-days for this shady-looking boa constrictor, there is fortunately a good possibility that trainers of the talent and force of Trotsky, and even of Souvarine, will ultimately get the better of the eminent reptile. For the moment, all we know is that he is on his way back from Constantinople in the company of the little bird Francis Gérard. Travel, which is so conducive to shaping the character of our youth, is not changing the shape of M. Naville Sr.'s pocketbook. It is also of prime importance to go and turn Leon Trotsky against the only friends he has. One last question, quite platonic, addressed to M. Naville: WHO is subsidizing *La Verité,* the organ of Communist opposition where your name grows larger week by week and is now displayed grandly on the first page? Thank you.

If I deemed it worthwhile to devote considerable time to such subjects, it was, first of all, in order to show that, contrary to what they would have us believe, all of our former collaborators, who today claim that as far as Surrealism is concerned it is good riddance to bad rubbish. have without exception been expelled by us: it seems not completely beside the point to inform the reader why. We also dwelt at some length on this matter in order to demonstrate that, if Surrealism considers itself ineluctably linked, because of certain affinities I have indicated, to the movement of Marxist thought and to that movement alone, it refuses and will no doubt long refuse to choose between the two very broad currents which, at the present time, pit against one another men who, although they may differ as to tactics, have nonetheless proved themselves to be out and out revolutionaries. It is not at the very moment when Trotsky, in a letter dated September 25, 1929, agrees that in the International "it is obvious that a change in the official direction toward the left is taking place," and when, for all intents and purposes, he fully and wholeheartedly supports the requests made by Racovsky, Cassior, and Okoudjava to be taken back into the fold, a request whose acceptance might lead to his own reintegration, it is not at such a moment that we intend to show ourselves to be more intractable than he. It is not at the very moment when the mere contemplation of the most painful conflict that exists leads to, on the part of such men—forgetting momentarily, at least publicly, their ultimate reservations— a new closing of ranks, that we intend, however peripherally, to aggravate the sentimental wound of repression the way M. Panaït Istrati is doing or the way M. Naville is doing by congratulating the former, while at the same time chiding him gently: "Istrati, it would have been preferable for you not to have published a fragment of your book in a magazine such as *La Nouvelle revue française*,"* etc. Our getting involved in such matters is meant merely to caution the serious-minded against a handful of individuals whom we know from experience to be fools, frauds, or artful schemers but who, in any case, have only the worst intentions as far as the revolutionary movement is concerned. This is about the extent of what we feel bound to say in this area for the present. We are the first to regret that it is so little.

In order for such divergences, about-faces, and betrayals of confidence to be possible on the very level on which I have

*Concerning Panaït Istrati and the Roussakov affair, see *La Nouvelle revue française*, October 1, 1929; and *La Verité*, October 11, 1929.

just put myself, things in general must most certainly be in a sorry state and one must come to the sad conclusion that it is hardly possible to count upon the disinterested involvement of more than a few men at one time. If the revolutionary task itself, with all the discipline that its accomplishment presupposes, does not inherently separate immediately the wheat from the chaff, the sincere from the insincere; if, to its own great detriment, it has no choice but to wait for a series of events to do the job of unmasking the latter and adorn the naked faces of the former with a reflection of immortality, how does anyone expect the situation not to be even worse when it comes to matters not directly related to this task and, to take a concrete example, when it comes to the Surrealist effort insofar as this latter does not coincide perfectly with the former, that is, the revolutionary, effort? It is normal for Surrealism to appear in the midst of, and perhaps *at the cost of,* an uninterrupted succession of lapses and failures, of zigzags and defections which require a constant reevaluation of its original premises, that is the reminder of the initial principle of its activity together with a questioning of the *fickle tomorrow* according to which hearts fall in and out of love. Not every effort has been made, I must say, to bring this venture to a successful conclusion, were it only by utilizing to their utmost the means which were defined as being specifically ours or by profoundly testing the modes of investigation which, at the beginning of the movement with which we are concerned, were advocated. The problem of social action, I would like to repeat and to stress this point, is only one of the forms of a more general problem which Surrealism set out to deal with, and that is *the problem of human expression in all its forms.* Whoever speaks of expression speaks of language first and foremost. It should therefore come as no surprise to anyone to see Surrealism almost exclusively concerned with the question of language at first, nor should it surprise anyone to see it return to language, after some foray into another area, as though for the pleasure of traveling in conquered territory. Nothing, in fact, can any longer prevent this country from being largely conquered. The hordes of words which, whatever one may say, Dada and Surrealism set about to let loose as though opening a Pandora's box, are not of a kind to withdraw again for no good purpose. They will slowly but surely make their way into the silly little towns and cities of literature such as it is still being taught in this day and age and, here confusing without any difficulty the poor and rich sections, they will calmly consume a great number of towers. The population, taking the tact that the only edifice which has, thanks to our efforts, been seriously shaken to date is that of poetry, is not overly on its guard; it is setting up insignificant little defensive dikes here and there. People pretend not to pay too much attention to the fact that the logical mechanism of the sentence alone reveals itself to be increasingly powerless to provoke the emotive shock in man which really makes his life meaningful. By comparison, the products of this spontaneous, or *more* spontaneous, direct or *more* direct, activity, such as those which Surrealism offers him in ever-increasing numbers in the form of books, paintings, and films, are products which he looked at dumbfounded at first, but which he now surrounds himself with, and begins, more or less timidly, to rely on to shake up his settled ways of thinking. I know: this man is not yet *every* man, and we have to allow him time to become so. But consider how far a handful of completely modern works, about which the very least one can say is that a particularly unhealthy atmosphere pervades them, has already wormed their way, admirably and perversely, into the public consciousness: Baudelaire, Rimbaud (despite the reservations I have mentioned), Huysmans, Lautréamont, to mention only poetry. Let us not be afraid to make a law of this insalubrity. It must never be said that we did not do everything within our power to annihilate this ridiculous illusion of happiness and *understanding* which, to its ever-lasting glory, the nineteenth century denounced. To be sure, we have not ceased to love with fanatical zeal these miasma-ridden rays of sunshine. But, at a time in history when the officials in France are getting ready to celebrate grotesquely the hundredth anniversary of romanticism with public ceremonies, we say, and insist on saying, that this romanticism which we are today willing to consider as the tail, *but then only as an amazingly prehensile tail,* by its very essence remains unmitigated in its negation of these officials and these ceremonies, and we say that to be a hundred is for it to be still in the flower of its youth, that what has been wrongly called its heroic period can no longer honestly be considered as anything but the first cry of a newborn child which is only beginning to make its desires known through us and which, if one is willing to admit that what was thought "classically" before it came into being, was tantamount to good, undeniably wishes *naught but evil.*

Whatever the evolution of Surrealism may have been in the realm of politics, however urgently the order may have been passed on to us to count only upon the proletarian Revolution for the liberation of mankind—*the primary condition of the mind*—I can say in all honesty that we did not find any valid reason to change our minds about the means of expression which are characteristically ours and which, we have been able to verify through usage, served us well. Let anyone who cares to condemn this or that specifically Surrealist image that I may have used at random in the course of a preface, it will not release him from further obligations as far as images are concerned. "This family is a litter of dogs."* When, by quoting such a sentence out of context, anyone provokes a good deal of gloat-

*Rimbaud.

ing, all he will actually have done is assemble a great many ignoramuses. One will not have succeeded in sanctioning neo-naturalistic procedures at the expense of ours, that is, in deprecating everything which, since naturalism, has contributed to the most important conquests the mind has made. I am here reminded of the answers I gave, in September 1928, to these two questions that were asked me:

1) Do you believe that literary and artistic output is a purely individual phenomenon? Don't you think that it can or must be the reflection of the main currents which determine the economic and social evolution of humanity?

2) Do you believe in a literature and an art which express the aspirations of the working class? Who, in your opinion, are the principal representatives of this literature and this art?

My answers were as follows:

1) Most certainly, the same goes for literary or artistic output as for any intellectual phenomenon, in that the only question one can rightly raise concerning it is that of the *sovereignty of thought.* That is, it is impossible to answer your question affirmatively or negatively, and all one can say is that the only observable philosophical attitude in such a case consists in playing up "the contradiction (which does exist) between the nature of human thought which we take to be absolute and the reality of that thought in a crowd of individuals of limited thought: this is a problem that can be resolved only through infinite progress, through the series, at least virtually infinite, of successive generations of mankind. In this sense human thought is sovereign and is not; and its capacity to know is both limitless and limited. Sovereign and limitless by its nature, its vocation, potentially, and with respect to its ultimate goal in history; but lacking sovereignty and limited in each of its applications and in any of its several states."* This thought, in the area where you ask me to

---

*Friedrich Engels, *La Morale et le droit. Vérités éternelles.*

consider such and such a specific expression in relation to it, can only oscillate between the awareness of its inviolate autonomy and that of its utter dependence. In our own time, artistic and literary production appears to me to be wholly sacrificed to the needs that this drama after a century of truly harrowing poetry and philosophy (Hegel, Feuerbach, Marx, Lautréamont, Rimbaud, Jarry, Freud, Chaplin, Trotsky) has to work itself out. Under these circumstances, to say that this output can or must reflect the main currents which determine the economic and social evolution of humanity would be offering a rather unrefined judgment, implying the purely circumstantial awareness of thought and giving little credit to its fundamental nature: both unconditioned and conditioned, utopian and realistic, finding its end in itself and aspiring only to serve, etc.

2) I do not believe in the present possibility of an art or literature which expresses the aspirations of the working class. If I refuse to believe in such a possibility, it is because, in any prerevolutionary period the writer or artist, who of necessity is a product of the bourgeoisie, is by definition incapable of translating these aspirations. I do not deny that he can get some idea of these aspirations and that, in rather exceptional moral circumstances, he may be capable of conceiving of the relativity of any cause in terms of the proletarian cause. I consider it to be a matter of sensitivity and integrity for him. This does not mean, however, that he will elude the remarkable doubt, inherent in the means of expression which are his, which forces him to consider from a very special angle, within himself and for himself alone, the work he intends to do. In order to be viable, this work demands to be *situated* in relationship to certain other already existing works and must, in its turn, open up new paths. Making all due allowances, it would, for example, be just as pointless to protest against the assertion of a poetic determinism, whose laws cannot

be promulgated, as against that of dialectical materialism. Speaking personally, I am convinced that the two kinds of evolution are strictly similar and, moreover, that they have at least this much in common: *they are both unsparing.* Just as Marx' forecasts and predictions—as far as almost all the external events which have transpired since his death are concerned—have proved to be accurate, I can see nothing which would invalidate a single word of Lautréamont's with respect to events of interest only to the mind. By comparison, any attempt to explain social phenomena other than by Marx is to my mind as erroneous as any effort to defend or illustrate a so-called "proletarian" literature and art at a time in history when no one can fairly claim any real kinship with the proletarian culture, for the very excellent reason that this culture does not yet exist, even under proletarian regimes. "The vague theories about proletarian culture, conceived by analogy with and antithesis to bourgeois culture, result from comparisons between the proletariat and the bourgeoisie, in which the critical spirit is wholly lacking. . . . There can be no doubt but that a time will come in the evolution of the new society when economics, culture, and art will have the greatest freedom of movement—of progress. But on this subject we can only offer the most fantastical conjectures. In a society which will have rid itself of the overwhelming concern of providing for its daily bread, where communal laundries will wash everyone's clothes, where the children—all the children—well fed, healthy, and happy will absorb the basics of science and art as they do the air and sunlight, where there will no longer be any 'useless mouths,' where man's liberated egotism—an extraordinary force—will be concerned only with the knowledge, the transformation, and the betterment of the universe—in this society, the dynamic nature of the culture will not be comparable to anything the world has ever known in the past. But we shall reach this stage only after a long and painful transition, which lies almost entirely before us."*

These admirable remarks seem to me to answer once and for all the charges made by certain fraudulent and wily characters who in France today, under the dictatorship of Poincaré, pass themselves off as proletarian writers and artists, under the pretense that in what they paint or write there is nothing but ugliness and misery, as well as to answer those who cannot conceive of anything beyond base reportage, the funerary monument, and the sketch of prison, who know of nothing else to do but wave the ghost of Zola in front of our eyes—Zola whom they pick over like vultures without however diminishing him to the slightest degree and who, shamelessly castigating here everything that lives and breathes, suffers, hopes, and despairs, are opposed to any kind of serious research, do their level best to prevent any discovery and, under the pretense of giving what they know cannot be received—the immediate and general knowledge of what is being created—are not only the worst contemners of the mind but also the most certain counterrevolutionaries.

It is unfortunate, I started to say a while back, that more systematic and sustained efforts, such as those Surrealism has consistently called for—have not been made in the sphere of automatic writing, for example, and the description of dreams. In spite of our insistence that texts of this kind be included in Surrealist publications, and despite the prominent place they do occupy in certain works, we are forced to admit that the interest they arouse is not always sustained, or that they seem a little too much like "virtuoso pieces." The appearance of an obvious cliché in the middle of one of these texts is also completely prejudicial to the

*Leon Trotsky, "Revolution and Culture," in *Clarté,* November 1, 1923.

kind of conversion we wanted to bring about through
them. The fault for this state of affairs stems from the rampant carelessness of the vast majority of their authors who
were generally content to let their pens run rampant over
the paper without making the least effort to observe what
was going on inside themselves—this disassociation being
nonetheless easier to grasp and more interesting to consider than that of reflected writing—or to gather together,
more or less arbitrarily, oneirical elements with a view to
emphasizing their picturesque quality rather than usefully
revealing their interplay. Such confusion, of course, is of a
kind calculated to deprive us of the full benefit that this
sort of thing might provide us with. The main value they
offer Surrealism, in fact, is that they are likely to reveal to
us specific *logical* expanses, or more precisely those in which
the logical faculty, hitherto exercised to the full extent of
its powers in the realm of consciousness, does not act. What
am I saying! Not only do these logical expanses remain unexplored, the fact is that we still know as little as we ever
did about the origin of the *voice* which it is everyone's prerogative to hear, if only he will, a voice which converses
with us most specifically about something other than what
we believe we are thinking, and upon occasion assumes
a serious tone when we feel most light-hearted or deals in
idle prattle when we are unhappiest. This voice, moreover,
does not submit to the simple need for contradiction. . . .
While I am alone at my table, it talks to me about a man
who emerges from a ditch without, of course, telling me
who he is; if I become insistent, it will portray him for me
fairly clearly: no, definitely, I do not know this man. The
time it takes to note this fact, and already the man is lost. *I
listen,* I'm far from the *Second Manifesto of Surrealism.* . . .
There's no point in offering a multitude of examples; it is
the voice that speaks in this way. . . . Because the examples
drink . . . Sorry, I don't understand either. What would be
truly interesting would be to know to what extent this

voice is authorized, for example, to find fault with me: there's no point in offering a multitude of examples (and we know, since *Les Chants de Maldoror,* how unfettered and marvelous these critical intrusions can be). When the voice answers me that the examples drink (?) is this a way for the power which assumes it to conceal itself, and if this is true then why does it conceal itself? Was it on the verge of making itself clear at the moment I hastened to take it by surprise without grasping it? A problem such as this is not only of interest to Surrealism. No one, when he expresses himself, does anything more than come to terms with the possibility of a very obscure reconciliation between what he knew he had to say with what, on the same subject, he didn't know he had to say and nonetheless said. The most controlled thought is incapable of doing without this aid which, from the viewpoint of rigor, is undesirable. There really is torpedoing of the idea in the midst of the sentence which is articulating it, even if the sentence were to be free of any charming liberty taken with its meaning. Dadaism had especially wanted to draw attention to this torpedoing. We know that Surrealism, through its appeal to automatism, was involved in sheltering from this torpedoing a building of some sort: something like a Flying Dutchman (the image, which certain people thought they could use against me, however overused it may be, seems good to me, and I use it once again).

It is incumbent on us, I was therefore saying, to try to see more and more clearly what is transpiring unbeknownst to man in the depths of his mind, even if he should begin to hold his own vortex against us. We are, in all this, a far cry from wanting to reduce the portion of what can be untangled, and nothing could be farther from our minds than being sent back to the scientific study of "complexes." To be sure, Surrealism, which as we have seen deliberately opted for the Marxist doctrine in the realm of social problems, has no intention of minimizing

Freudian doctrine as it applies to the evaluation of ideas:
on the contrary, Surrealism believes Freudian criticism to
be the first and only one with a really solid basis. While it
is impossible for Surrealism to remain indifferent to the debate which, in its presence, pits qualified practitioners of
various psychoanalytical tendencies against one another—
just as it is obliged to consider daily and with impassioned
interest the struggle taking place within the leadership of
the International—it need not interfere in a controversy
which, it would seem, cannot long pursue a useful course
except among practitioners. This is not the area in which
Surrealism intends to point up the result of its personal experiments. But since by their very nature those individuals
who are drawn to Surrealism are especially interested in
the Freudian concept which affects the greater part of their
deep concerns as men—the concern to create, to destroy
artistically—I mean the definition of the phenomenon
known as "sublimation,"* Surrealism basically asks these

*The more one delves into the pathology of nervous illnesses,
says Freud, the more one perceives the connections which link them
to other phenomena of man's psychic life, even to those to which we
attach the greatest importance. And in spite of what we pretend, we
see how little reality satisfies us; thus, beneath the pressure of our
interior repressions, we create within ourselves a whole fantasy life
which, by carrying out our desires, makes up for the insufficiencies
of our actual existence. The energetic person who succeeds ["who
succeeds": it goes without saying that I leave to Freud the responsibility for this terminology] is the one who manages to turn these
desire-fantasies into reality. When this transmutation fails either
because of external circumstances or the weakness of the individual,
the person turns away from reality: he retires into the happier world
of his dreams: in case of sickness, he transforms the contents of them
into symptoms. Under certain favorable conditions, he can still find
some other way to move from his fantasies to reality, instead of stray-
ing definitively away from it by regression into the realm of infancy;
I believe that if he has *any artistic gift,* which is psychologically so
mysterious, he can, rather than transform his dreams into symptoms,
transform them into artistic creations. Thus can he escape the fate
of neurosis and, through this detour, make contact with reality.

people to bring to the accomplishment of their mission a new *awareness,* to perform an act of self-observation, which in their case is of very exceptional value, to compensate for what is insufficient about the penetration of so-called "artistic" states of mind by men who for the most part are not artists but doctors. Moreover, Surrealism demands that, by taking a path opposite from the one we have just seen them follow, those who possess, in the Freudian sense, the "precious faculty" we are referring to, bend their efforts toward studying in this light the most complex mechanism of all, "inspiration," and, from the moment they cease thinking of it as something sacred, Surrealism demands that, however confident they are of its extraordinary virtue, they dream only of making it shed its final ties, or even— something no one had ever dared conceive of—of making it submit to them. There is no point in resorting to subtleties on this point; we all know well enough what inspiration is. There is no way of mistaking it; it is what has provided for the supreme needs of expression in every time and clime. It is commonly said that it is either present or it is not, and if it is absent, nothing of what, by way of comparison, is suggested by the human cleverness that interest, discursive intelligence, and the talent acquired by dint of hard work obliterate, can make up for it. We can easily recognize it by that total possession of our mind which, at rare intervals, prevents our being, for every problem posed, the plaything of one rational solution rather than some other equally rational solution, by that sort of short circuit it creates between a given idea and a respondent idea (written, for example). Just as in the physical world, a short circuit occurs when the two "poles" of a machine are joined by a conductor of little or no resistance. In poetry and in painting, Surrealism has done everything it can and more to increase these short circuits. It believes, and it will never believe in anything more wholeheartedly, in reproducing artificially this ideal moment when man, in the grips of a particular emotion, is suddenly seized by this something "stronger than himself" which projects him, in self-defense, into immortality. If he were lucid, awake, he would be terrified as he wriggled out of this tight situation. The whole point for him is not to be free of it, for him to go on talking the entire time this mysterious ringing lasts: it is, in fact, the point at which he ceases to belong to himself that he belongs to us. These products of psychic activity, as far removed as possible from the desire to make sense, as free as possible of any ideas of responsibility which are always prone to act as brakes, as independent as possible of everything which is not "the passive life of the intelligence"— these products which automatic writing and the description of dreams represent* offer at one and the same time the ad-

---

*If I feel bound to emphasize so strongly the value of these two procedures, it is not because they seem to constitute in themselves the intellectual panacea but because, for a practiced observer, they are less prone to confusion and trickery than any others and because they are still the best thing we have found to give man some fair idea of his resources. It goes without saying that the conditions which life imposes upon us make it all but impossible to perform without interruption a thought-exercise apparently so gratuitous. Those who have indulged in such attempts unreservedly, no matter how far some of them may subsequently have fallen, will not have been one day projected so fruitlessly into the heart of *interior fairyland*. Compared to this enchanted world, a return to any premeditated activity of the mind, however much their contemporaries swear by it, will seem to them but a sad spectacle.

These very direct means, once again available to everyone, which we persist in promoting the moment it is a question, not basically now of producing works of art, but of casting light upon the unrevealed and yet revealable portion of our being wherein all beauty, all love, all virtue that we scarcely recognize in ourselves, shine with great intensity—these direct means are not the only ones. In particular, it seems that at the present time there are great expectations for certain techniques of pure deception whose application to art and life will result in fixing the attention, not any longer on what is real, or on the imaginary, but, how shall I express it, *on the other side of reality*. One enjoys imagining novels that cannot

vantage of being unique in providing elements of appreciation of great style to a body of criticism which, in the realm of art, reveals itself to be strangely helpless, of permitting a general reclassification of lyrical values, and of proposing a key capable of opening indefinitely that box of many bottoms called man, a key that dissuades him from turning back, for reasons of self-preservation, when in the darkness he bumps into doors, locked from the outside, of the "beyond," of reality, of reason, of genius, and of love. A day will come when we will no longer allow ourselves to use it in such cavalier fashion, as we have done, with its palpable proofs of an existence other than the one we think we are living. We will then be surprised to realize that, having come so close to seizing *the truth,* most of us have been careful to provide ourselves with an alibi, be it literary or any other, rather than throwing ourselves, without knowing how to swim, into the water, and without believing in the phoenix, plunging into the fire to reach this truth.

The fault, I repeat, will not have been all ours indiscriminately. In dealing with the lack of discipline and purity in

---

end, as there are problems without solutions. When will we see a novel in which the characters, copiously defined by a few unimportant characteristics, will act in a completely predictable manner toward an unpredictable result, or, conversely, another novel in which psychology will give up trying perfunctorily to perform its great useless duties, at the expense of people and events in order really to *hold* a fraction of a second between two blades and to surprise there the seeds of the incidents; or that other novel in which the verisimilitude of the setting will, for the first time, stop concealing from us the strange symbolic life which objects, the most commonplace as well as the most clearly defined, have only in dreams; or another in which the construction will be extremely simple but the words generally used to describe weariness will be employed to describe a scene of kidnapping, or *happy* words used to describe, with great precision, a storm, etc. Anyone who is of the opinion that it is high time to put an end to these insulting "realistic" insanities will have no problem making up his own selection.

which these elementary efforts have to some extent foundered, I intend fully to point out what, at the present time, is contaminated in what passes, throughout far too many works, as the valid expression of Surrealism. I refuse to accept, for the most part, the suitability of this expression to this idea. It will fall to the innocence and to the anger of some future men to extract from Surrealism what cannot fail to be still alive, to restore, at the cost of considerable confusion, Surrealism to its proper goal. Meanwhile, it will be enough for my friends and me to straighten up, to some slight degree, as I am doing here, the silhouette of Surrealism uselessly burdened with flowers but still proud. The very slight extent to which Surrealism now eludes us is not, moreover, something which ought to make us fear that it may be used against us by others. It is, of course, a great pity that Alfred de Vigny was such a pretentious person and so utterly stupid, that Théophile Gautier's old age was marred by his senility, but it is not a great pity for *romanticism*. It saddens us to think that Mallarmé was a petit bourgeois of the first water or that there were actually people who believed that Moréas was a serious artist, but, assuming that symbolism was something, one would not feel sad *for symbolism,* etc. By the same token, I do not believe there is any serious problem as far as Surrealism is concerned because it has suffered the loss of this individual or that, however brilliant, and especially in the case of the one who, after he has left the fold, is no longer whole and indicates by his every action that he is desirous of returning to normality. Thus it is that, after having allowed him an incredible amount of time to recover from what we hoped was only a temporary abuse of his critical faculties, I believe that we are now forced to say to Robert Desnos that, as we no longer expect anything whatsoever from him, we have no choice but to free him from any commitments he may have made in the past with us. I must confess that it saddens me to some degree to do this. In contrast to the early traveling companions, whom we have never thought of trying to retain, Desnos played an essential, an unforgettable, role in the evolution of Surrealism, and the present moment is probably more ill chosen than any other to deny it. (But Chirico too, isn't that true, and yet . . .). Books such as *Deuil pour deuil, La Liberté ou l'amour, C'est les bottes de sept lieues cette phrase: Je me vois,* and everything that myth, which is less beautiful than reality, will grant Desnos in recompense for an activity that was not devoted solely to writing books, will long militate in favor of what he is now in a position to combat. Let it suffice to recall that this happened four or five years ago. Since then, Desnos, ill served in this respect by those same powers who for a while had supported him, and about whom he seems still unaware that they were forces of dark-ness, unfortunately took it into his head to act on the plane of reality where he was no more or less than a man poorer and more alone than the next, like those who have seen, I say, *seen* what others are afraid to see and who, rather than live what is, are condemned to live what "was" and what "will be." "Lack of philosophical background," as he declares today, ironically—not lack of philosophical background but perhaps *lack of philosophical spirit* and also, as a result, lack of knowing how to prefer one's inner character rather than this or that exterior historical character who—really! what a childish idea: to be Robespierre or Hugo! All those who know him know that this is what will have kept Desnos from being Desnos—he thought he could indulge with impunity in one of the most dangerous activities that exists, journalism, and, because of it, fail to respond personally to a handful of serious demands which Surrealism, in the course of its evolution, found itself faced with: for instance, to go along with Marxism or not. Now that this individualistic method has proved itself, now that this journalistic activity of Desnos' has completely consumed the other, we have no choice but to draw our own conclusions on the subject, however cruel it may be to us. I say that this activity, which presently exceeds the limits within which it was already barely tolerable *(Paris-Soir, Le Soir, Le Merle)* needs to be denounced as highly confusing. The article entitled "The Mercenaries of Opinion," tossed as a gift of joyful accession into the remarkable garbage pail known as *Bifur,* is in itself sufficiently eloquent: in it Desnos passes judgment on himself, and in what a style! "An editor's habits are many and varied. He is generally an employee, relatively punctual, reasonably lazy," etc., etc. In it one finds due homage paid to M. Merle, to Clemenceau, and this confession, more distressing than all the rest, to wit: "The newspaper is an ogre that kills all who make it live."

After that, how can one be surprised to read in some newspaper or other this ridiculous item of gossip: "Robert Desnos, the Surrealist poet, whom Man Ray asked to write the screenplay of his film, *Etoile de mer,* made a trip with me last year to Cuba. And do you know what Robert Desnos recited to me beneath the tropical stars? Alexandrine verses, Al-ex-an-drines! And what is more (but don't breathe a word of this to anyone, for you might ruin the reputation of this charming poet), when these Alexandrines were not by Jean Racine, they were his own."

Actually, I think that these Alexandrines go hand in glove with the prose that appeared in *Bifur.* This joke, which ended up by no longer being even dubious, began the day when Desnos, vying with M. Ernest Raynaud in this parody, thought that he could invent out of whole cloth a poem by Rimbaud which had never been found. This poem, with no indication that it was of spurious origin, unfortunately appeared under the title "Les Veilleurs" by Arthur Rimbaud as the lead poem in *La Liberté ou l'amour.* I do not believe that this poem, or any of those of the same kind that followed, add one whit to Desnos' glory. I leave it up to the specialists, not only to determine whether or not these verses are bad (false, padded, and *empty*), but also to assert that, from the Surrealist point of view, they give every indication of a ridiculous ambition and an unforgivable lack of understanding of the goals of poetry today.

This lack of understanding on the part of Desnos and a few others is in fact taking such an aggressive turn that it absolves me from carping at him at length. As final proof, I shall merely note in passing the unspeakable idea they had to use as a sign for a "nightclub" in Montparnasse, the customary haunt of their nocturnal exploits, the only name which, since time began, constituted a pure challenge to everything stupid, base, and loathsome on earth: *Maldoror*.

"It seems that things are at sixes and sevens with the Surrealists. Messieurs Breton and Aragon are reported to have become unbearable by the way in which they act as if they were a couple of commanding officers. I even have it on good authority that their conduct can only be compared to two old top sergeants who have just reenlisted. You know how it is. There are some people who don't like that kind of thing. In short, a few of them got together and decided to open a new nightclub in Montparnasse which they baptized *Maldoror*. They come right out and say that *Maldoror*, for a Surrealist, is like Jesus Christ for a Christian, and that seeing a sign like that is certainly going to shock and offend these two gentlemen, Breton and Aragon."* The author of the above lines, who paid a visit to the premises, with no malice intended and in the casual style that befits his observations, further reports: " . . . Just then a Surrealist arrived, which made one more customer. And what a customer! It was none other than Robert Desnos! He was a great disappointment, for all he ordered was a freshly squeezed lemonade. In response to the general consternation, he explained in a thick voice:

**Candide,* January 9, 1930.

'Thas all I can take. Haven't breathed a sober breath
in two days.' "

What a pity!

Obviously it would be far too easy for me to turn to
good account the fact that today they think they cannot
attack me without at the same time "attacking" Lautréamont, that is the unattackable.

Desnos and his friends will surely not mind if I reproduce here, with complete equanimity, the few basic
sentences which constitute my reply to an already ancient
inquiry by the *Disque verte*, sentences whose wording I
need not change at all and whose sentiments, they cannot
deny, they then approved of wholeheartedly:

"Whatever you may attempt, very few people let
themselves be guided by that unforgettable light: *Maldoror*, and the hermetic *Poems*, that light one need not
have known in order truly to make one's way, and to be.
The opinion of others matters little. Lautréamont a man,
a poet, even a prophet: come now! The so-called literary
necessity to which you appeal will not succeed in divesting
the Mind of that *summons*, the most dramatic that ever
existed, and, of that which remains and will always remain the negation of all sociability, of all human constraints, it will not succeed in creating a precious exchange
value and a random stepping stone of progress. Literature
and philosophy today struggle vainly in order not to take
into account a revelation which condemns them. It is the
whole world which, without realizing it, is going to suffer
the consequences, and it is for no other reason that the
most clear-sighted, the purest, among us owe it to themselves to die *in the breech*. Liberty, Sir . . ."

There is, in a negation as vulgar as the association of
the word "Maldoror" with the existence of a cheap bar
enough to restrain me from this time forth from voicing
the least judgment as to what Desnos may write. Let us
look no further, in the realm of poetry, than that spree of

quatrains.* This, then, is where the excessive use of the verbal gift can lead to, when it is destined to veil a serious lack of thought and to renew ties with the ridiculous tradition of the poet "in the clouds"; at a time when this tradition is broken and, whatever a few belated rhymers may think, well broken, when it has given way before the combined efforts of these men whom we put forward because they really wanted *to say* something—Borel, the Nerval of *Aurélia,* Baudelaire, Lautréamont, the Rimbaud of 1874-1875, the early Huysmans, the Apollinaire of the "poèmes-conversations" and the "Quelconqueries," it is painful to think that one of those whom we took to be one of our own decided to play a "Bateau ivre" game with us, completely from the outside, or to lull us back to sleep to the sound of the "Stances." It is true that the problems of poetry have, over the past few years, ceased to be posed from a basically formal angle, and, to be sure, we are more interested in judging the subversive quality of a work such as that of Aragon, Crevel, Eluard, or Péret, bearing in mind the poem's own internal light and what, because of that light, the impossible yields to the possible, the allowable steals from the forbidden, than in knowing why such and such a writer occasionally makes up his mind to begin a new paragraph. One reason less why anyone should come and talk to us in this day and age about the caesura: why shouldn't there also be among us partisans of a specific technique of "vers libre," and why should we not go dig up the corpse of Robert de Souza? Desnos cannot be serious: we are not ready to reassure the world so easily.

Every day brings us new indications of disappointments which we must have the courage to admit, if for no other reason than as a measure of mental hygiene, and inscribe

*Cf. *Corps et biens* (Nouvelle Revue Française, 1930), the final pages.

in the horribly debit side of the ledger of life. With all too
few exceptions, they concern people in whom, far too generously, we placed our trust and hope. Free Duchamps was
not to give up the game he was playing, in the vague vicinity of the war years, for an interminable game of *chess*
which may give a strange idea of a mind loath to serve but
also—always the execrable Harrar—seeming afflicted with a
generous dose of skepticism insofar as it refuses to say why.
Even less do we forgive M. Ribemont-Dessaignes for having offered as a successor to *L'Empereur de Chine* a series
of odious little detective stories, which he even openly signs
"Dessaignes," in the most vulgar cinema magazines. Finally, I am concerned to hear that Picabia might be on
the verge of renouncing an attitude of almost pure provocation and rage which we found difficult at times to reconcile with our own but which, at least in poetry and
painting, always seemed to make admirable sense: "To
buckle down to one's work, to bring to it the sublime, the
aristocratic 'craftsmanship' which has never stood in the
way of poetic inspiration and which alone allows a work
to remain young after the passage of centuries . . . we must
be *careful* . . . we must close ranks and, among conscien-
tious souls, not try to play dirty tricks on one another . . .
we must favor the flowering of the ideal," etc. Even making
certain allowances for *Bifur,* where these lines appeared,
is this really the Picabia we know who is speaking in this
manner?

This said, we would by way of compensation like to give
due credit to a man from whom we have been separated
for many long years, the expression of whose thought still
interests us, a man whose concerns, to judge by what we
have still been able to read by him, are not all that far
from our own, and, under these circumstances, there is
perhaps good reason to think that our misunderstanding

with him was not based on anything quite so serious as we may have been led to think. It is entirely possible that Tzara, who, early in 1922, at the time of the liquidation of "Dada" as a movement, no longer saw eye to eye with us insofar as the practical methods we should use in the pursuit of a common goal were concerned, was the victim of excessive charges which we, because of this lack of agreement, leveled against him—as he leveled equally outrageous charges against us—and that, during the notorious performance of the *Coeur à barbe,* in order for our rupture to take the turn we know it did, all that was required was for him to make some untoward gesture, the meaning of which, he claims—*and I only recently learned this*—we misinterpreted. (It must be admitted that the main object of "Dada" spectacles was always to create as much confusion as possible, and that in the mind of the organizer the whole idea was to bring the misunderstanding between participants and public to its highest pitch. It should be borne in mind that not all of us, that evening, were on the same side.) Personally, I am perfectly willing to accept this version, and I see no other reason, therefore, not to insist, insofar as all those who were involved are concerned, that these incidents be forgotten. Since they took place, I am of the opinion that, as Tzara's intellectual attitude has never ceased to be unequivocal, we would be acting with undue narrow-mindedness not to tell him so publicly. As far as we are concerned—my friends and I—we would like to show by this reconciliation that what governs our conduct in every circumstance is in no wise the sectarian desire to impose at any cost a viewpoint which we do not even ask Tzara to share completely, but rather the concern to recognize value—what we think of as *value*—wherever it exists. We believe in the *efficacity* of Tzara's poetry, which is the same as saying that we consider it, apart from Surrealism, as the only really "situated" poetry. When I speak of its efficacity, I mean to imply that it is operative in the broadest possible area and that it represents a notable step forward today in the direction of human liberation. When I say that it is "situated," the reader will understand that I am comparing it with all those works which might just as well have been written yesterday or the day before: in the front rank of the things that Lautréamont has not rendered absolutely impossible there is Tzara's poetry. *De nos oiseaux* having just appeared, it is fortunately not the press's silence which will succeed in stopping the damage it can do.

Therefore without having to ask Tzara to get hold of himself, we would simply like to suggest that he make what he is doing more obvious than it was possible for him to do over these past few years. Knowing that he himself is desirous of joining forces with us, as in the past, let us remind him that, by his own admission, he once wrote "to look for men, and nothing more." In this connection, let him not forget, we were like him. Let no one think that we found ourselves, then lost ourselves.

I look around us, searching to see who else we might exchange a sign of understanding with, but to no avail: there is nothing. Perhaps it is befitting, at the very most, to point out to Daumal, who, in *Le Grand jeu,* begins an interesting inquiry about the devil, that nothing could prevent us from applauding a large portion of the declarations he signed, by himself or together with Lecomte, were it not for the fairly disastrous impression of his failing in a specific circumstance that we can still recall.* It is unfortunate, on the other hand, that Daumal has hitherto avoided stating in no uncertain terms his personal position, and that of *Le Grand jeu,* or that part of it for which he is responsible, with respect to Surrealism. One is hard put to understand that something which prompts these paeans of

*Cf. "A suivre," in *Variétés,* June 1929.

praise for Rimbaud does not provoke deification pure and simple when it comes to Lautréamont. "The ceaseless contemplation of a dark Evidence, absolute maw": we agree, this is what we are condemned to. Why, then, basely play one group off against the other? Why, unless vainly to distinguish oneself, to act as though one had never heard of Lautréamont? "But the great, black anti-suns, wells of truth in the basic plot, in the gray veil of arching sky, come and go and suck each other up, and men call them Absences."* He who speaks in this manner having had the courage to say that he is no longer in control of himself, has no reason to prefer being away from us, as he will soon find out.

Alchemy of the word: this expression which we go around repeating more or less at random today demands to be taken literally. If the chapter of *Une Saison en enfer* that they specify does not perhaps completely justify their aspiration, it is nonetheless a fact that it can be authentically considered to be the beginning of a difficult undertaking which Surrealism is alone in pursuing today. We would be guilty of some sort of literary childishness if we were to claim that our debt to this famous text was anything less than great. Is the admirable fourteenth century any less great as regards human hope (and, of course, of human despair) because a man of Flamel's genius received from a mysterious power the manuscript, which already existed, of Abraham the Jew, or because the secrets of Hermes had not been completely lost? I do not believe so for one minute, and I think that Flamel's efforts, with all their appearance of concrete success, lose nothing by having been helped and anticipated. In our own time, everything comes to pass as though a few men had just been possessed, by supernatural means, of a singular volume

*René Daumal, "Feux à volonté," in *Le Grand jeu,* Spring 1929.

resulting from the collaboration of Rimbaud, Lautréamont, and a few others, and that a voice said to them, as
the angel said to Flamel, "Come, behold this book, look
well, you will not understand a line in it, neither you nor
many others, but you will one day see therein what no one
could see."* They are no longer in a position to steal away
from this contemplation. I would appreciate your noting
the remarkable analogy, insofar as their goals are concerned, between the Surrealist efforts and those of the alchemists: the philosopher's stone is nothing more or less
than that which was to enable man's imagination to take a
stunning revenge on all things, which brings us once again,
after centuries of the mind's domestication and insane

*Three weeks after this passage of the *Second Manifesto of
Surrealism* had been written I learned of Desnos' article entitled "Le
Mystère d'Abraham juif" which had just appeared two days before,
in issue number 5 of *Documents*. "There can be no doubt," I wrote
on November 13, "that Desnos and I, at about the same time, were
involved in the same experiment, although we were *acting completely
independently* from each other. It would be worthwhile determining
whether one of us might have heard more or less opportunely about
what the other was up to, and I believe I can state categorically that
the name of Abraham the Jew was never mentioned by either one of
us in the presence of the other. Two of the three figures which illustrate Desnos' text (and whose vulgarity I must personally take to
task; for one thing, they date from the seventeenth century) are precisely those by Flamel that I cite later on. This is not the first time
that something of this kind has happened to Desnos and me. (See,
for example, "Entrée des médiums," "Les mots san rides," in *Les Pas
perdus*, published by La Nouvelle Revue Française.) There is nothing
to which I have attached greater importance than the manifestation
of such mediumistic phenomena which can actually survive affective
bonds. In this connection, I am not about to change, as I believe I
demonstrated adequately in *Nadja*."

    Since then, M. G.-H. Rivière has informed me, in *Documents*,
that when the magazine asked him to write on Abraham the Jew
it was the first time that he, Desnos, had heard of him. This piece of
information, which virtually obliges me to abandon the hypothesis
of a direct transmission of thought, in no way invalidates, it seems
to me, the general sense of my observation.

resignation, to the attempt to liberate once and for all the imagination by the "long, immense, reasoned derangement of the senses," and all the rest. Perhaps we have thus far only managed to decorate modestly the walls of our abode with figures which, at first glance, seem beautiful to us, again in imitation of Flamel before he discovered his prime agent, his "matter," his "furnace." He liked to portray thus "a King with a great cutlass, who was having a multitude of infants killed before his eyes, infants whose mothers were sobbing at the feet of the heartless gendarmes, whilst the blood of said children was then gathered by other soldiers and put into a large vessel, in which the Sun and the Moon of heaven came to bathe," and close beside it was "a young man with wingèd feet, with Mercury's wand in his hand, wherewith he struck a salade which covered his head. Against him came running and flying with wings outspread a tall old man who wore a clock affixed to his head." Doesn't this sound like *the* Surrealist painting? And who knows whether we are going to find ourselves at some future date faced with the necessity, in the light of some new evidence or not, of making use of completely new objects, or objects considered completely obsolete? I do not necessarily think that we will resume the habit of swallowing the hearts of moles or of listening, as to the beating of our own heart, to the rhythm of the water boiling in a boiler. Or rather I don't really know, I'm waiting. All I do know is that man's sorrow is far from over, and all I hail is the return of this *furor,* four kinds of which Agrippa perceived, fruitlessly or not. With Surrealism, it is indeed solely with this *furor* that we have to deal. And let it be clearly understood that we are not talking about a simple regrouping of words or a capricious redistribution of visual images, but of the re-creation of a state which can only be fairly compared to that of madness: the modern authors whom I quote have sufficiently expounded on this point. We couldn't care less that Rim-

baud decided to apologize for what he calls his "sophisms";
that that, to borrow his own expression, "happened" is not
of the slightest interest to us. All we see in this is a very
ordinary piece of petty cowardice which in no way affects
the fate that a certain number of ideas can have. "I know
today how to greet beauty": Rimbaud cannot be forgiven
for having wanted to make us believe in a second flight on
his part when he went back into prison. "Alchemy of the
Word": we can also regret that the "Word" is here taken
in a somewhat limiting sense, and Rimbaud, moreover,
seems to recognize that "outmoded poetics" plays too important a role in this alchemy. The Word is more, and, for
the cabalists, it is nothing less, for example, than that in
the image of which the human soul is created; we know
that it has been traced back to the point of being the initial
example of the cause of causes; it is, therefore, as much in
what we fear as in what we write, as in what we love.

I say that Surrealism is still in its period of preparation, and
I hasten to add that this period may last as long as I (*as I*
to the very faint degree that I am not yet of a mind to admit that a certain Paul Lucas encountered Flamel in Brusa
at the beginning of the seventeenth century, that this same
Flamel, accompanied by his wife and one son, was seen at
the Paris Opera in 1761, and that he made a brief appearance in Paris during the month of May 1819, at which
time he was purported to have rented a store at 22, rue de
Cléry, in Paris). The fact is that the preparations are,
roughly speaking, "artistic" in nature. Nonetheless, I foresee that they will come to an end, and when they do the
revolutionary ideas that Surrealism harbors will appear
to the accompaniment of an enormous rending sound and
will give themselves free rein. Great things can come of
the modern shunting of certain wills in the future: assert-

ing themselves in the wake of ours, they will make them-selves more implacable than ours. In any case, we shall in my opinion have done enough by having helped dem-onstrate the scandalous inanity of what, even when we arrived on the scene, *was being thought,* and by having maintained—if only maintained—that it was necessary for what had been thought to give way at last to the *thinkable.*

One has a right to wonder *who* precisely Rimbaud was trying to discourage when he said that those who tried to follow in his footsteps would be struck dumb or driven insane. Lautréamont begins by warning the reader that "unless he brings to his reading a strict logic and a well-steeled mind at least equal to his defiance, the mortal emanations of this book—*Les Chants de Maldoror*—will impregnate his soul, as water does sugar." This question of malediction which till now has elicited only ironic and hare-brained comments, is more timely than ever. Sur-realism has everything to lose by wanting to remove this course from itself. It is necessary to emphasize once again and to maintain here the "Maranatha" of the alchemists, set at the threshold of the work to stop the profane. This, it strikes me, is the most urgent matter to bring to the at-tention of some of our friends who appear to me to be a trifle too preoccupied with placing and selling their paint-ings, for instance. "I should be grateful," wrote Nougé recently, "if those among us whose name begins to mean something, would erase it." Without actually knowing who he has in mind, I think in any case that it is not ask-ing too much of the former or of the latter to stop showing off smugly in public and appearing behind the footlights. The approval of the public is to be avoided like the plague. It is absolutely essential to keep the public from *entering* if one wishes to avoid confusion. I must add that the public must be kept panting in expectation at the gate by a sys-tem of challenges and provocations.

I ASK FOR THE PROFOUND, THE VERITABLE OCCULTATION OF
SURREALISM.*

I proclaim, in this matter, the right of absolute severity. No concessions to the world, and no grace. *The terrible
contract in hand.*

Cursed be they who would give out the baleful bread
to the birds.

"Anyone who, desirous of attaining the supreme goal of
the soul, sets out in search of the Oracle," we read in the
Third Book of Magic, "must detach his mind completely
from commonplace things, in order to reach it, he must
purify his mind of any malady, any weakness, spite, or
similar defects, and of any state contrary to the reason
which follows it, as rust follows iron," and the Fourth Book
specifies in no uncertain terms that the hoped-for
revelation further requires that one keep oneself in a
"pure, bright place, wherein white wall hangings are every-

---

*But I expect people to ask me how one can bring about this
occultation. Independently of the effort which consists in impairing
this parasitical and "French" tendency which would like Surrealism,
in its turn, to end with some songs, I think we would not be wasting
our time by probing seriously into those sciences which for various
reasons are today completely discredited. I am speaking of astrology,
among the oldest of these sciences, metapsychics (especially as it concerns the study of cryptesthesia) among the modern. It is merely a
question of approaching these sciences with a minimum of mistrust,
and for that it suffices, in both cases, to have a precise—and positive—
idea of the calculus of probabilities. The only thing is, we must never
under any circumstances confide to anyone else the task of making
this computation in our place. This said, I am of the opinion that we
cannot remain indifferent to the question of knowing, for example,
whether certain subjects are capable of reproducing a drawing placed
in an opaque envelope and closed in the absence of the person who
drew it and of anyone who might have any knowledge of it. In the
course of various experiments conceived as "parlor games" whose
value as entertainment, or even as recreation, does not to my mind
in any way affect their importance: Surrealist texts obtained simultaneously by several people writing from such to such a time in the

where apparent," and that one confront the evil Spirits as well as the good only to the degree of "dignification" one has attained. He stresses the fact that the book of evil Spirits is written "on a very pure paper that has never been used for any other purpose," a paper which is commonly referred to as "virgin parchment."

---

same room, collaborative efforts intended to result in the creation of a unique sentence or drawing, only one of whose elements (subject, verb, or predicate adjective—head, belly, or legs) was supplied by each person ("Le cadavre exquis," cf. *La Révolution surréaliste,* nos. 9 and 10; *Variétés,* June 1929), in the definition of something not given ("Le Dialogue en 1928," cf. *La Révolution surréaliste,* no. 11), in the forecasting of events which would bring about some completely unsuspected situation ("Jeux surréalistes," cf. *Variétés,* June 1929), etc., we think we have brought out into the open a strange possibility of thought, which is that of its *pooling.* The fact remains that very striking relationships are established in this manner, that remarkable analogies appear, that an inexplicable factor of irrefutability most often intervenes, and that, in a nutshell this is one of the most extraordinary *meeting grounds.* But we are only at the stage of suggesting where it is. It is obvious, moreover, that in this area we would be making a foolish display of vanity by counting on our own resources, and nothing more. Aside from the demands of the calculus of probabilities, which in metapsychics is almost always out of proportion to the benefit that one can derive from the least allegation and which would reduce us, to start with, to waiting for our ranks to be swelled ten or a hundredfold, we must also reckon with the gift of dissociation and clairvoyance, which is especially poorly shared among people all of whom, unfortunately, are more or less impregnated with academic psychology. Nothing would be less useless in this connection than to try to "follow" certain *subjects,* taken both from the normal world and from the other, and to do so in an attitude which defies both the spirit of the sideshow and that of the doctor's office, and is, in a word, the Surrealist attitude. The result of these observations ought to be set down in a naturalistic manner, obviously excluding any exterior poeticizing. I ask, once again, that we submit ourselves to the mediums who do exist, albeit no doubt in very small numbers, and that we subordinate our interest—which ought not to be overestimated—in what we are doing to the interest which the first of their messages offers. Praise be to hysteria, Aragon and I have said, and to

There is no evidence that the Magi failed to keep their clothing and their souls in anything less than an impeccable state of cleanliness, and, expecting what we expect of certain practices of mental alchemy, I would likewise fail to understand how we could, in this same connection, be any less demanding than they. And yet this is precisely what we are most roundly taken to task for, and it is this aspect that M. Bataille, who is currently waging an absurd campaign against what he terms "the sordid quests for every integrity," seems less willing to forgive

---

its train of young, naked women sliding along the roofs. The problem of woman is the most wonderful and disturbing problem there is in the world. And this is so precisely to the extent that the faith a noncorrupted man must be able to place, not only in the Revolution, *but also in love,* brings us back to it. I insist on this point, all the more so because this insistence is what seems to have hitherto garnered for me the greatest number of recriminations. Yes, I believe, I have always believed, that to give up love, whether or not it be done under some ideological pretext, is one of the few unatonable crimes that a man possessed of some degree of intelligence can commit in the course of his life. A certain man, who sees himself as a revolutionary, would like to convince us that love is impossible in a bourgeois society; some other pretends to devote himself to a cause more jealous than love itself; the truth is that almost no one has the courage to affront with open eyes the bright daylight of love in which the obsessive ideas of salvation and the damnation of the spirit blend and merge, for the supreme edification of man. Whosoever fails to remain in this respect in a state of expectation and perfect receptivity, how, I ask, can he speak *humanly?*

Recently I wrote, as an introduction to an inquiry carried out by *la Révolution surréaliste:*

"If any idea seems hitherto to have eluded all efforts to reduce it, to have resisted down to the present time even the most out-and-out pessimists, we think it is the idea *of love,* which is the only idea capable of reconciling any man, momentarily or not, with the idea of *life.*"

This word—"love"—which all sorts of practical jokers have strained their wits to subject to every generalization, every possible corruption (filial love, holy love, love of country, etc.), is used by us

than any other of our alleged shortcomings. M. Bataille interests me only insofar as he imagines that he is comparing the harsh discipline of the mind to which we intend purely and simply to subject literally everything—and we see no problem in making Hegel primarily responsible for it— to a discipline which does not even manage to seem more cowardly, for it tends to be that of the nonmind (and it is there, in fact, that Hegel awaits it). M. Bataille professes to wish only to consider in the world that which is vilest, most discouraging, and most corrupted, and he invites man, *so as to avoid making himself useful for anything specific,* "to run absurdly with *him*—his eyes suddenly become dim and filled with unavowable tears—toward some haunted provincial houses, seamier than flies, more depraved, ranker than barber shops." If I sometimes happen

---

here, it goes without saying, in its strictest sense, we are restoring it to its meaning which threatens a human being with total attachment, based upon the overwhelming awareness of the truth, of *our truth,* "in a soul and a body" which are the soul and body of that person. What we are referring to, in the course of this pursuit of the truth which is the basis of all meaningful activity, is the sudden abandonment of a system of more or less patient research for the help and on behalf of an evidence which our work has not produced and which, with such features on such and such a day, mysteriously became incarnate. What we have to say about it is, we hope, of a nature to dissuade the "pleasure" specialists from answering us, as well as the collectors of amorous adventures, the dashers after sensual delight (assuming they are inclined to disguise their mania lyrically), the scorners and "faith healers" of the so-called love madness, and the perpetual love-hypochondriacs.

It was indeed by others, and by them alone, that I have always hoped to make myself heard. More than ever—since what we are discussing here are the possibilities of occultation of Surrealism—I turn toward those who are not afraid to conceive of love as the site of ideal occultation of all thought. I say to them: there are real apparitions, but there is a mirror in the mind over which the vast majority of mankind could lean without seeing themselves. Odious control does not work all that well. The person you love lives. The language of revelation says certain words to itself, some of which are loud.

to relate such remarks, it is because they seem to implicate not only M. Bataille but also certain ex-Surrealists who wanted to be fully free to involve themselves anywhere and everywhere. Perhaps M. Bataille is sufficiently forceful to bring them together, and if he succeeds in this effort the results, in my opinion, will be extremely interesting. Already lined up at the starting gate for the race which, as we have seen, M. Bataille is organizing, are: Messrs. Desnos, Leiris, Limbour, Masson, and Vitrac. We haven't been able to figure out why M. Ribemont-Dessaignes, for exam-

---

others soft, from several sides all at once. We must resign ourselves to learning it in snatches.

.   .   .   .

When, on the other hand, we think of what is expressed astrologically in Surrealism of a very preponderant "Uranian" influence, how can one not wish to see, from the Surrealist viewpoint, a sincere critical work devoted to Uranus appear which would, in this respect, fill in the serious gap from the past. One may as well say that nothing has yet been undertaken in this sense. The astrological chart of Baudelaire, who was born under the remarkable astrological conjunction of Uranus and Neptune, thereby remains as it were uninterpretable. About the conjunction of Uranus with Saturn, which took place from 1896 to 1898 *and occurs only once every forty-five years*—about this conjunction which presided at the time of Aragon's birth, Eluard's, and my own we know from Choisnard simply that, although it has not been the subject of any extensive astrological studies, "it would reasonably seem to signify a deep attachment to the sciences, an inquisitive interest in the mysterious, and a profound need to learn." (Of course, Choisnard's vocabulary is questionable.) "Who knows," he adds, "whether the conjunction of Saturn with Uranus may not give birth to a new school in the realm of science? This relative position of the planets, properly placed in a horoscope, could correspond to the make-up of a man endowed with the qualities of reflection, sagacity, and independence, a man capable of becoming a first-class investigator." These lines, taken from his work *L'Influence astrale* were written in 1893, and in 1925 Choisnard noted that his prediction seemed to be coming true.

ple, is not yet there. I maintain that it is extremely significant to see reunited all those whom a defect of one sort or another has removed from a given initial activity because there is a good possibility that all they have in common is their dissatisfaction. I am amused, moreover, to think that one cannot leave Surrealism without running into M. Bataille, so great is the truism that the dislike of discipline can only result in one's submitting oneself anew to discipline.

In M. Bataille's case, and this is no news to anyone, what we are witnessing is an obnoxious return to old anti-dialectical materialism, which this time is trying to force its way gratuitously through Freud. "Materialism," he says, "direct interpretation, *excluding all idealism*, of raw phenomena, so as not to be considered as materialism in a state of senility, ought to be based immediately on economic and social phenomena." Since "historical materialism" is not defined here (and indeed how could it be?), we are obliged to point out that from the philosophical point of view of expression it is vague, and that from the poetic point of view as to its novelty, it is worthless.

What is less uncertain is the use M. Bataille intends to make of a small number of specific ideas he has about which, considering what they are, it is a question of ascertaining whether they derive from medicine or from exorcism, for, insofar as "the appearance of the fly on the orator's nose" is concerned (Georges Bataille, "Figure humaine," *Documents*, No. 4), the ultimate argument against the "ego," we all know the ridiculous Pascalian argument, which Lautréamont did justice to long ago: "The mind of the greatest man (underscore three times "the greatest man") is not so dependent that it is liable to be upset by the slightest din going on around him. It does not take the silence of a cannon to stop him from thinking. It does not take the noise of a weathervane, of a pulley. The fly's thought-processes are disturbed at present. A man is buzzing in its ears." A man who is thinking, as well as on the mountain top, can land on the nose of a fly. The only reason we are going on at such length about flies is that M. Bataille loves flies. Not we: we love the miters of old evocators, the miters of pure linen to whose front point was affixed a blade of gold and upon which flies did not settle, because they had been purified to keep them away. M. Bataille's misfortune is to reason: admittedly, he reasons like someone who "has a fly on his nose," which allies him more closely with the dead than with the living, but *he does reason.* He is trying, with the help of the tiny mechanism in him which is not completely out of order, to share his obsessions: this very fact proves that he cannot claim, no matter what he may say, to be opposed to any system, *like an unthinking brute.* What is paradoxical and embarrassing about M. Bataille's case is that his phobia about "the idea," as soon as he attempts to communicate it, can only take an ideological turn. A state of conscious deficiency, in a form tending to become generalized, the doctors would say. Here, in fact, is someone who propounds as a principle that "horror does not lead to any pathological complaisance and only plays the role of manure in the growth of plant life, manure whose odor is stifling no doubt but salutary for the plant." Beneath its appearance of infinite banality, this idea is in itself dishonest or pathological (it remains to be proved that Lully, and Berkeley, and Hegel, and Rabbe, and Baudelaire, and Rimbaud, and Marx, and Lenin acted very specifically like pigs in the lives they led). It is to be noted that M. Bataille misuses adjectives with a passion: befouled, senile, rank, sordid, lewd, doddering, and that these words, far from serving him to disparage an unbearable state of affairs, are those through which his delight is most lyrically expressed. The "unnamable broom" to which Jarry refers having fallen into his plate, M. Bataille declares that he is delighted.* He who, for hours on end during the day, lets his librarian fingers wander over old and sometimes charming manuscripts (it is common knowledge that he exercises this profession at the Bibliothèque Nationale), at night wallows in impurities wherewith, in his image, he would like to see them covered: witness the *Apocalypse de Saint-Sever* to which he devoted an article in the second issue of *Documents,* an article which is the prototype of false testimony. Let the reader be so kind as to refer to the plate of the "Flood" reproduced in this same issue and tell me whether, objectively, "a jolly and unexpected feeling appears with the goat which is shown at the bottom of the page and with the raven whose beak is plunged into the meat"—here M. Bataille's enthusiasm knows no bounds—"of a human head." To endow various architectural elements with human features, as he does throughout this study and elsewhere, is again nothing other than a classic sign of psychasthenia. The fact of the matter is that M. Bataille is simply very tired, and when he makes the discovery, which for him is overwhelming, that "the inside of a rose does not correspond at all to its exterior beauty, and that if one tears off all the petals of the corolla, all that remains is a sordid looking tuft," all he does is make me smile as I recall Alphonse Allais' tale in which a sultan has so exhausted the subjects of amusement that, despairing of seeing him grow bored, his grand Vizier can think of nothing better to do than to bring him a very beautiful damsel who begins to dance, at first completely covered with veils, for him alone. She is so beautiful that the sultan orders her to drop one of her veils each time she stops dancing. No sooner is she naked than the sultan signals idly for her to be stripped: they quickly flay her

*In his *Différence de la philosophie de la nature chez Democrite et Epicure,* Marx tells us how, in every age, there thus come into being hair-philosophers, fingernail-philosophers, *toenail-philosophers, excrement-philosophers,* etc.

alive. It is none the less true that the rose, stripped of its petals, remains *the rose* and, moreover, in the story above, the dancing girl goes on dancing.

    If anyone brings up as an argument the story about "the ambiguous gesture of the Marquis de Sade who, locked up with the insane, has the most beautiful roses brought to him in order to dip their petals in the liquid shit of a drainage ditch," I shall reply by saying that, in order for the story to lose any of its extraordinary implications it would suffice that the gesture be done, not by a man who has spent twenty-seven years of his life in prison *for his beliefs,* but by a staid librarian. There is, in fact, every reason to believe that Sade, whose desire for moral and social independence is, in contrast to that of M. Bataille, irrelevant, merely wished by that gesture to attack the poetic *idol,* that conventional "virtue" which willynilly makes a flower—to the extent that anyone can offer it—the brilliant vehicle of the most noble as well as the most ignoble sentiments, all this in an effort to try to make the human mind get rid of its chains. Besides, it behooves us to reserve judgment about such a fact which, even if it is not completely apocryphal, would in no way harm the impeccable integrity of Sade's life and thought, and the heroic need that was his to create an order of things which was not as it were dependent upon everything that had come before him.

Surrealism is less inclined than ever to dispense with this integrity, or to sit idly by while this person or that thinks he is free to abandon it, under the vague, the odious pretext that he has to live. We want nothing to do with this dole of "talents." What we are asking is, we think, such as to bring about an acquiescence, an utter refusal, and not to indulge in words, to sustain erratic hopes. Does one or does one not want to risk everything for the mere pleasure of perceiving in the distance, at the bottom of the crucible into which we propose to cast our slim resources, what is still left of our good reputation and our doubts, together pell-mell with the pretty, "sensitive" glassware, the radical notion of impotence and the foolishness of our so-called duties, *the light that will cease to fail?*

We submit that the Surrealist endeavor can only hope to be crowned with success if it is carried out under conditions of moral asepsis which very few people in this day and age are interested in hearing about. Without these conditions, it is, however, impossible to arrest the spread of this cancer of the mind which consists of thinking all too sadly that certain things "are," while others, which well might be, "are not." We have suggested that they must merge into each other, or very perceptibly impinge upon each other at their respective limits. It is a matter, not of remaining there at that point, but *of not being able to do less than to strain desperately toward that limit.*

Man, who would wrongly allow himself to be intimidated by a few monstrous historical failures, is still free to *believe* in his freedom. He is his own master, in spite of the old clouds which pass and his blind forces which encounter obstacles. Doesn't he have any inkling of the brief beauty concealed and of the long and accessible beauty that can be revealed? Let him also look carefully for the key to love, which the poet claimed to have found: he has it. It is up to him and him alone to rise above the fleeting sentiment of living dangerously and of dying. Let him, in spite of any restrictions, use the avenging arm of the idea against the bestiality of all beings and of all things, and let him one day, vanquished—*but vanquished only if the world is the world*—welcome the discharge of his sad rifles like a salvo fired in salute.

BEFORE, AFTER

Before

Preoccupied with morality, that is with the meaning of life, and not with the observation of human laws, André Breton, by his love of exact life and adventure, once again gives its real meaning to the word "religion."

ROBERT DESNOS
Intentions

My dear friend, my admiration for you is not dependent on any perpetual reference to your "virtues" or your faults.

GEORGES RIBEMONT-DESSAIGNES
Variétés

My dear Breton, it is possible I may never return to France. This evening I insulted everything you can insult. I am undone. Blood flows from my eyes, my nostrils, and my mouth. Do not abandon me. Defend my cause.

GEORGES LIMBOUR
July 21, 1924

Arriving Paris. Thank you.

GEORGES LIMBOUR
July 23, 1924

. . . I know exactly what I owe you, and I also know that that it was the various ideas you taught me in the course of our conversations that enabled me to come to these realizations. We are following parallel paths. I would like you to know that my friendship for you is not a superficial matter.

JACQUES BARON
1929

I am one of André Breton's friends because of the confidence he has in me. But it is not confidence. No one has it. It is a grace. I wish it upon you. It is grace that I wish upon you.

ROGER VITRAC
Le Journal du peuple

After

And the final vanity of this ghost will be to stink eternally among the foul smells of paradise promised at the certain and not-far-distant conversion of the pheasant André Breton.

ROBERT DESNOS
Un Cadavre, 1930

The Second Manifesto of Surrealism is not a revelation but it is a success.

It is impossible to produce anything better in the category of hypocrite, double crosser, sacristan and, to be candid: cop and parish priest.

GEORGES RIBEMONT-DESSAIGNES
Un Cadavre

I would enjoy seeing your nose bleed.

GEORGES LIMBOUR
December 1929

He was Breton the honest, the fervent revolutionary, the disciplined moralist.

Oh, sure, quite a fellow!

A farmyard esthete, this cold-blooded animal has never contributed anything but the rankest confusion to whatever he has been involved in.

JACQUES BARON
Un Cadavre

As for his ideas, I do not believe that anyone ever took them seriously, save for a few indulgent critics that he fawned upon, a handful of schoolboys somewhat overaged, and a few women pregnant with monsters.

ROGER VITRAC
Un Cadavre

Fully determined at every opportunity to use, and even to abuse, the authority which the conscious and systematic practice of written or other expression confers, in agreement with André Breton on all points and resolved to apply the conclusions which are self-evident from the reading of THE SECOND MANIFESTO OF SURREALISM, we the undersigned, who have no illusion as to the impact of "artistic and literary" magazines, have decided to lend their support to a periodical publication which, bearing the title:

LE SURRÉALISME
AU SERVICE DE LA RÉVOLUTION

not only will allow them to reply with some immediacy to the riff-raff who make a profession of thinking, but also to prepare the definitive dissuasion of the intellectual forces living today in behalf of revolutionary fatality.

MAXIME ALEXANDRE
ARAGON
JOE BOUSQUET
LUIS BUNUEL
RENÉ CHAR
RENÉ CREVEL
SALVADOR DALI
PAUL ELUARD
MAX ERNST
MARCEL FOURRIER
CAMILLE GOEMANS
PAUL NOUGÉ
BENJAMIN PÉRET
FRANCIS PONGE
MARCO RISTITCH
GEORGES SADOUL
YVES TANGUY
ANDRÉ THIRION
TRISTAN TZARA
ALBERT VALENTIN.

1930

A LETTER TO SEERS
(1925)

Mesdames,

The time has come; I beg you to do justice. At this very hour girls as lovely as the day are bruising their knees in the hiding places to which the ignoble white drone draws them one by one. They accuse themselves of sins that on occasion are charmingly mortal (as if there could be sins) while the other prophesies, stirs, or *pardons.* Who is being deceived here?

I dream of these girls, these young women who ought to put all their confidence in you, the only tributaries and the only guardians of the Secret. I am speaking of the great Secret, of the Unrevealable. They would no longer be obliged to lie. In your presence, as elsewhere, they might be the most elegant ones, the maddest ones. And listen to you, have a slight presentiment of you, with a luminous hand and crossed legs.

I think of all the men lost in echoing courts of justice. They believe that they must answer, here for an affair of the heart, there for a crime. They search their memory in vain: what can have happened? They can never hope for anything beyond partial acquittal. All boundlessly unhappy. Because they have done what in all simplicity they believed they had to do, because once again they have not taken *the orders of the marvelous* (usually because they did not know how to take them), they have here started down a path that they will come to feel, with the greatest pain, was not theirs, and come to feel that whether they would refuse to go farther in this direction or not depended on help from the outside, which was extremely problematical. Life, undesirable life, goes on ravishingly. Each one goes at it with the idea of his own freedom that he has managed to frame for himself, and God knows that generally this idea is a timid one. But it is not the man of today who would consent to search in the stars for the head of the pin, the famous pin he can't get out of the game anyhow.* He has patiently accepted his lot, poor man, has even been, I do believe, endlessly patient. He makes it a duty to disregard the miraculous intercessions in his favor which might be forthcoming. His imagination is a theater in ruins, a baleful perch for parrots and crows. This man will no longer do anything except to please himself; at every moment he boasts of bringing the source of his authority into the light of day. An absurd pretentiousness is perhaps the cause of his many disappointments. He nonetheless willingly deprives himself of the help of what he does not know, I mean what he cannot know, and uses any sort of argument to justify himself for so doing. He scarcely believes in the invention of the Philosophers' Stone by Nicolas Flamel, for the simple reason that the great alchemist seems not to have got rich enough from it. Outside of the religious scruples he might have had about taking such a vulgar advantage, however, one may well wonder how the obtaining of more than a few bits of gold could have interested him, when it had been above all a matter of building up a spiritual fortune. This need for industrialization, which is uppermost in people's objection to Flamel, is to be found almost everywhere: it is one of the principal factors in the defeat of the spirit. It is what has given birth to this

---

* The expression "tirer l'épingle du jeu," literally "to get the pin out of the game," figuratively means "to get out of something without a loss."—*Tr.*

frantic mania for control, which it will be Surrealism's only glory to have denounced. Naturally they would all like to have been behind Flamel when he made this decisive experiment, which doubtless would have been decisive only for him. The same goes for mediums, whom people immediately wanted to submit to the observation of doctors, "scholars," and other illiterates. And for the most part, mediums have let themselves be caught red-handed in the act of committing vulgar hoaxes, which to me is a proof of their probity and their taste. Of course once official science had been reassured, with one damning report coming to reinforce many other reports, the terrible Evidence once again compelled recognition. So it was with us, with those of us who have been acknowledged to have some "talent," if only to deplore that we make such bad use of it or that the love of scandal—or, as is also said, of publicity—brings us to such culpable extremes. All this at a time when there are such nice novels to be written, and even poetry which might be read in our lifetime and might be, we are promised, highly appreciated after our death.

But what does it really matter? Mesdames, today my mind is wholly on your disgrace. I know that you no longer dare to use your voice, no longer deign to use your all-powerful authority except within the woeful "legal" limits. I can see in my mind's eye the houses you live in, on the fourth floor, in districts more or less remote from the cities. Your existence and what little toleration you receive, despite how well you are seen to behave, help me to bear the extraordinary emptiness of this time and keep from despairing. What is a barometer which records the "variable," as if time could be uncertain? Time is certain: already the man that I will be has the man that I am by the throat, but the man that I have been leaves me in peace. This is called my mystery, but I do not believe in (I do not prize) the impenetrability of this mystery, and no one wholly believes in it for himself. The great veil that falls over my childhood only half conceals the strange years that will precede my death. And I shall one day speak of my death. Inside my-

self I am several hours ahead of myself. The proof is that
what happens to me surprises me only to the exact degree
that I need not be surprised *any more.* I want to know
everything: I can tell myself everything.

I have not spoken of your immense power gratuitously, although nothing today equals the moderation with which
you use it. The least difficult among you could rightfully
exert their superiority over us; we would hold it to be the
only undeniable one. I know: given the horrible conditions
that time imposes on us—past, present, future—who can
prevent us from living from day to day? It is suddenly a
question of an *assurance* (in a domain where up to now
not the least possibility of assurance has been admitted),
without which a great part, the most annoying part, of
human agitation would have died down. Yet you keep this
assurance, Mesdames, endlessly at our disposal; it has few
ambiguities. Why must you give it to us *for what it is
worth?*
    For you are not too annoyed if one contradicts you on
one point or another where the information of another
may appear to be incontrovertible, for instance if you took
a notion to tell me that I respect work. It is probable, moreover, that you would not say this, that you are forbidden to
do so: the fact remains that the consequences of your intervention could not be at the mercy of an apparent error of
this order. It is not by chance that I speak of intervention.
Everything that is revealed to me about the future falls in
a marvelous field which is nothing other than that of absolute possibility, and develops there at all costs. Whether or
not reality takes it upon itself subsequently to verify the
assertions that I receive from you, I shall not consider this
arithmetical proof to be of prime importance, as would all
those who had not tried the same operation for themselves.
It may happen that I decide to passionately deduce what I
shall do from this trial-and-error calculation which causes
me to suppose at every moment that the problem of my life
is resolved, adopting for that purpose results that you are
kind enough to submit to me, that may or may not be arbi-

A Letter to Seers 201

trary, but are always great. It appears that I must go to China around 1931 and run great dangers there for twenty years. Two times out of two, I let myself be told this, which is rather troubling. I also learned indirectly that I was to die before that time. But I do not think that "it must be one way or the other." I have faith in everything you have told me. I would not try to resist the temptation you have aroused in me, let's say to wait for myself in China, for anything in the world. For thanks too to you, I am already there.

It is your role, Mesdames, to make us confuse the accomplishable fact and the accomplished fact. I will go even further. This difference, considered irreducible, between the probable sensations of an aeronaut and his real sensations, that someone once boasted of holding to be essential and being able to evaluate precisely, even taking it into his head to deduce from it extreme consequences as regards human attitudes—this difference ceases to hold or holds quite differently as soon as it is no longer myself that *proposes*, that intends, and I allow you to *dispose* of me. As soon as it is a question for me of China, and not for example Paris or South America, I transport myself in thought to China much more easily than elsewhere. Movies have lost a great deal of their interest for me! On the other hand, it is as if doors were opening in the Orient, as if the echo of an all-enfolding agitation reached me, as if a breath, which might well be that of Freedom, suddenly makes the old chest of Europe, on which I had gone to sleep, resound. It is likely that I needed only to be pushed down onto the ground by you and stretch out full-length, not as one does to spy on something, but as one does to embrace, to cover all the shadow ahead of one. It is true that almost anything can happen without me, that left to itself my power of anticipation exercises itself less in depth than in breadth, but if you state in advance that the aeronaut is *me*, that the man who is going to live in China is *me*, if this powerful active datum comes to grip these inert travelers, good-bye meticulous fine difference and "indifference"! It can be seen that action seduces me also in its own way, and that I have the highest possible opinion of experience, since I endeavor to experience what I have not done! There are people who claim that the war taught them something; even so they aren't as far along as I am, since I know what the year 1939 has in store for me.

Out of hatred for memory, for that combustion that it feeds in all the places where I no longer want to see anything, I want to have dealings only with you. Because it is to you that it has been given to keep in us that admirable *detector* without which we would lose even the sense of our continuity, since you alone know how to cause there to spring forth from us a personage similar in all respects to ourselves who, beyond the thousands and thousands of beds on which we shall, alas, lie, beyond the table with innumerabe covers around which we shall carry on our vain secret meetings, will go forth victoriously before us.

It is to this end that I am addressing myself to all of you, because there is not one among you who could not render us this immense service. Provided that you do not overstep the infinitely vast framework of your powers, any distinction of merit between one and another of you seems otiose to me; in my opinion you are all equally qualified. What is will *be*, by virtue of language alone: nothing in the world can stop it. I grant that that may be more or less well stated, but that is all.

Your one error is to have accepted the scandalous condition that is forced upon you, a relative poverty that obliges you to be "visited" at such and such an hour, like doctors; and to have become resigned to the outrages that opinion, materialist opinion, reactionary opinion, public opinion, bad opinion does not spare us. May it be that age-old persecutions will forever deter you from spreading through the world the great annunciation, despite those who do not wish to hear it? Would you so doubt your right and your power that you would long want to appear to do as others do, as those who make their living from a trade do? We have seen poets steal away out of disdain for the struggle, but now they are getting hold of themselves, in the name of that small bit of clairvoyance, hardly different from your own, that they possess. Enough of particular truths, enough of splendid lights kept in rings! We are searching for, we are on the track of, a moral truth of which the least that one can say is that it forbids us to act circumspectly. This truth must become blinding. What are you thinking of, here it is, the next eruption of Vesuvius! They tell me that you have offered your services to further certain police investigations, but this is not possible: there has been an encroachment on your rights, or the news is false. I am not the dupe of what the newspapers sometimes print about the revelations that you supposedly consent to pass on to some editor of theirs: you are certainly being slandered. But even though you are women, it is time, I entreat you, to give up this passivity. They will invade your homes on the eve of the happy catastrophe. Do not abandon us; we will recognize you in the crowd by your unbound hair. Give us stones, brilliant stones, to drive off the infamous priests. We no longer see this world as it is, we are absent. Here is *love* now, here are the soldiers of the past!

POLITICAL POSITION
OF SURREALISM
(1935)

Extracts

Preface
(1935)

Without going so far as to wish to paraphrase the dark and cynical phrase: "How beautiful the Republic was during the Empire!" I believe that one can have a real feeling of nostalgia for that already far-off period which extends from the founding of the First International to the first days of the stabilization of Soviet power. Socialism, which for a long time had been nothing but a noble aspiration, had just sunk deep and firm roots into the earth; it was, in its period of most rapid growth, the tree that could not fail one day to light the world with its flowers, something like those big royal poincianas that I saw last May bathing the windows of the Canary Islands in transparent blood. And this very blood, to the extent that it was necessary at first to shed it over a long period at the foot of this tree in order to bring about the advent of socialism, this blood was luminously infused with the awareness that it was fulfilling its highest destiny—men had at last discovered a cause for which they would not fall in vain, the whole question of bettering the lot of mankind was at stake; from this blood there rose a perfume of deliverance.

The Marxist theory of Revolution, not yet having been

tested by the facts, enjoyed a growing prestige to the very extent that, taking as a point of departure the least imperfect solution of the social problem that had been proposed up to the time of its formulation, it was able to maintain a great degree of flexibility in adapting itself to later events, and enjoyed an unprecedented dynamic force. Then the proletariat, daily more aware of the historical necessity of its ultimate triumph over the bourgeoisie, rallied to its cause in the struggle a small number of intellectuals who, through the free exercise of their reason, had become sufficiently aware of the course of human evolution to make a complete break with the bourgeois class from which most of them had come. The task of these intellectuals was to help the proletariat by constantly teaching it what it had done and what it still had to do in order for it to bring about its liberation. It was also their task to constantly update the particulars of the problem, to make certain new factors relating to these particulars were introduced, to make the system operate if necessary in such a way as to keep it in a state of constant readiness. I cannot overly emphasize the fact that for an enlightened determinist like Lafargue, economic determinism is not the "absolutely perfect tool" that "can become the key to all the problems of history." On this point, Lafargue approves of scientists for admitting that "from the practical point of view, it is of secondary importance whether theories and hypotheses are correct, provided that they guide us to results that are in accordance with the facts," and he adds: "Truth, after all, is merely the hypothesis which works the best; error is often the shortest route to a discovery. *Such an attitude, in politics as in any other area, is the only one that men who think can claim as their own. A system is alive only to the extent that it does not pretend to be infallible, definitive, but on the contrary sets great store by what appears to be most contradictory to it in the light of ensuing events, either in order to overcome this contradiction or to start all over again and try to make itself less precarious, taking this contradiction as its point of departure if it proves to be insurmountable. The urgent appeal to the violent overthrow of the social order which dates from the Com*munist Manifesto *of 1848 was able to begin being implemented in 1917 only because others had continued Marx's efforts in the direction of impassioned accommodation, confrontation, and coordination.*

From Marx to Lenin, this period of gestation which lasted

more than half a century sustained such a great effervescence of ideas, the problem of its outcome gave rise to so many debates, the points of view relating to it clashed with one another on all occasions with such violence, and, finally, the view that was to carry the day did prevail so forcefully that I cannot help but consider the constitution—both through men and events— of scientific socialism as a model school. As a school of an ever more profound understanding of human need which must aim, in all areas and on the largest possible scale, at finding satisfaction, but also as a school of independence where each person must be free to express in any and every circumstance his way of seeing things, and must be ready to justify endlessly the non-domestication of his spirit.

For years now, however, a great deal of time and effort has gone into telling us that times have changed on five-sixths of the globe (since a catchword prompts us to subtract) the revolutionary has no longer basically to look to himself for the re-creation of the reasons which militate in favor of social transformation, and to try to accelerate, from the point where he now finds himself, this transformation by every possible means. He is invited to leave that up to other men—men who have "made the Revolution" in the U.S.S.R. and who, some day or other, will presumably be called upon to fill a providential role everywhere else. The unbridled exaltation over whatever these men undertake, be it great or small, takes the place of judgment with respect to the possibilities which are theirs. We are witnessing the formation of a taboo, of the deplorable crystallization of what may be the most moving and most protean in the essence of human demands. Can we be asked to toss onto the dunghill this unlimited capacity to say no which is the whole secret of human progress in order to watch and wonder unreservedly at what is going on without us at the other end of the world? No, this contemplative, ecstatic attitude is totally irreconcilable with the revolutionary sentiment.

The worst of it is that all those who go about popularizing this attitude are not necessarily dupes of their own game, no more than are all of those who hesitate to rebel against it. Certain of the former, alas, are all too content with the double life that they are materially free to lead, concealing an obvious willingness to temporize endlessly beneath frenzied praise for the Soviet regime, interspersed with violent verbal attacks upon the capitalist society. Many others, who if they are not paralyzed by the fear of "furnishing arms to reaction," are at least reluctant to see themselves relegated to an ineffectual opposition, prefer to still their doubts even if they are obliged to admit, in low tones, that those who do not share their reservations are right. In the wings, a whole host of political nonentities—who are also flirting seriously with fascism—profit from this to gravitate in the most alarming way, forever ready to hail Stalin as a "statesman," proclaiming his "realistic genius" each time he abandons more overtly and more seriously the principles that led to the Revolution, honoring him above all for having had the wisdom and foresight to reduce to nothing the democratic tendencies of the working class. These latter are not the least ardent defenders of what is most partial, and therefore most debatable, in what the U.S.S.R. offers for us to admire: thus the progress realized there in the industrial sector has never seemed as exciting to them as it has following Stalin's declaration to Laval in May, of which the least that one can say is that it unleashed on the revolutionary world the winds of catastrophe.

This book, which in certain respects aims at the elucidation of very special intellectual problems, is not free from traces of the malaise caused by this state of affairs. Still in all, if I consider the lapse of time—a few months—during which the fragments which compose it were fashioned, I am far from disturbed by the fact that there are certain fluctuations apparent therein. I am confident, in fact, that these fluctuations are in keeping with the especially tumultuous course of recent history. I furthermore believe that any living thought must have both constants and variables if it is to serve as the basis for any undertaking whatsoever. It is only on this condition that it assumes its full functional value.

Moreover, I could not possibly allow matters to stand as they are. Beyond the considerations that follow, which are those to which my preoccupation over the past ten years has led me, namely to reconcile Surrealism as a method of creating a collective myth with the much more general movement involving the liberation of man who tends first to change fundamentally the bourgeois form of property, the problem of action, of the immediate action to be taken, remains intact. In the light of the stupefying reevaluation—by the very persons whose job it was to defend them—of revolutionary principles which have hereto-

fore been considered as intanglble, the abandonment of which cannot be justified by any serious materialist analysis of the world situation, in the light of the impossibility of any longer believing in any impending improvement in this sense of the ideology of the parties of the left, in the light of the insolvency of these parties, which suddenly became apparent at the time of the Italian-Ethiopian conflict when their watchwords met with no success, and of its possible generalization, I believe that this question of what action to take must receive, from me as well as from all those who are of a mind to put an end to an abject laisser-faire *policy, an unequivocal reply. You will find this reply, in October 1935, in my participation in the foundation of* Contre-Attaque, *the Union for Combat of revolutionary intellectuals.*

POLITICAL POSITION OF TODAY'S ART
(1935)

[Lecture delivered by Breton on April 1, 1935, in Prague]

Comrades,

When my friends Vitezslav Nezval and Karel Teige informed me that I was invited to speak to your group, the "Leftist Front," and questioned me about the subject that would be most appropriate for me to speak on before you, I fell to thinking about the very name of your organization. This word "front," whose use in this sense is a recent phenomenon that has very rapidly become widespread, is enough in itself to remind me of the hard, occasionally tragic, and at the same time exciting realities of this hour. These banners that have suddenly begun to flap over Europe, setting a common or social front, a single front or a red front over against a national front, the last battle formation of capitalism, are of a sort to imbue me more and more deeply with the idea that we live in an era in which man belongs to himself less than ever, in which he is held responsible for the totality of his acts, no longer before a single conscience, his own, but before the collective conscience of all those who want to have no more to do with a monstrous system of slavery and hunger.

Before being a moral conscience, this conscience is a psychological conscience.

On the one hand the reinforcement of the mechanism of oppression based on the family, religion, and the fatherland, the recognition of a necessity of man to enslave man, the careful underhanded exploitation of the urgent need to transform society for the sole profit of a financial and industrial oligarchy, the need also to silence the great isolated appeals through which the person who up until now has been intellectually privileged manages, sometimes after a long space of time, to rouse his fellowmen from their apathy, the whole mechanism of stagnation, of regression, and of wearing down: this is night. On the other hand the destruction of social barriers, the hatred of all servitude (the defense of liberty is never a servitude), the prospect of man's right truly to dispose of himself—with all profit to the workers, the assiduous attention to grasping the whole process of dissatisfaction, of moving rapidly forward, of youth, so as to grant it the greatest possible right to grasp the entire range of human demands, from whatever angle it presents itself: this is day.

In this regard, it is impossible to conceive of a clearer situation.

Thus the words "leftist front" told me quite a bit. But as I took the trouble to inform myself about the way your association was set up, as I learned that it brought intellectuals together in close association to fight back against fascism and war, I could not help but think of the double problem that faces today's leftist intellectuals, particularly poets and artists. The very word "leftist" nevertheless urged me on, because of the way it designates, in politics on the one hand and in art on the other, two approaches which until further notice may appear to be very different.

We know that the adjective "revolutionary" is generously applied to every work, to every intellectual creator who appears to break with tradition. I say "appears to break," for that mysterious entity, tradition, that some attempt to describe as being very exclusive, has proved for centuries to have a boundless capacity for assimilation. This adjective, which hastily takes into account the indisputable nonconformist will that quickens such a work, such a creator, has the grave defect of being confused with one which tends to define a systematic action aiming at the transformation of the world and implying the necessity of concretely attacking its real bases.

A most regrettable ambiguity results from this. Thus

Monsieur Paul Claudel, the French ambassador in Brussels, who is dedicating the leisures of his old age to putting lives of saints in verse as he sees fit, thus Monsieur Paul Claudel, who in another connection is the apostle of "going the whole hog" in time of war (this ignoble phrase unfortunately expresses all too well the idea behind it) is considered, because of certain formal innovations in his poetry, to be an avant-garde writer, and it is not without a shudder that we learn that his *L'Annonce faite à Marie* has been translated and staged in the U.S.S.R.

Thus too, authors whose technique is unbelievably behind the times, but who do not neglect a single occasion to proclaim themselves to be in perfect accord with the ideology of the left or the extreme left, find a great number of willing ears when they take it into their heads to lay the law down about this very technique, scorning what constitutes the historic necessities of its development.

There is no reason to close our eyes to the fact that Monsieur Claudel's case on the one hand, and the attitude of these authors on the other, both cast great discredit on modern art, a discredit which in leftist political circles today goes, if not so far as to cause suspicion to be cast on the good faith of innovating writers and artists who may be truly attached to the cause of the proletariat, at least so far as to put the quality and the efficacy of the services that they can render this cause in grave doubt.

In the face of the difficulties that have been encountered, in France, for example, by the Surrealists' adherence to various revolutionary organizations, difficulties that have proved to be insurmountable for a certain number of us, it is not at all an exaggeration to say, if one can still speak of intellectual drama in a world shaken from top to bottom by a drama of another nature, that the situation of these innovating writers and artists is dramatic. They find themselves, in fact, in the face of a dilemma: either they must give up interpreting and expressing the world in the ways that each of them finds the secret of within himself and himself alone—it is his very chance of enduring that is at stake—or they must give up collaborating on the practical plan of action for changing this world. Although a few symptoms of greater tolerance have begun to appear within the last few months, it would appear that for a long time they had nothing but a choice between these two abdications. It has become a commonplace, moreover, to point out that leftist political circles appreciate in art only time-honored, or even outworn, forms: a few years ago *L'Humanité* made a specialty out of translating Mayakovsky's poems into doggerel; in the sculpture section of the Association of Revolutionary Writers and Artists of Paris, they began by offering a bust of Stalin for competition—whereas rightist circles are remarkably cordial, peculiarly friendly in this respect. Monsieur Léon Daudet, the editor of the royalist journal *L'Action française,* is pleased to repeat that Picasso is the greatest living painter; a large daily paper a few days ago reported in a three-column article that with the patronage of Mussolini primitives, classic painters, and Surrealists were soon going to occupy the Grand Palais simultaneously in a huge exhibition of Italian art.

What to do? Avant-garde art, caught between this total lack of comprehension and this completely relative, self-seeking comprehension, cannot in my opinion long put up with such a compromise. Those among the modern poets and artists—the vast majority, I think—who realize that their work confuses and baffles bourgeois society, who very conscientiously aspire to help bring about a new world, a better world, owe it to themselves to swim against the current that is dragging them into passing for mere entertainers, whom the bourgeoisie will never let up on (they tried to make Catholic poets out of Baudelaire, out of Rimbaud, once they were dead).

Is there, properly speaking, is there or is there not an art of the left capable of defending itself, and I mean by that one capable of justifying its "advanced" technique by the very fact that it is in the service of a leftist state of mind?

Is it vain to seek to discover a cause-and-effect relationship between this state of mind and this technique? It is dismaying, really, that this is the point we have reached, at the very moment when scientific experimentation, by contrast, can not only be pursued without hindrance but also, because of adventurous speculations that it gives rise to, is watched *from the left* with the most constant solicitude.

And we barely escape being asked why we don't write in alexandrines any more, why we don't paint historical scenes, or at least apples, like Cézanne.

I say that this art can find its justification only through searching analysis and systematic objectification of its resources. I think that this latter task is the only one that will allow us to clear up this detestable misunderstanding that has lasted far too long. It is only by coming back, each time it is possible, to the actual particulars of the artistic problem and by not neglecting any occasion to bare the reasons that lead the artist to adopt a new technique that we will manage to put things to rights once again. I am persuaded that in this way we will soon have done with the very evident differences of opinion that have impaired judgment up to now.

And let us first of all take the elementary precaution of repeating that we are in the West, that is to say that far from witnessing and participating, as our Russian comrades do, in the building of a new world, of a world whose evolution opens an unlimited field to human hope (and it is quite natural that in these conditions the first temptation of Soviet writers and artists was to reflect it in and for all things, and their first ambition to make it known), we live in open conflict with the immediate world that surrounds us, an ultrasophisticated world, a world which, no matter what aspect of it is put to the question, proves in the face of free thought to be *without an alibi*. In whatever direction I turn, there is in the functioning of this world the same appearance of cold and hostile irrationality, the same outer ceremony beneath which it is immediately obvious that the sign survives the thing signified. It is a matter of all intellectual values being persecuted, all moral ideas falling to pieces, all the benefits of life being condemned to corruption and becoming indiscernible. The contamination of money has covered everything over. What is designated by the word fatherland, or the word justice, or the word duty has become foreign to us. A gaping wound opens before our eyes; we are witnesses of the fact that great evil continues to be perpetuated, and our first task is merely to measure our participation in it. To be objectors in every respect to whatever particular obligation this world attempts to reduce us. The most disgusting derision is the key to all the procedures by which this world has the gall to try and win us over to its cause. We have only to open a newspaper and we are immediately at grips with this frightful delirium of a dying man: here dogs are being blessed; there, always in the same place, we are not spared for a single day the bewildering paradox: "He who wants peace prepares war"; a bit farther on they are seeking to awaken the old and sordid instinct for mob lynching, against a man whom abysmal social contradictions, more treacherous for him than for another, have pushed into committing a misdeed or a crime. All this wantonly supported by a greedy imposition of servitude, whose aim it has become to trample human dignity underfoot, each day a bit more knowingly. People seek on all sides to bring about a dismal resignation, with the help of many bits of foolishness— recitals and spectacles. The most elementary logical notions do not manage to escape this onslaught of baseness unharmed: during a recent trial in France, a psychiatric expert was heard to declare that the accused man belonged to a category of abnormal people whose responsibility was not thereby diminished in any way but indeed was to be considered to be increased. And this idiot, who was also doubtless a scoundrel, could calmly walk out of the courtroom, proud as can be of his sadistic shrewdness. He deserved well, of course, of the bourgeois world, in whom this idea of responsibility, which is still firmly rooted in public opinion however unclear it may be, remains the only thing that paralyzes its odious system of oppression. This constant need to pile one savagery, one absurdity atop another suffices to substantiate the fact that we are going through a real crisis of judgment, this being of course a function of the economic crisis. Men who profess to think necessarily feel more affected by this former crisis than by this latter. There is no doubt that the initial symptoms of this might be sought rather far back in time, in a good number of Romantic or post-Romantic writers and artists, if we are aware of their completely spontaneous hatred of the typical bourgeois, who was so energetically derided and opposed in France by men such as Pétrus Borel, Flaubert, Baudelaire, Daumier, or Courbet. These five names alone would point to a common will not to compromise in any way whatsoever with the reigning class, which from 1830 to 1870 is ridiculed and stigmatized by artists for its morals above all else. It is only after 1871, the date of the first revolution of the proletariat, that the half-comic bourgeois bogeyman begins to be considered as the symbol of an encroaching peril, doomed to grow continuously worse and worse, of a sort of leprosy against which—if one wishes to prevent the real meaning of the most precious human attainments from being distorted and from contributing only to the greater and greater debasement of the human condition—it was no longer sufficient merely to brandish the whip; rather, it will some day be necessary to apply a red-hot iron to it.

We should notice that the last artist that I have named, Gustave Courbet, is already convinced of this, and plays a role in the foreground of the great popular uprising of the Commune. As you know, it was at his instigation that the Vendôme column, the symbol of Napoleon's victories, was condemned to destruction, and Courbet is there in his shirtsleeves, magnificently robust and alive, watching it fall onto its bed of manure. The serious, childlike expression on the face of this man at this moment, a man who is also a very great artist, has always captivated me. This head, in fact, is the one in which there takes place a wholly original explosion of the contradiction that still possesses us Western writers of the left when it is a question of giving our work the meaning we would like our acts to have, with the aid of certain outside circumstances. I leaf through a Courbet album today: here are forests, here are women, here is the sea, here are priests coming back drunk and staggering from some solemn rite beneath the gibes of fieldhands, but here also is the magic scene entitled "Le Reve," where the realism, however deliberate it is, manages to hold its own only in the execution, since there is not the slightest trace of it in the general conception. As can be seen, the majority of the pictorial themes taken up by Courbet do not differ essentially from those that the artists of his time chose to treat. I emphasize the fact that in them we can discover no clear trace, so to speak, of his social preoccupations, even though they were active concerns with him. For purposes of general exaltation, we may no doubt regret that Courbet has not given his personal vision of this episode or that in the great insurrection in which he took part, but in the end we must resign ourselves to the fact that he did not attempt to do so.

Such a remark becomes all the more meaningful from the fact, for example, that we owe the graphic portrayal of some of the most striking scenes of the first French Revolution to a painter who was an academician if there ever was one, or in other words an artist who technically was as impersonal as possible, and by that very fact very much behind his own times: David. It is nonetheless true that Courbet's work proved to be particularly capable of withstanding time, and that by virtue of its technique alone it has had such a vast influence that it would not be stretching the truth to maintain today that the whole of modern painting would be different if this body of work had not existed. David on the other hand has had no influence at all, and today it takes all the indulgent curiosity of the historian to get his grand classic backgrounds, against which figures with no feelings whatsoever are frozen, exhumed from time to time. Moreover, David the official painter of the Revolution is potentially David the official painter of the Empire. We relapse, once again, into inauthenticity.

As far as Courbet is concerned, we must recognize that everything happens as if he had decided that there must be some way to reflect his profound faith in the betterment of the world in everything that he tried to evoke, some way to make it appear somehow in the light that he caused to fall on the horizon or on a roebuck's belly. . . . Here, then, was a man of mature sensibilities and, most importantly, one at grips with certain of the most intoxicating circumstances in all of history. These circumstances lead him, as a man, to risk his life without hesitation; they do not lead him to give directly polemical meaning to his art.

I shall take another example from the same period. Arthur Rimbaud too is there to confront the new-born Commune with all his seventeen-year-old genius. How will he behave toward it? His biographers are insistent on one point. His enthusiasm the first day is boundless: on his way from Charleville to Paris, he loses not a single chance to try to communicate this enthusiasm to all those he meets, knowing that the uprising he dreams of taking part in aims at changing their lot for the better. To judge from the conversations he had at this juncture, as reported by Ernest Delahaye, Rimbaud from this moment on had a very clear idea of the profound causes and aims of the great workers' movement. His whole will to change the world radically, a will that no one ever took farther than he did, was suddenly channeled, was immediately offered up to become one with the workers' will to emancipation. It is as if human happiness, which his previous work at once denies and exasperatedly searches for, suddenly revealed itself to him, ready to let itself be won. Days pass, the Commune suffers a crushing defeat. The blood of its victims takes with it all the hope of a generation, blocks the ascent of a century toward the sun. For a long time to come, truth will again have to go underground, having been reduced to tatters along with life. Why shouldn't we try and delve deeply and fervently to find out what trace all this may have left in Rimbaud's work? What reason would there be not to catch ourselves wishing that it would reflect for all men this initial hope that lives on despite everything, and that it would draw from despair itself the strength to inspire confidence in the outcome of future struggles? But if one questions Rimbaud's complete works on this point, one finds on the one hand that the poems written under the direct pressure of events of the Commune are four in number, "Les Mains de Jeanne-Marie," "Le Coeur volé," "Paris se repeuple," "Chant de guerre parisienne" (two others have apparently been lost), and that their tenor in no way differs from that of the other poems; on the other hand, that all Rimbaud's later poetry unfolds in a direction that implies no appreciable lack of continuity with the poetry that went before. The verbal experiments, of a quality that is extremely rare, which characterize his later poetry from one end to the other confer on these four poems I have mentioned a cast that is no less hermetic than that conferred on his other poems that at first sight seem the most difficult. The central preoccupation that comes to light in them is still obviously of a technical order. As in the preceding case, it is clear here that his great ambition was to translate the world into a new language, that this ambition tended to override all others along the way, and one cannot help but see in this the reason for the totally unique influence that this work enjoys on the poetic plane, and perhaps on the moral plane, and for the exceptional renown that it continues to enjoy.

It can be seen that the beginning, then the end, of the profoundly exciting state of affairs that went to make up the life of the Paris Commune, for example, for all practical purposes left art face to face with its own problems, and that afterward, as before, the great themes that presented themselves to the poet and the artist continued to be the round of the seasons, nature, women, love, dreams, life, and death. The fact is that art, somewhere during its whole evolution in modern times, is summoned to the realization that its quality resides in imagination alone, independently of the exterior object that brought it to birth. Namely, that *everything depends on the freedom with which this imagination manages to express and assert itself and to portray only itself.* The very condition of objectivity in art is that it appear to be detached from every specific circle of ideas and forms. In that way alone will it conform to the primordial necessity that belongs to it alone, which is the necessity of being totally *human.* In it all the interests of the heart and mind together find a means of entering into play. Rimbaud moves us, wins our hearts just as much when he undertakes to make us see a child given over to the care of two "Seekers of Lice" as when he uses all his sublime capacity for bitterness to depict for us the entry of troops from Versailles into Paris. True spirit must show itself everywhere at once. There are still a great many of us in the world who think that putting poetry and art in the exclusive service of an idea, however much that idea moves us to enthusiasm by itself, would be to condemn them in a very short time to being immobilized, and amount to sidetracking them. I have said that I wanted to put forth no idea that does not follow from the analysis of the very resources of poetry and art. Let us therefore stop to consider this analysis for a few moments.

It is common knowledge that true poetry and art are a function of two essential things, that they bring into play in man two special means, the power of emotion and the gift of expression. No one considers it a revelation to discover that every great poet or artist is a man of exceptional sensitiveness, and in its search for the biographical particulars of his life, a search often carried to greater lengths than is reasonable, the public customarily attributes to him reactions that have a violence proportionate to his genius. A very great thirst for pathos here seeks to satisfy itself in a rather theoretical manner. The exceptional gift of expression of a Shakespeare, a Goethe, or a Baudelaire is something no less universally recognized. Men of all conditions, all classes, who find splendid justification in their works, who find in them a temporarily triumphant awareness of the meaning of their joys and sorrows, do not lose sight of the fact that a unique privilege now and then permits artistic subjectivity to become identical with true objectivity; they render homage to the individual faculty that sheds light on the great ignorance, the great collective obscurity. But if in general it is quite clear that the power of emotion and the gift of expression must both be present in the man from whom we may expect a *work of art,* people commonly have, on the other hand, a completely false idea of the relationships that obtain between these two great means in the born artist. Positivist rationalism soon gave people to believe that the second tended to put itself directly in the service of the first: as a poet, you experience a violent emotion, which I suppose to be private in nature, in the course of your life; you will write the work that counts for something, you are told, under the immediate influence of this emotion. This statement need only be examined more closely to see that it is wrong on all counts. Even if it were granted that a small number of genuine poetic works came about under these conditions (in France we could find a few examples in the work of Victor Hugo), most often such a method results only in a work that does not make much of a mark, for the simple reason that poetic subjectivity has here gotten the upper hand, *that it has not been brought back to that one living focal point from which it can radiate outward,* from which alone it is able to penetrate to the depths of men's hearts. Determining this living focal point should, in my opinion, be the central concern of all the critical speculation that art gives rise to. I say that subjective emotion, whatever its intensity, is not directly creative in art, that it has value only insofar as it is reinstated in, and indistinctly incorporated into, the emotional depths which the artist is called to draw upon. Generally, it is not by divulging to us the circumstances in which he lost a loved one forever that he will manage to move us in turn, even if his emotion at this moment is at its height. Nor is it by sharing with us, in whatever lyric mode, the enthusiasm aroused in him by such and such a spectacle, let us say the spectacle of Soviet victories, that he will arouse or keep alive the same enthusiasm in us. He can thereby write an eloquent work, and that is all. On the other hand, if this pain is very deep and very keen, this enthusiasm very lively, they will be of such a nature as to intensify extremely that living focus of which I was speaking. Every later work, whatever the pretext for it, will thereby increase all the more in stature; one can even say that providing it avoids the temptation to communicate the emotional process directly, it will gain in humanity what it loses in severity.

When I was drawing up these notes a few days ago in the country, my bedroom window overlooked a vast sun- and rain-drenched countryside in the southwest of France, and from it I could see a very beautiful rainbow whose end touched the ground very close to me, in a little walled enclosure open to the sky and overgrown with ivy. This very low house, long in ruins, with its walls which seemed never to have supported a roof, its worm-eaten beams, its moss, its dirt filled with weeds and rubbish, and the little animals that I imagined were crouching in its corners, took me back to my earliest memories, to the very first emotions of my childhood, and it seemed to me a very beautiful thing that this rainbow should come forth from it at that very moment to illustrate what I was saying. Yes, this rainbow seemed at that moment to be the very trajectory of emotion through space and time. The best and the worst of what I had myself experienced, plunged, then plunged again, as it pleased, into this house which was no longer a house, on which twilight was now descending, and above which a bird sang. And the colors of the spectrum had never been as intense as when they played over this little house. It was as if the whole rainbow effect had truly come to birth there, as if everything that such a building had once meant to me, the discovery of mystery, beauty, fear had been necessary for whatever understanding I may have of myself when I undertake to unveil the truth to myself. This little house was the crucible, the *living focus* that I wanted to show here. It was in this house that everything in my life that had disheartened and enchanted me had melted away, had been shorn of everything that was incidental. It alone stood before this luminous and endless wheel.

The state of social laceration in which we live leaves the man who is not an art specialist little inclination to admit that the problem of expression is posed in these terms. In general, he confines himself to the manifest content of the work of art, and to the degree that he has taken sides politically, he is ready to find in it all sorts of virtues or defects, depending on whether it outwardly militates in favor of the cause that he has made his own or not. The very urgency of the task of changing the world, such as it appears to us, commonly leads people to believe that all available means ought to be enlisted in its service, that the pursuit of all other intellectual tasks should be postponed. "You are stirring up post-revolutionary problems," people have said; "if such problems should ever be posed, it can only be within a classless society." I believe that in the last part of my *Vases communiquants* I have already treated this objection as it deserves:

So long as the decisive step has not been taken toward general liberation, the intellectual—we are told—should make every effort to act on the proletariat to raise its level of awareness as a class and develop its fighting spirit.

This completely pragmatic solution does not stand up under examination. It is no sooner formulated than objections that are by turn essential and incidental are raised against it.

It takes far too little account, in the first place, of the permanent conflict within the individual between the theoretical idea and the practical idea, both of which are inadequate by themselves and doomed to mutually limit each other. It does not discuss the reality of the circuitous path man is forced to follow because of his very nature, which makes him depend not only on the form of existence of the collectivity, but also on a subjective necessity: the need for both himself and his species to survive. This desire that I attribute to him, that I know is within him, the desire to have done as soon as possible with a world where what is most valuable in him each day becomes more incapable of showing what it can accomplish, this desire in which his noble aspirations must be concentrated and coordinated to the utmost—how could it keep on being an active desire if it did not at each second mobilize all the personal past, all the personal present of the individual? . . . It is important that there be some of us on this side of Europe to keep this desire ready to be endlessly created anew, and properly centered on eternal human desires if it is not to become impoverished by becoming the prisoner of its own rigor. Once viable, this desire must not prevent every sort of question from being posed, and the need to know in all fields *from taking its course. It is a fortunate thing that Soviet expeditions, after so many others, are heading for the Pole today. This too is a way for the Revolution to advise us of its victory. Who would dare to accuse me of delaying the day when this victory must be seen to be total by pointing out a few other no less venerable and no less beautiful areas of attraction? A hard and fast rule, such as the one requiring of the individual an activity strictly appropriate to a revolutionary aim and forbidding him all other activities cannot fail to replace this revolutionary aim in the category of abstract good, that is to say a principle that is not enough to motivate the being whose subjective will no longer tends of and by itself to identify itself with this abstract good. . . .*

The incidental objections that seem to me to be of the sort to reinforce these essential objections have to do with the fact that the revolutionary world today finds itself for the first time divided into two sections which aspire, certainly, with all their might to unite, and which will unite, but which find between them a wall so many centuries thick that nothing can be done but destroy it. This wall is so opaque and resistant that because of it the forces which, on both sides of it, militate for its being torn down, are in large part reduced to guesswork, to presuppositions. This wall, which naturally is subject to very serious cracks, is peculiar in that in front of it people are boldly building, organizing life, whereas behind it the revolutionary effort is applied to destruction, to the necessary disorganization of the existing state of affairs. There results from this a remarkable unevenness within revolutionary thought, an unevenness whose spatial, completely episodic nature gives it a most unpromising character.

Since revolutionary reality is not able to be the same for men who are differently situated, some on this side of armed insurrection, and others beyond it, it may appear somewhat hazardous to seek to institute a community of duties for men with different orientations to such an essential concrete fact. . . . Our ambition is to unite—with an indestructible knot, a knot whose secret we will have passionately sought to penetrate so that it may be truly indestructible—this activity of transformation with this activity of interpretation. . . . We want this knot to be tied, we want it to give rise to the wish to undo it and the discovery that it cannot be undone. . . . If in the new society we wish to prevent private life, with its opportunities and its disappointments, from continuing to be both the great distributor and the great depriver of energies, we must see to it that subjective existence finds splendid revenge in the field of knowledge, of consciousness that is neither weak nor ashamed. Every error in the interpretation of man gives rise to an error in the interpretation of the universe: it is, consequently, an obstacle to its transformation. Now it must be pointed out that a whole world of unavowable prejudices gravitates around the other world, the world which can be dealt justice only with a red-hot iron from the moment that we observe a minute of suffering under high magnification. It is made up of cloudy, distorting bubbles which keep coming up from the marshy bottom, from the unconscious of the individual. The transformation of society will be truly effective and complete only when we have put an end to these corrupting germs. We will put an end to them only by agreeing to rehabilitate the study of the ego so as to be able to integrate it with that of collective being.

May I be permitted to point out that these theses, which at that time were held to be *unacceptable,* to be quite contradictory, if only to the resolutions of the Kharkov Congress, today are beginning to receive splendid confirmation? May I be permitted to maintain that they were within the line laid down for poetry and art in 1935 by the first Congress of Soviet Writers, *even before this line was laid down?* May I be permitted to claim that, along with my Surrealist friends, I was the only one that was not mistaken?

I came back more explicitly to these theses, as a matter of fact, in a text that appeared in issue number six of the *Minotaure,* under the title: "La Grande actualité poétique," where by turn I record the reinforcement of the position I have just defined on the plane of world poetry, and the symptoms of an early end to the conflict which seem, happily, to have finally materialized in the last few months.

It is impossible, in my opinion, not to be convinced that a sort of very unusual consultative voice has suddenly been attributed to the poet as night falls on a world, a voice that he will keep and rightfully use in another world, as day breaks. It is not just in France that this consultative voice is beginning to be granted the poet, not without great reticence. It seems as if bourgeois civilization on every hand finds itself more inexorably condemned because it totally lacks poetic justification. To restrict myself here to two evidences of this, a text by Stephen Spender, and another by C. Day Lewis, which have just been translated from English by Flavia Léopold, I shall add along with them that today's poet, thoroughly convinced of the greatness of his own role, is less ready than ever to renounce his prerogatives where expression is concerned:

Communists today [C. Day Lewis writes], "picture us as being slaves to the formula of art for art's sake, and poetry as a trifle, or at the very most an infidel, so long as it is not the servant of revolution. Don't believe a word of it. No real poet has ever written in obedience to a formula. He writes because he wants to make something.

" 'Art for art's sake' is as senseless a formula for him as the formula 'Revolution for revolution's sake' would be in the eyes of the true revolutionary. The poet gives his universe, and translates into his own language, the language of individual truth, the coded messages that he receives. In a capitalist regime these materials cannot help but have a capitalist tinge. But if this regime is dying, or as you would have it, is already dead, its poetry is bound to point this out: it will have a funereal sound, but this is not to say that it will therefore cease to be poetry. If we are on the threshold of a new life, you may rest assured that the poet will have something to say about it, for he has sharp senses."

And Spender, after having spoken his mind about this propaganda poetry where the writer comes up against this impossible challenge, on the one hand to try to "create a poem which forms a whole," and on the other hand "to try to draw us out of poetry so as to lead us into the real world" and having adjured poetry to remain what it is, "an important function of language and feeling," remarks:

. . . The antipathy of Communists for bourgeois art stems above all from the fact that they imagine, quite wrongly, that bourgeois art necessarily propagates bourgeois "ideology." When the proletariat has produced its own literature, it will obviously rediscover the literature of today. Thus in Russia Tolstoi has numerous readers today, and the people will soon discover writers who were contemporaries, because a literature without a historic link with the literature of the past and even of the immediate past cannot exist. It will be realized, when the time comes, that bour-

geois art is not bourgeois propaganda, but simply the depiction of that phase of our society when the bourgeois class possessed culture. . . . It is quite true that bourgeois art is the work of bourgeois writers who speak of bourgeois and address themselves to bourgeois, but it is not true that this art is nothing but counterrevolutionary propaganda. It might seem much closer to the truth to maintain that bourgeois art has played a large part in the downfall of capitalist society, but this opinion would be as erroneous as the one I have just mentioned: art has merely placed already existent forces working to pull the regime down into contact with each other. Art has not played a role in propaganda, but it has contributed to psychoanalysis. For this reason it is very important that we always have good artists and that these artists do not stray off into militant politics, for art may allow revolutionary militants to see clearly those events in history that have the most political meaning, in the deepest sense of the word.

These very vigorous protests, which are current in various countries as they are in France, are provoked, we know, by a series of more or less unfortunate attempts to codify poetry and art in Soviet Russia, a codification that was paradoxically and imprudently applied immediately to all other countries by political zealots. In this respect the misdeeds of the RAPP (Association of Proletarian Writers), dissolved in April 1932, cannot be emphasized too strongly. The history of Russian poetry since the Revolution, moreover, leads one not only to question the correctness and the harshness of the cultural line that was followed, but also to think that the results obtained are, on the political plane, the exact opposite of what was being sought. Essenin's suicide, shortly before Mayakovsky's, if one remembers that in the field of poetry these two names are the greatest that the Russian Revolution can put forward, even considering the "bad company" the former kept, and certain "bourgeois holdovers" of the latter, cannot help but give credence to the opinion that they were the objects of serious persecution, and that in their lifetime they were understood only very superficially. As we look back, it may seem that everything was done to obtain from them more than they were able to give, and it is quite significant to hear Trotsky deplore the fact that in the first period of "revolutionary reconstruction" the technique of Mayakovsky—who had thought it his duty to devote all his lyric powers to celebrating this reconstruction—had become banal. It is also necessary to state today that the cultural policy of the U.S.S.R. has shown itself to be not only quite disastrous but also perfectly vain on this point, as is amply witnessed, on the one hand, by the current downfall of the *false* so-called proletarian poets, and, on the other hand, by the growing success of a Boris Pasternak, who, we are carefully told, is "always irrational," always spontaneous, and "knew how to create a universe of his own," a universe that is far from owing everything to the specific preoccupations of his surroundings and his time, since "memories and objects, love and dreams, words and meditation, nature and play" are presented to us as "the elements that people his creation."

The First Congress of Soviet Writers, which was held from August 17 to September 1 in Moscow, appears to mark the beginning of a period of thaw in this respect. Is this to say that somewhere in the world there has come a time when the personality of man is going to be able to give its full measure in lyric poetry as well as elsewhere? This cannot be, of course, and it is hardly worth recalling that the Revolution is merely preparing itself, to repeat Trotsky's phrase, to "win every man's right not only to bread but to poetry." This conquest belongs to classless world society. However, it cannot help but be a most hopeful sign when we see a preponderant tendency to study seriously every aspect of the human problem manifesting itself in Moscow in 1934, and it can only be comforting to pay close attention to certain characteristic aspects of the Congress. While poetry in the other countries is condemned to having an almost shameful marginal existence, and can aspire only to be a distant echo (outside of the framework of existence of the poet), it is a *sign of the times* when a director of Soviet policy, Bukharin, who is also a ranking *dialectician,* takes it upon himself to present the report on poetry to a First Congress of Writers, and it is also a sign of the times when this report concludes that there is no antagonism between the image (the recourse to the irrational) and the idea, that there is no antagonism between the "new eroticism" and the "meaning of the collectivity" within the framework of a "socialist realism" which "can have no other objective than man himself." It is impossible at the present time to measure the scope of such declarations coming from such a source. The least that we can say is that because of them poetry turns out to be more necessary, more alive than ever, and that its prestige cannot fail to be considerably enhanced on the international scale.

It is also a *sign of the times* when André Malraux, who was warmly applauded, can give a sensational and decisive speech in Moscow, from which I excerpt the following passages:

Does the image of the U.S.S.R. that is given us in its literature express it?

In the outer facts, yes.

In ethics and psychology, no.

Because you do not always extend to writers the full share of confidence that you extend to everyone else.

Why?

Because of a misunderstanding about culture, it seems to me.

What do all the delegations who have come here so that their members can bring this human warmth here, this unique friendship in which your literature believes, say to you?

"Express us, show us."

It is necessary to know how.

Yes, the Soviet Union must be expressed. . . . But be warned, comrades, that by expressing a powerful civilization one does not necessarily create a powerful literature, and that for a great literature to be born photographing a great era here will not suffice. . . .

If "writers are the engineers of souls," do not forget that the highest function of an engineer is to invent.

Art is not a submission, it is a conquest.

The conquest of what?

Of feelings and the means to express them.

About what?

About the unconscious, almost always; about logic, very often.

Marxism is the consciousness of the social; culture is the consciousness of the psychological.

To the bourgeoisie that said: the individual; communism will reply: man. And the cultural watchword that communism will set in opposition to those of the greatest eras of individualism, the watchword which in Marx's works links the first pages of the German Ideology *to the last drafts of* Capital *is: "More awareness."*

"More awareness"—this is, in all truth, the watchword par excellence that we like to remember from Marx and would like to remember from this first Congress. More awareness of the social always, but also more awareness of the psychological. Such a consideration necessarily leads us back to the problem of how to acquire this greater awareness, and here it seems to me indispensable to call upon the specialist whose authority can be considered the least exceptionable on the subject:

The question "How does something become conscious?" may be advantageously replaced, Freud says, by this question:

"How does something become preconscious?" The answer: "thanks to the association with the corresponding verbal representations," *and a little further on he says more explicitly:* "How can we bring repressed elements into (pre)consciousness?—by reestablishing through the work of analysis those intermediate preconscious members, verbal memories."

Now these verbal representations, which Freud tells us are "mnemonic traces stemming principally from acoustic perceptions" are precisely what constitutes the raw material of poetry. "Poetic rubbish," Rimbaud reveals, "had a great part in my alchemy of the word." Surrealism's whole effort in particular for the last fifteen years has been to obtain from the poet the instantaneous revelation of these verbal traces whose psychic charges are capable of being communicated to the perception-consciousness system (and also to obtain from the painter the most rapid projection possible of optical mnemonic traces). I shall never tire of repeating that *automatism* alone is the dispenser of the elements on which the secondary work of emotional amalgamation and passage from the unconscious to the preconscious can operate effectively.

I have recently been accused of seeking to establish a sort of united front of poetry and art; people have written that automatism, such as it has been practiced by Surrealism, could be considered to be nothing but a tic, nothing but a superannuated bias of a literary school that was wrongly considered to be a means of knowledge. If what I am accused of is the will to dig out and defend whatever there may be that is common and inalienable in the aspirations of those whose role it is today to sharpen human sensibilities again, beyond all the differences that separate them, most of which I consider to be reducible in the near future, yes, I am for the constitution of this united front of poetry and art. As regards the conception that each of them has of his own role, I see no fundamental antagonism between, for example, Pierre-Jean Jouve, who believes that "in its experience today, poetry is in the presence of multiple condensations through which it manages to touch the *symbol*—no longer controlled by the intellect but rather rising from the depths, redoubtable and real," Tristan Tzara, according to whom "the notions of identity and of imitation, whose senseless use in the interpretation of the work of art constitutes the principal argument of those who would like to assign it the role of a tool for propaganda, are now replaced by those having specifically to do with a process of *symbolization*," and André Malraux, declaring that "the work of the Western artist consists of creating a personal myth through a *series of symbols*." If I discover no essential obstacle to the formation of this "united front," it is because it seems obvious to me that the elucidation of the means proper to today's art that is worthy of this name and the very elaboration of the personal myth that has just been mentioned can in the end result only in the denunciation of the conditions in which this art and this myth are called upon to develop themselves, and in the unconditional defense of a single cause, that of the *emancipation of man*. This has obviously been the case with Surrealism, whose systematic action resulted in the creating, among young intellectuals, of a current that clearly opposed inertia in politics and the need for escape from the real that was almost the one distinguishing characteristic of the whole postwar psychosis.

If Surrealism went to Moscow, people have said that it was because it hoped to find indispensable support for the spread of its poetry in social revolution, that is to say the possibility, in the leisure that had been won for the liberated proletarian man, of living off a personal activity that for lack of a better word we still call poetic. This transposition of the Surrealist act to the political plane has resulted in acquainting contemporary young people with the U.S.S.R. and making it possible to hold the opinion that in theory the Soviet regime was a viable regime, perhaps the only one. Surrealism was the first to take this path, which others— Gide and Malraux—have followed.*

Psychic automatism—is it really indispensable to return to this subject?—has never constituted an end in itself for Surrealism, and to claim the contrary is to show bad faith. The premeditated energy in poetry and in art that has as its object the rediscovery, at any price, of the naturalness, the truth, and the originality it once had, in a society that has come to the end of its development and is on the threshold of a new society, necessarily had some day to discover the immense reservoir from which symbols spring completely armed and spread to collective life through the work of a few men. It was a question of foiling, foiling for-

* P. O. Lapie, "L'Insurrection surréaliste," *Cahiers du sud,* January, 1935.

ever, the coalition of forces that seek to make the unconscious incapable of any sort of violent eruption: a society that feels itself threatened on all sides, as bourgeois society does, rightly thinks that such an eruption may be the death of it. The technical procedures that Surrealism has developed for that purpose could, of course, have value in its eyes only as a sounding-line, and there is no way to turn them to account except as such. But regardless of what has been said of them, we persist in maintaining that they are within the reach of everyone and that once they have been defined, anyone who cares to can trace on paper and elsewhere the apparently hieroglyphic signs that at least express the first instances of what has been called, by contrast to the *ego,* the *id,* meaning thereby all the psychic elements in which the ego (which is conscious by definition) is prolonged and in which people have been led to see "the arena of the struggle that brings Eros and the death instinct to grips." We should not linger over the signs in question because of their immediate strangeness or their formal beauty, for the excellent reason that it has now been established that they are *decipherable.* Personally, I believe that I have sufficiently insisted on the fact that the automatic text and the Surrealist poem are no less interpretable than the dream narrative, and that nothing must be neglected to carry through such interpretations each time that we can be put on the track of them. I do not know if these are postrevolutionary problems, but I do know that art, which for centuries has been forced to stray very little from the beaten path of the *ego* and *superego,* cannot help but be eager to explore the immense and almost virgin territory of the *id* in all directions. It is now too committed to this to give up this far-distant expedition, and I see nothing rash in this to prejudice its future evolution. I said at the beginning that we live in an era in which man belongs to himself less than ever; it is not surprising that such an era, in which the anguish of living has reached its peak, sees these great floodgates opening in art. The artist, in turn, is beginning to give up the personality that he was so jealous of before. He is suddenly in possession of the key to a treasure, but this treasure does not belong to him; it becomes impossible for him to arrogate it to himself, even by surprise: *this treasure is none other than the collective treasure.*

In these conditions, thus, art is no longer a question of the creation of a personal myth, but rather, with Surrealism, *of the creation of a collective myth.* For this fact to be questionable, it would have been necessary, as I have already said, for Surrealism to be opposed, for the postwar period in the West, by a movement of a completely different character that would have had the same attraction for young minds, and it is clear that such a movement has found no favorable terrain for itself in the last fifteen years. It is no less obvious that Surrealism has continued to go farther and farther beyond the strict framework within which certain of us have struggled fiercely to maintain it, to avoid seeing it turn aside onto an apolitical plane where it would lose all its historical meaning, or commit itself exclusively to the political plane, where it would merely be redundant. I certainly do not flatter myself today that I have seen to it that no one is now rebuffed by the aggressiveness Surrealism still has, which is absolutely necessary to keep it alive. I was shown, some time ago, a still life of Manet's that the jury unanimously refused just after it was painted, on the pretext that it was impossible to make anything out in it at all. This little canvas represents nothing more or less than a dead rabbit hung head down, painted with a clarity and a precision that leave it no reason to envy photography. The poetic works of the end of the last century that were considered the most hermetic or the most delirious are becoming clearer day by day. When the majority of the other works that offer no resistance to immediate comprehension have grown dim, when those voices in which a very large audience was pleased to recognize effortlessly its own voice have been stilled, it is strikingly clear that these difficult works have contradictorily begun to speak *for us.* Their darkness, pierced in the beginning by a single phosphorescent point that only very experienced eyes could see, has been replaced by a light that we know will one day be total. It is now beyond question that Surrealist works will share the same lot as all previous works that are *historically situated.* The climate of Benjamin Péret's poetry or Max Ernst's painting will then be the very climate of life. Hitler and his acolytes are, unfortunately, very well aware that it was necessary not only to persecute Marxists but also to forbid all avant-garde art in order to stifle leftist thought even for a short time. It is up to us to unite in opposing him through the invincible force of that which *must be,* of *human becoming.*

SPEECH TO THE CONGRESS OF WRITERS
(1935)

It is surely not by chance that we find ourselves assembled here in this hall in June 1935, and that for the first time such a discussion is embarked upon in Paris. It would be absolutely useless to disregard the circumstances that brought it about in this particular time and place. It would be absolutely false to attempt to eliminate from the debate everything that is not strictly relevant to the proper means for reassuring the defense of culture. Were we to do so, only the most disgusting sort of prophesying would result. Let us on the contrary emphasize that this discussion is taking place just after the signing of the Franco-Soviet pact of assistance and Stalin's declaration which L'Humanité *said was "hard" to resign ourselves to, and reverberated "like a clap of thunder." In my opinion every man who has not lost soundness of judgment out of political passion cannot help but condemn the means employed to bring about, from one day to the next, a complete reversal of opinion on this subject in the U.S.S.R. and in France. What steps were not taken for years to accustom us to the idea of possible aggression by France, the principal beneficiary of the Treaty of Versailles (how could we cease to be for the revision of this iniquitous treaty?)?*

Is it not true that a France armed to the teeth, an ultra-imperialist France still stunned at having hatched the Hitlerian monster, is this same France that suddenly has been recently justified in world opinion, that is even invited, in exchange for problematical aid to be granted to the U.S.S.R. in case of war, to speed up her production of armaments? On this point everything demonstrates that it is not our agreement that is being sought, but our submission. If the Franco-Soviet rapprochement appears to the directors of the U.S.S.R. to be a necessity, a hard necessity at present, if revolutionaries must convince themselves of this necessity as they had to convince themselves some years ago of the necessity of the N.E.P., they still must not let themselves be led by blind men, nor delightedly lend themselves to a still greater sacrifice than the one that is demanded of them. Beware of fideism lurking! If Franco-Soviet rapprochement is essential, this is less than ever the moment to part with our critical sense: it is up to us to keep extremely close watch on the lines along which this rapprochement is reached. Let us be on our guard from the moment that bourgeois France takes an interest in it: as intellectuals it is up to us to continue to be rather particularly suspicious of the forms that its cultural rapprochement with the U.S.S.R. may take.

Why? It is obvious that we are entirely won over to the idea of close collaboration between the two peoples on the scientific and artistic plane. We have never ceased to maintain that because proletarian culture must, in the very words of Lenin, "appear as the natural result of the knowledge acquired by humanity under the capitalist and feudalist yoke," the attentive consideration of Western literature, even contemporary literature, is just as essential to the Soviet writer as the attentive consideration of Soviet literature is to the revolutionary Western writer. Just as this latter must, in the words of Romain Rolland, embrace "the great tableaux of collective life presented by the principal Soviet novels," which are a school for action, so must the former continue to keep an eye on what Romain Rolland, again, calls "the great provinces of inner life" that Western literature reflects. It is quite significant that Romain Rolland, discussing the "role of the writer in today's society," reaches this lapidary formula: "We must dream, Lenin said; we must act, Goethe said." Surrealism has never claimed otherwise, except that all its effort has tended toward resolving this opposition dialectically. "The poet of the future," I wrote in

1932, "will go beyond the depressing idea of the irreparable divorce between action and dream. . . . He will bring together, at whatever cost, the two terms of the human relationship which, if destroyed, would instantly cause the most precious conquests to become a dead letter: the objective awareness of realities and their internal development, *insofar as it is magic (until we are otherwise notified), by virtue of individual feeling on the one hand and universal feeling on the other." This interpenetration of action and dream, being a function in particular of the interpenetration of Soviet literature and that of countries that are still capitalist, though it still awaits the fusion of these two literatures in that of the classless society, is everything that we have sought, everything we will continue to seek to render more profound and more effective.*

But this attitude, which we have long defined as ours, puts us particularly on our guard, I repeat, against the turn that the Franco-Soviet cultural rapprochement may take from the moment that the bourgeois government of this country takes it up as its own cause, but only from the outside, *and gives us reason to think that it will attempt to turn it against us, that it will attempt to twist it so as to make us abandon ideas regarding which until very recently it was important for revolutionaries to prove themselves unshakeable, that it will attempt, through the ploy of exchanging innocuous intellectual merchandise, to aim a blow at the morale of the working class. Here suddenly, caught in the tightening grasp of contradictions which obviously do not spare it any more than they do the other capitalist nations, here suddenly France is rehabilitated, here is Monsieur Laval back with his little accommodation bill. Here is France about to be able to put on airs as the elder sister of the Soviet Republic, and by that I mean airs as its protector: French imperialism needed only this mask to become even more insolent. On the intellectual plane, if I may say so, we may expect that the propaganda services of the Quai d'Orsay will take advantage of the situation to flood the U.S.S.R. with the insanities and vulgarities that France makes available to other peoples in the form of newspapers, books, films, and tours of the Comédie Française. We will not be very happy to see all that joining the complete works of Maupassant, the plays of Scribe, Claudel, and Louis Verneuil, which have already been brought into that country with impunity. These various considerations oblige us to keep ourselves in a state of* alert.

We proclaim this state of alert because it seems to us that people have been in too much of a hurry in their willingness to justify the abandonment of certain of the most venerable Bolshevik watchwords, and it seems to us that grave mistakes have been made which might have serious consequences. From the Marxist point of view it is, for example, extremely distressing to read in L'Humanité: "*If proletarians, to repeat Marx's expression, 'have no country,' the internationalists nonetheless have something to defend: the cultural patrimony of France, the spiritual riches accumulated through everything that its artists, its artisans, its workers, its thinkers have produced.*" *Who is there who will not see in this an attempt to revive—in complete contradiction to Marx's doctrine—the idea of the fatherland, a very passable definition of which is given in the last part of the sentence that I have just quoted? It is clearly specified here that the French worker is to defend the cultural patrimony of France, and what is worse, it is unquestionably hinted that he is to defend it against Germany. While in all recent armed conflicts it has been impossible to determine who was the aggressor, the French proletariat is now being prepared to bear all the responsibility of a new world war against Germany; it is being trained, in fact, to fight against the German proletariat, as in the grandest days of 1914.*

We Surrealists "don't love our country." As writers or artists, we have said that we have no intention whatsoever of rejecting the cultural heritage of centuries. It is annoying that today we are obliged to recall that for us it is a universal *heritage, which makes us no less dependent on German thought than on any other. Better still, we can say that it is above all in philosophy written in the German tongue that we have discovered the only effective antidote against the positivist rationalism which continues to wreak its ravages here.* This antidote is none other than dialectical materialism as a general theory of knowledge. *Today, as yesterday, it is positivist rationalism that we continue to oppose. That is what we have fought intellectually, that we will continue to fight as the principal enemy, as* the enemy in our own country. *We remain firmly opposed to any claim by a Frenchman that he possesses the cultural patrimony of France alone, and to all extolling of a feeling of Frenchness in France.*

For our part we refuse to reflect, in literature as in art, the ideological about-face which in the revolutionary camp of this country was recently taken to mean the abandonment of the watchword: transform imperialist war into civil war. Although it appears fallacious to us to maintain that a war that would set Germany on the one hand against France and the U.S.S.R. on the other would not be an imperialist war (as if French imperialism, merely because of the Moscow pact, could cease to be itself in such a circumstance! Must it be admitted that this war would be half imperialist?), we will not work for the strangling of German thought—of German thought which, as we have said, was so active yesterday and cannot help but be the source of German revolutionary thought tomorrow—by revising our attitude concerning the French cultural patrimony. It is from this point of view that we unreservedly countersign the manifesto of March 25, 1935, of the Vigilance Committee of Intellectuals against any return to "sacred union." Like the Vigilance Committee, we think that "telling the German people that Hitler (and only he among all capitalist and fascist governments!) wants war is not a good way to persuade them." We demand that Germany not be excluded, under any pretext, from future international deliberations for disarmament and peace. We will not work for the strangling of German thought, we will oppose it insofar as it might serve to sanction the feeling that there will inevitably be a war that French workers would be all the happier to leave for because they would be preceded not only by the tricolor, but by the tricolor and the red flag.

On this occasion we have no intention whatsoever of modifying the line which has been ours for ten years. We have already said that our ambition was to show the use that could legitimately be made of our cultural heritage in our era and in the West. In the realm of poetry and in the realm of the plastic arts which are our special province, we still think (1) that this cultural heritage must be constantly inventoried; (2) that it must be decided what is deadwood in it so as to rapidly eliminate it; (3) that the only acceptable part furnished by the remainder must be used not only as a factor in human progress, but also as an arm which inevitably turns against bourgeois society as that society degenerates. *To light our path through the labyrinth of existing human works the judgment of posterity is, in all truth, a fairly sure guide since the spirit of man ever feels its way along, but also ever goes forward. It is not a question here of substituting desires for realities: independently of whatever* constitutes its "manifest content," the work of art lives to the degree that it ceaselessly re-creates emotion, and to the degree that an ever more general sensibility from day to day draws from it a more and more necessary sustenance. This is the case, for example, of a body of work such as that of Baudelaire; I cannot imagine his prestige ceasing to grow in the eyes of new generations of poets, even Soviet poets. This property, possessed here and there by certain artistic works, can appear to us only as a function of their very particular situation in time, of that air of being figureheads at the prow of a ship that they assume in relation to the historical circumstances that unleashed them. They bring about a perfect balance between the inner and the outer: it is this balance that objectively confers authenticity upon them; it is this balance that causes them to be called to pursue their dazzling career without being affected by social upheavals. A cultural heritage in its acceptable form is above all the sum of such works with an exceptionally rich "latent content." These works, which today in poetry are those of Nerval, Baudelaire, Lautréamont, and Jarry and not the many so-called "classic" works (the classics that bourgeois society has chosen for itself are not ours), remain above all else messengers and their influence ceaselessly increases in such a way that it would be useless for a poet of our time to oppose their being so chosen. Not only can literature not be studied outside the history of society and the history of literature itself; it also cannot be written, in each era, unless the writer reconciles two very different concrete facts: the history of society up to his time, and the history of literature up to his time. In poetry a body of work such as that of Rimbaud is a perfect example of this, and from the point of view of historical materialism revolutionaries must make it their own, not partially, but totally. I am assured that at the last commemoration of the dead of the Commune, the Paris Association of Revolutionary Writers paraded past the wall under the banner "To the Militants of the Commune: Rimbaud, Courbet, Flourens." The use here made of Rimbaud's name is improper. Revolutionaries must not answer the disloyalty of their adversaries by disloyalty on their part. To represent Rimbaud—the artist and the man at grips with all his problems—as having arrived in May 1871, at a conception of his role that could be contrasted with that of today's poetic researchers is to falsify the facts. To do that, or brazenly *to claim that Rimbaud fell silent "for lack of an audience"—in the same way that by playing on a simple coincidence of names people once tried to make us confuse the author of the* Chants de Maldoror, *Isidore Ducasse, with the Blanquist agitator Félix Ducasse—is knowingly to bear false witness. The first act of courage for a revolutionary must be to prefer life to legend. The real Rimbaud of that period, who was, certainly, won over socially to the revolutionary cause, is not only the author of "Les Mains de Jeanne-Marie," but also the author of "Le Coeur volé." Nor is he exclusively, as some would lead us to believe, the very young "sharpshooter of the Revolution" of the barracks of Babylon; he is also the man fully occupied with problems apparently external to the Revolution, the man who is wholly revealed in the so-called "Lettre du voyant," quite characteristically dated May 15, 1871.*

In the present period, one of our first cultural duties, one of our first duties on the literary plane, is to shelter such works full of sap against all falsification from the right or from the left which would result in their being impoverished. If we cite the work of Rimbaud as an example, let it be plainly understood that we could also cite that of Sade, or with certain reservations, that of Freud. Nothing can force us to deny these names, just as nothing will force us to deny the names of Marx and Lenin.

From where we stand, we maintain that the activity of interpreting the world must continue to be linked with the activity of changing the world. We maintain that it is the poet's, the artist's role to study the human problem in depth in all its forms, that it is precisely the unlimited *advance of his mind in this direction that has a potential value for changing the world, that this advance—insofar as it is an evolved product of the superstructure—cannot help but reinforce the necessity to change this world economically. In art we rise up against any regressive conception that tends to oppose content to form, in order to sacrifice the latter to the former. If today's authentic poets were to go in for propagandistic poetry, which as presently defined is completely exterior, this would mean that they were denying the* historical conditions of poetry itself. To defend culture *is above all to take over the interests of that which intellectually resists serious materialist analysis, of that which is viable, of that which will continue to bear fruit. It is not by stereotyped declarations against fascism and war that we will manage to liberate either the mind or man from the ancient chains that bind him and the new chains that threaten him. It is by the affirmation of our unshakeable fidelity to the powers of emancipation of the mind and of man that we have recognized one by one and that we will fight to cause to be recognized as such.*

"Transform the world," Marx said; "change life," Rimbaud said. These two watchwords are one for us.

Paris, June 1935.

ON THE TIME WHEN THE SURREALISTS
WERE RIGHT
(1935)

In notifying the "International Congress for the Defense of Culture" of their collective support, Surrealist writers, who looked forward to participating in a real discussion, had two principal goals in mind: (1) drawing attention to how unconditional and dangerous the words "defense of culture," taken by themselves, can be; (2) preventing all the sessions that had been set up from dribbling away into antifascist soapbox preaching that would be more or less vague, and seeing to it that there was debate on a certain number of questions that are still disputable, questions which, if left systematically in shadow, would assure that any affirmation of a common outlook, any will to convergent action, would remain mere words at this juncture.

In their letter of April 20 to the organizers, Surrealist writers made it clear that for them there can be no question of defending and upholding culture in a capitalist regime. We are interested, they stated, only in the *development* of this culture, and this very development necessitates above all the transformation of society through proletarian Revolution.

They demand in particular that the following questions be put on the agenda of the Congress: the right to pursue, both in literature and in art, the search for new means of expression;

the right of the artist and writer to continue to study the human problem in all its forms (demanding the freedom of the subject, refusing to judge the quality of a work by the present size of its audience, resisting all attempts to limit the field of observation and action of any man who aspires to create intellectually).

This wish to have a say on specific questions encountered nothing but obstacles: after the participating Surrealist writers were persuaded, without difficulty, to let only one of their number speak for them, they were constantly kept away from the work of organizing the congress, and on the ridiculous pretext that a personal difference that had nothing to do with the congress was being settled—by the person whom the Surrealists had designated to express their point of view—none of their names appeared on the poster or on the program.*

It was only because of the very insistent entreaties of René Crevel and doubtless because of the act of despair, whose

---

* More than a week before the opening of the Congress, André Breton, meeting Mr. Ehrenburg by chance in the street, apparently committed the error of recalling a few passages of his book, *Seen by a Writer of the U.S.S.R.,* and giving him a severe dressing down. Mr. Ehrenburg's quips may be remembered: "The Surrealists are kindly disposed both to Hegel and Marx and to the Revolution, but what they refuse to do is work. They have things to keep them busy. They study pederasty and dreams, for example. . . . They apply themselves to gobbling up an inheritance here, a wife's dowry there. . . . They begin with obscene words. Those of their number who are less sly admit that their program consists of making amorous advances to girls. Those who know more or less what's what understand that they won't get very far that way. For them a woman means conformism. They preach a completely different program: onanism, pederasty, fetishism, exhibitionism, and even sodomy. But it is hard to astonish anybody in Paris even with such a program as this. So . . . Freud comes to the rescue and ordinary perversions are covered with the veil of the incomprehensible. The stupider it is, the better!"

How surprised we were to learn that there was no longer a place for Breton at the Congress, from the moment that the Soviet delegation sided with the man who insulted us! Organizers of the Congress censured what Breton had done and asked him "whether he meant to say that recourse to brutality was the synonym of culture." Breton replied: "Recourse to brutality is no more a 'synonym of culture' to me than recourse to the most contemptible calumny is. In the present case the former can be viewed only as a natural consequence of the latter. It is as impossible for me to admit that I offended the Soviet delegation in the person of Mr. Ehrenburg as it is for me to consider myself offended by this delegation when a book entitled *Seen by a Writer of the U.S.S.R.* appears. I did not know, need I say, that Mr. Ehrenburg, who usually lives in Paris, was a member of this delegation, and all I saw in him was a false witness like any other." We are of the opinion that the question is now closed.

causes are not clear,* committed by him the following night, that Paul Eluard on June 25, at the very end of the session, was allowed to read the text that in the beginning Breton was scheduled to read. The president, moreover, saw fit to interrupt him at one certain sentence to warn the public, whose opinion at that juncture was quite divided but with hostile elements having the upper hand, that since the hall was only rented until 12:30 the lights might go out in a few minutes and that the end of the speech, and any reply to it, would be postponed until the following day. The reply—as noisy, servile, and nonexistent as one could wish for, but permitting no other—which opened the closing session on June 26 again brought out the total lack of impartiality with which the debates had been conducted from beginning to end.

After that we are not surprised to see the following scandalous statement in M. Barbusse's paper, in the report on the work of the Congress: "Eluard declared that he was against the Franco-Soviet pact and against cultural collaboration between France and the U.S.S.R."

The "International Congress for the Defense of Culture" was held under the sign of systematic suppression: the suppression of real cultural problems, the suppression of voices not recognized as being those of the ruling clique. Addressed as it was to that majority of confirmed new conformists, the sentence from Gide's opening speech: "In the capitalist society in which we live today, it seems almost impossible for literature of value to be anything but a literature of protest" took on a rather cruel and enigmatic meaning. There was partial suppression of the speeches of Magdeleine Paz, of Plisnier, pure and simple skipping of that of the Chinese delegate, and complete withdrawal of Nezval's right to speak (and how many others, having learned of these methods, had chosen not to be there!), but in the meantime, on the other hand, there were moving declarations such as those of Malraux, Waldo Frank, or Pasternak— a veritable bath of useless repetitions, infantile considerations,

---

*Commune, the organ of the A.E.A.R., naturally takes it upon itself to draw "the lesson of a lifetime, interrupted only because of René Crevel's despair at not being physically able to maintain himself at the level of that immediate sense of reality that he intended to give all his attention to." We leave the responsibility for this completely gratuitous, crudely pragmatic, and fundamentally dishonest statement on the shoulders of its anonymous authors. What a contrary "lesson" Commune would justify our drawing from the suicide of Mayakovsky!

and toadying: those claiming to be saving culture chose an unhealthy climate for it. The way in which this Congress, supposedly a revolutionary one, was dissolved is the exact counterpart of the way in which it was announced. It was announced by posters with certain names standing out in larger letters in red; it ended with the creation of an "International Association of Writers for the Defense of Culture" directed by a board of 112 members, having at its head a presidium—a board which to all appearances elected itself, since neither the participants nor members of the audience were consulted on its composition.

We can do no more than formally notify this board, this association, of our mistrust.

We foresee the attempt that will be made to use such a declaration against us. Being bent on the ruin of the ideological position that was theirs for some time and still is ours, the former Surrealists who have become functionaries of the Communist Party or aspire to become such, people who, doubtless in order to get themselves forgiven for their past trouble-making, have abandoned all critical sense and are anxious to be examples of the most fanatic obedience by being ever ready to contradict on order what they have affirmed on order—these former Surrealists will of course be the first to denounce us as professional malcontents, as systematic opponents. Everyone knows the revolting content people have managed to read into this latter grievance: declaring that one disagrees on such and such a point with the official party line is not only to perform an act of ridiculous purism, but also to do a disservice to the U.S.S.R., to try to snatch militants away from the Party, to give arms to the enemies of the proletariat, to behave "objectively" as counter-revolutionaries. "We in no way consider Marx's theory as something perfect and unassailable; on the contrary, we are persuaded that it has provided only the bases of a science that Socialists must necessarily perfect in every way if they do not wish to lag behind life": Lenin, who expressed himself in this fashion in 1899, thereby gives us every reason to think that in this regard Leninism today is undergoing the same fate as Marxism. At the very least this assurance does not dispose us to accept the present watchwords of the Communist International without examination and to approve of the way in which they are applied a *priori*. We would think that we were failing our duty as revolutionary intellectuals if we were to accept these watchwords before having thought them over. If there are some that we do not accept in the end, we would again fail in this duty if we did not point out that our entire being balks at them, that we need to be convinced in order to *follow* with the same heartfelt enthusiasm.

We deplore, once again, the more and more habitual recourse to certain ways of discrediting people which in the revolutionary struggle result in strengthening particular resistances rather than destroying them. One of these ways, which merely comes to the rescue of the preceding method, consists of representing the various opposition elements as an organic, almost homogeneous whole moved by feelings that are wholly negative, in short as a single instrument of sabotage. Merely expressing a doubt about an instruction that has been received suffices to relegate you to the category of public malefactors (at least that is what they ridiculously try to make you out to be in the eyes of the masses): you are under orders from Trotsky, if not of Doriot. Socialism is being built in only one country, you are told; consequently you must have blind confidence in the leaders of that country. Whatever it may be that you object to, any hesitation on your part is criminal. This is the point we have reached, this is the intellectual freedom that is left us. Any man who thinks in a revolutionary way today is faced with a system of thought that is not his own, that at best it is up to his ingenuity to foresee, that at best it is up to his flexibility to try to justify from day to day.

In this frenetic need for orthodoxy, it is impossible, both for an individual and for a party, to see anything but the mark of a feeble self-awareness. "A party establishes itself as a victorious party by dividing itself, or by being able to bear division," Engels said, and also: "The solidarity of the proletariat is everywhere realized in groupings of different parties which engage in a life and death struggle as did the Christian sects in the Roman Empire during the worst persecutions." The spectacle of the divisions of the Workers' Social Democratic Party in Russia in 1903 and of the numerous and lengthy conflicts between tendencies that followed, *in conjunction with the extreme possibilities of regrouping the most divergent—but intact—minds to bring about a truly revolutionary situation* furnishes the most striking proof of these words. Disregarding insults and attempts to intimidate us, we shall continue to try to keep ourselves intact and to that end safeguard at any cost the independence of our judgment, without for all that aspiring to keep ourselves free of error in any and every circumstance.

We lay entire claim to this right, so extensively employed by "professional revolutionaries" in the first part of the twentieth century, for all revolutionary intellectuals, *on condition that they participate actively in the efforts to unite that the present situation, dominated by the awareness of the fascist menace, may necessitate.* Our collaboration in the *Call to Struggle* of February 10, 1934, appealing to all workers, organized or not, to bring a unity of action into being as quickly as possible, and apply to this process "the very broad spirit of conciliation demanded by the seriousness of the present hour," our immediate adherence to the Intellectuals' Vigilance Committee, our survey on unity of action of April 1934, our presence in the street during all the great workers' demonstrations suffice, we believe, to confound those who still dare speak of our "ivory tower." We nonetheless persist in defining ourselves as specifically as possible on the intellectual plane; we intend not to be forced to give up anything that appears valuable to us and proper to us on this plane, just as we reserve the right, if need be, in the presence of such a decision, to say: "In our opinion this is unjust, this is false" of any measure that clashes with what lies deepest within ourselves, and to do so with all the more reason if the approval of any collectivity, which is always easy to exploit, is behind it. We maintain that the free statement of all points of view and the permanent confrontation of all tendencies constitute the most indispensable ferment of the revolutionary struggle. "Everyone is free to say and to write what he pleases," Lenin stated in 1905; "freedom of speech and freedom of the press must be total." We shall consider any other conception to be reactionary.

Opportunism today unfortunately tends to annihilate the two essential ingredients of the revolutionary spirit such as it has always manifested itself till now: the refractory nature—dynamic and creative—of certain beings, and their careful and complete fulfillment of their pledges to themselves and to others during common action. Whether in the field of politics or in the field of art, two forces—the spontaneous refusal of the conditions of life offered man and the imperative need to change them, on the one hand, and enduring fidelity to principles or moral rigor on the other—have carried the world forward. One cannot hem them in with impunity, and even combat them for years, only to replace them with the messianic idea of what is being accomplished in the U.S.S.R. and cannot help but be accomplished by the U.S.S.R., an idea that necessitates an *a priori* sanction of a policy of more and more serious compromises. We say that by traveling farther and farther along this road the revolutionary spirit cannot help but become blunted and corrupted. On this point, we again assure ourselves that we have Lenin on our side, for on September 3, 1917, he wrote: "The duty of a revolutionary party is not to proclaim an impossible renunciation of all sorts of compromises but to know how, *in the course of all compromises,* insofar as these are inevitable, to keep one's fidelity to one's principles, one's class, one's revolutionary aim, and to prepare the revolution and the education of the masses that must be led to victory." If these latter conditions were not fulfilled, we believe that it would no longer be a question of compromises, but of a surrender of principle. Need we grant that they have been fulfilled?

No. We were moved, in fact, as so many others were, by the declaration stating, on May 15, 1935, that "Stalin understands and fully approves the national defense policy promulgated by France to keep its armed forces up to the standards required by its security." If at the very beginning we insisted on considering this to be only another particularly painful compromise on the part of the head of the Communist International, we nonetheless immediately expressed, with all the force of our desire, the most explicit reservations about the possibilities of accepting the instructions that people here hastened to deduce from it: the abandonment of the watchword "transformation of imperialist war into civil war" (the condemnation of revolutionary defeatism), the denunciation of the Germany of 1935 as the one instigator of a war that is soon to come (the discouraging of all hope of fraternization in the event of war), and the reawakening among French workers of the idea of loyalty to one's country. The position we took against these directives, from the very first day, is well known. This position is consonant in all respects with that of the Intellectuals' Vigilance Committee: it is against any policy of encirclement and isolation of Germany, for the examination by an international committee of the concrete offers of limitation and reduction of armaments made by Hitler, and for the revision of the treaty of Versailles, the principal obstacle to continued peace, through political negotiations. It is hardly necessary to emphasize that since that time the signing of the Anglo-German convention allowing German naval rearmament has sanctioned this way of looking at things, in the very measure that this convention can be regarded only as a consequence of the policy of increasingly barring Germany from power, a policy which the Franco-Soviet pact has suddenly made even more painful for her.

By itself such a consideration does not dispose us to accept the idea of loyalty to one's country, in whatever transitional form it is put before us. Any sacrifice on our part to this idea and to the famous duties which result from it would immediately conflict with the very definite initial reasons for becoming revolutionaries that we know we had. Long before becoming aware of economic and social realities, outside of which the struggle against everything that we wish to overthrow would have been pointless, we were struck by the absolute inanity of such concepts, and on this point nothing will ever force us to make honorable amends. What is happening in the U.S.S.R. and what has happened there in the past? No denial has come to us to dissipate the dense shadow that Vaillant-Couturier, Thorez and Company have cast over events. We have spoken of how this shadow hung over the International Congress of Writers (whose speakers' stand was the scene of the symbolic parading of the author of this wildly chauvinistic declaration: "I have again been told: 'It is you who have forced Germany to rearm, because of the humiliation that you have subjected her to for twenty years with your treaty.' I say in reply that she had to accept this humiliation. Germany wanted war [I mean the German people, if it is true that a people ever want anything] and lost it. They must pay the price for these things. I have no taste for forgiveness.").*

If we violently object to all attempts to rehabilitate the idea of loyalty to one's country, against all appeals to national sentiment in a capitalist regime, it is not only, I insist, because in the deepest and remotest part of ourselves we feel ourselves totally incapable of subscribing to it, it is not only because we see in it the stirring up of a sordid illusion that only too often has set the world on fire, but above all because *even with the best will in the world* we cannot avoid taking these concepts as a symptom of a general evil that can be described. This evil is definable from the moment that such a symptom can be compared with equally morbid symptoms and form a homogeneous group with them. We were often reproached, once upon a time,

*Julien Benda (*Nouvelle revue française,* May 1935).

for having echoed the protests raised by the spectacle of certain Soviet films, such as *Road of Life,* that tended to stupid moral preaching. "The wind of systematic cretinization that blows from the U.S.S.R.," one of our correspondents was not afraid to write about them. A few months ago, the fact of our having read in *Lu* some of the answers to a survey conducted by Soviet papers on the present conception of love and the common life of men and women in the U.S.S.R. (there was a choice of confidential replies by men and women, each more heartbreaking than the last) made us ask ourselves for a moment whether the attitude just mentioned—that until then we had not sided with—was that extreme. Let us pass rapidly over the disappointment caused us by the wretched products of "proletarian art" and "Socialist realism." Nor have we ceased worrying about the *idolatrous cult* through which certain selfish zealots are trying to secure the loyalty of the working masses not only to the U.S.S.R. but also to the person of its chief (the "everything thanks to you, great educator Stalin" of the former bandit Avdeenko brings to mind the "so long as it is your desire, general" of the ignoble Claudel). But if we still entertained some doubt about the hopeless outcome of such an evil (it is not a question of not knowing what the Revolution has been, what it has done; it is a question of knowing what state of health it is in if it is still alive), this doubt, we declare, could not possibly withstand the reading of the letters which *Lu* reprinted from *Komsomolskaya Pravda* in its issue of July 12, 1935, under the title:

RESPECT YOUR PARENTS

On March 23 *Komsomolskaya Pravda* published the letter of a worker in the Ordjonikidze factory. This letter criticized the attitude of a young worker named Tchernychev who was arrogant to his parents. A hard worker at the factory, he was unbearable at home. The paper has received a great many letters on the subject:

I WAS ASHAMED

I showed my parents the letter about the young communist Tchernychev. I was ashamed: this letter could also apply to me. My mother said to me: "You see, Alexandre, you're like Tchernychev in several ways.

You think I don't understand anything, you don't let me get a word in, you don't respect your brothers and sisters, and you don't want to help them with their studies. My father agreed: yes, your attitude is hardly that of a Young Communist.

It was unpleasant for me to hear such reproofs, but they were justified. At a family reunion, I gave my word that I would change my habits. I promised to keep an eye on my brother Leo who is a bad student and sometimes drinks with his schoolmates; I also promised to keep an eye on the progress of my sisters at school and to help them if they need help. I am the head of the Young Communist organization. If I don't keep my word, if I don't reform, what will the rank and file say? It is I who must furnish an example.

Smolov, Kolkhoz Frounzé.

RESPECT YOUR ELDERS

I love my mother very much, I always help her, and now that I am independent, I do not forget to write her long detailed letters. It is a joy to have such a dear and beloved being somewhere and always be able to tell that person about your life.

The attitude of many of my fellow students toward their parents always used to surprise me.

I often heard these words:

"I haven't written my parents for two months."

I remember the following incident. I had just written a letter. Young Communist Savine said to me: "Who are you writing to?" "My mother." "Isn't your letter too long?" "Only eight pages." "Eight pages!" he said, astonished. "I never write more than a page. I put 'Am in good health' and that's all. How can my mother understand anything, she's a peasant on a collective farm."

My mother is a simple peasant on a collective farm too. Nonetheless she'll be happy to receive a detailed letter from her son, who has become a brigadier in the shock troops and a student.

No, Tchernychev is not a civilized man. He does not deserve this title because he doesn't respect his parents.

Krachennikov, student.

It is almost useless to emphasize the ultra-conformist wretchedness of such elucubrations, which a privately owned paper in France would hardly make space for. The least that can be said of them is that they give a semblance of belated justification to the famous "Moscow the dotard," an expression coined by one of those personages who today are quite at home serving Moscow, dotard or not, on their knees, in return for a few small advantages. Let us limit ourselves to noticing the process of rapid regression that would have it that after the fatherland it is the family that escapes the dying Russian Revolution without a scratch (what does André Gide think of that?). For the finest victories of socialism to be sent down the drain all that remains to be done is to reestablish religion there—why not?—and private property. Even at the cost of arousing the fury of their toadies, we ask if there is any need of drawing up another balance sheet in order to judge a regime by its works—in this case the *present* regime of Soviet Russia and the all-powerful head under whom this regime is turning into the very negation of what it should be and what it has been.

We can do no more than to formally notify this regime, this chief, of our mistrust.

André BRETON, Salvador DALI, Oscar DOMINGUEZ, Paul ELUARD, Max ERNST, Marcel FOURRIER, Maurice HEINE, Maurice HENRY, Georges HUGNET, Sylvain ITKINE, Marcel JEAN, Dora MAAR, René MAGRITTE, Léo MALET, Marie-Louise MAYOUX, Jehan MAYOUX, E.-L.-T. MÉSENS, Paul NOUGÉ, Méret OPPENHEIM, Henri PARISOT, Benjamin PÉRET, Man RAY, Maurice SINGER, André SOURIS, Yves TANGUY, Robert VALANÇAY.

Paris, August 1935.

SURREALIST SITUATION OF THE OBJECT
Situation of the Surrealist Object
(1935)

[Lecture delivered in Prague March 29, 1935]

I am very happy to be speaking today in a city outside of France which yesterday was still unknown to me, but which of all the cities that I had not visited, was by far the least foreign to me. Prague with its legendary charms is, in fact, one of those cities that electively pin down poetic thought, which is always more or less adrift in space. Completely apart from the geographical, historical, and economic considerations that this city and the customs of its inhabitants may lend themselves to, when viewed from a distance, with her towers that bristle like no others, it seems to be the magic capital of old Europe. By the very fact that it carefully incubates all the delights of the past for the imagination, it seems to me that it would be less difficult for me to make myself understood in this corner of the world than in any other, since in choosing to speak to you tonight about Surrealist poetry and art, I am endeavoring to make you the judges of the very possibility of present and future delights. "The art object," as someone has nicely put it, "lies between the sensible and the rational. It is something spiritual that seems to be material. Insofar as they address themselves to our senses or to our imagination, art and poetry deliberately create a world of shadows, of phantoms, of fictitious likenesses, and yet for all that they cannot be accused of being powerless and unable to produce anything but empty forms of reality."* Let me say that for me it is a special pleasure to bring the world of new shadows that goes by the name of Surrealism and the sky of Prague together. But I must admit that it is not only the more phosphorescent color of this sky at a distance as compared to that of so many others that makes me feel that my task is particularly easy: I also know that for many long years I have enjoyed perfect intellectual fellowship with men such as Vitezslav Nezval and Karel Teige, whose trust and friendship is a source of pride to me. I know too that through their efforts here everything about the origins and the successive stages of the Surrealist movement in France has been made perfectly clear to you, this being a movement whose development they have never ceased to follow very closely. Constantly interpreted by Teige in the most lively way, made to undergo an all-powerful lyric thrust by Nezval, Surrealism can flatter itself that it has blossomed in Prague as it has in Paris. It is thus above all friends and collaborators whom I greet in this hall in the person of Toyen, Stirsky, Biebl, Makovsky, Bronk, Honzl, Jezek.

I want to emphasize that nothing distinguishes the action they are engaged in, whatever their field of endeavor, from my own, and that it is through a growing closeness of the ties that bind us (at the same time that they bind us to a very mobile nucleus of poets and artists, a nucleus that has already been formed or is in the process of being formed in each country) that I expect genuine concerted action involving all of us to become possible. Such action is necessary if we wish Surrealism one day soon to speak as a master in its own domain, where those very persons who deplore it as a symptom of a more or less curable social evil are obliged to admit that nothing very significant can really be marshalled against it.

The publication in this country of admirably complete and well-documented texts such as Karel Teige's *Suèt, ktéry vonî,* the recent translation into Czech of my two works, *Nadja* and *Les vases communiquants,* several conflicting lectures given in Prague by our friends, the very objective reports of the debates which Surrealism has given rise to in recent years in *Surréalismus v diskusi,* several exhibitions of paintings and

*Hegel, Introduction to the *Poetics.*

sculpture, and finally the very recent founding of the review *Surréalismus* under the direction of Vitezslav Nezval, are responsible for my having the good fortune, in accepting the invitation of the Manes Society, to be addressing an audience that for the most part is very well informed. I therefore feel no need to trace the history of the Surrealist movement from 1920 to the present for you. It is our most recent preoccupations that I wish to speak of.

I shall remind you that when I spoke a little less than a year ago in Brussels, I mentioned, very summarily, that a *fundamental crisis of the object* was taking place in the wake of Surrealism. "It is essentially on the object that the more and more clear-sighted eyes of Surrealism have remained open in recent years," I wrote. "It is the very attentive examination of the numerous recent speculations that this *object* has publicly given rise to (the oneiric object, the symbolic object, the real and virtual object, the found object, etc.), and this examination alone, that will allow one to understand all the implications of the present temptation of Surrealism. It is essential that interest be focused on this point." This conclusion has lost none of its pertinence six months later. A recent proposal by Man Ray is excellent proof of this. I shall explain it with a brief commentary so as to make it perfectly understandable to you. Perhaps the greatest danger threatening Surrealism today is the fact that because of its spread throughout the world, which was very sudden and rapid, the word found favor much faster than the idea and all sorts of more or less questionable creations tend to pin the Surrealist label on themselves: thus works tending to be "abstractivist," in Holland, in Switzerland, and according to very recent reports in England, manage to enjoy ambiguous neighborly relations with Surrealist works; thus the unmentionable Monsieur Cocteau has been able to have a hand in Surrealist exhibitions in America and in Surrealist publications in Japan. To avoid such misunderstandings or render such vulgar abuses impossible in the future, it would be desirable for us to establish a very precise line of demarcation between what is Surrealist in its essence and what seeks to pass itself off as such for publicity or for other reasons. The ideal, obviously, would be for every authentic Surrealist object to have some distinctive outer sign so that it would be immediately recognizable; Man Ray thought it should be a sort of hallmark or seal. In the same way that, for example, the spectator can read on the screen the inscription "A Paramount Film" (leaving, in this case, the insufficient guarantee of quality that results from it out of the discussion), the amateur, who up to now has not been sufficiently forewarned, would discover on the poem, the book, the drawing, the canvas, the sculpture, the new construction before him a mark that would be inimitable and indelible, something like: "A Surrealist Object." The slyly humorous turn Man Ray has recently given this idea does not make it less appropriate. Supposing that it could be worked out, we must be confident that there would not be the least arbitrariness in the considerations that would decide whether the mark was to be affixed or not affixed in any case. The best way of securing agreement on this question seems to me to be to seek to determine the exact situation of the Surrealist object today. This situation is, of course, the correlative of another, the Surrealist situation of the object. It is only when we have reached perfect agreement on the way in which Surrealism represents the object in general—this table, the photograph that that man over there has in his pocket, a tree at the very instant that it is struck by lightning, an aurora borealis, or, to enter the domain of the impossible, a flying lion—that there can arise the question of defining the place that the Surrealist object must take to justify the adjective Surrealist. I want to make it clear that in the expression *Surrealist object,* I take the word *object* in its broadest philosophical sense, considering it for the moment apart from the very special meaning that has had currency among us recently: you know that people have fallen into the habit of meaning by "Surrealist object" a type of little nonsculptural construction, whose great importance I hope to show you later, but which for all that cannot claim that title exclusively, but rather has had to be called that for lack of a more appropriate designation.

In this regard I cannot repeat too often that Hegel, in his *Esthetics,* attacked all the problems that on the plane of poetry and art may today be considered to be the most difficult, and that with unparalleled lucidity he solved them for the most part. It takes nothing less than the current lack of knowledge of almost the whole of Hegel's brilliant work, a lack of knowledge that is deliberately perpetuated in various countries, for various obscurantists for hire here and there to still find in such problems either reasons for anxiety or pretexts for endless controversy. It also takes nothing less than the blind submission of too large a number of Marxists to what they summarily take to be the right interpretation of Marx and Engels for Soviet Russia and the cultural bodies placed in other countries under its control to raise their voices in deplorable chorus with those whom I just mentioned, allowing certain people to reopen, and what is worse, to fly into passions over debates which are impossible after Hegel. You cite Hegel and in revolutionary circles you immediately see brows darken. What, Hegel, that man who tried to make dialectics walk on its head! You are suspect, and since the Marxist theses on poetry and art, which are very rare and not very convincing, were all improvised long after Marx, the first Philistine to come along feels free to garner applause for himself by throwing the words "a fighting literature and painting," "class content," and the like at your head.

Yet Hegel did come along. He came along and before our day made short work of these vain quarrels people keep picking with us. His views on poetry and art, the only ones up to the present to have stemmed from an encyclopedic fund of knowledge, are still above all those of a marvelous historian; no systematic bias can be considered *a priori* as having vitiated them, and despite everything this bias would be noticeable in the course of argument even if in the eyes of the materialist reader it entailed only a few easily rectifiable errors. The essential point is that a truly unique summa of knowledge was put to work in such a case, and that it was submitted to the action of a machine which was then completely new, since Hegel was the inventor of it, a machine whose power has proved to be unique: the dialectical machine. I say that even today it is Hegel whom we must question about how well-founded or ill-founded Surrealist activity in the arts is. He alone can say whether this activity was predetermined in time; he alone can teach us whether its future duration is likely to be measured in days or centuries.

It is appropriate to recall, first of all, that Hegel, who places poetry above all the other arts (according to him they are ranked in the following order, *proceeding from the poorest to the richest:* architecture, sculpture, painting, music, poetry), who sees in poetry the 'true art of the spirit," the only "universal art" likely to produce in its own domain all the modes of representation that belong to the other arts, and foresaw its present destiny very clearly. In the measure that poetry tends in time to predominate over the other arts, Hegel's magnificent analysis revealed that it increasingly manifests, *contradictorily,* the need to attain, first by its own means and secondly by new means, the precision of sensible forms. Freed as it is of all contact with weighty matter, enjoying the privilege of representing, both materially and morally, the *successive situations* of life, realizing the perfect synthesis of sound and idea, to the benefit of the imagination, poetry in the modern era, beginning with its great emancipation by the Romantics, has never ceased affirming its hegemony over the other arts, penetrating them deeply, and reserving a domain for itself that day by day grows larger. To tell the truth, it is in painting that it appears to have discovered the vastest field of influence: it is so well established there that painting can today claim to share, in large measure, its vastest objective, which is, Hegel again tells us, to reveal the powers of spiritual life to consciousness. At the present time there is no fundamental difference between the ambitions of a poem by Paul Eluard or Benjamin Péret and the ambitions of a canvas by Max Ernst, Miró, or Tanguy. Liberated from the need to reproduce forms essentially taken from the outer world, painting benefits in its turn from the only external element that no art can get along without, namely inner representation, *the image present to the mind.* It confronts this inner representation with that of the concrete forms of the real world, seeks in turn, as it has done with Picasso, to seize the object in its generality, and as soon as it has succeeded in so doing, tries to take that supreme step which is the poetic step par excellence: excluding (relatively) the external object as such and considering nature only in its relationship with the inner world of consciousness. The fusion of the two arts tends to become so complete in our day that it becomes a matter of indifference, so to speak, whether men such as Arp and Dali express themselves in poetic or plastic forms of expression, and if in the case of Arp these two forms of expression can be considered to be necessarily complementary, in the case of Dali they each coincide so perfectly that the reading of certain fragments of his poems merely gives a bit more animation to visual scenes to which the eye, to its surprise, lends the usual brilliance of his paintings. But if painting was the first to pass through a great number of the degrees that separated it from poetry as a mode of expression, it is important to note that it was followed in this respect by sculpture, as the experience of Giacometti and Arp demonstrates. What is remarkable is that architecture, that is to say the most elementary of all the arts, also seems to have been the first really to move in this direction. In spite of the particularly violent reaction that followed it, it cannot be forgotten that the architectural and sculptural art of 1900, art nouveau, completely changed the idea that people had come to have of human construction in space, that it expressed with unique, sudden, and totally unexpected intensity the "desire for ideal things" that up to that time was not considered to be part of its domain, at least in the civilized world. As Salvador Dali first put the matter in 1930 in passionately enthusiastic terms, "no collective effort has managed to create a world of dreams as pure and disturbing as these art nouveau buildings, which by themselves constitute, on the very fringe of architecture, true realizations of solidified desires, in which the most violent and cruel automatism painfully betrays a hatred of reality and a need for refuge in an ideal world similar to those in a childhood neurosis." It is to be noted that toward the end of the nineteenth century in France a completely uneducated man, whose social function was to deliver the mail to a few villages in Drôme, the mailman Cheval, built—without anyone's help, with a faith that did not falter for forty years, and with only the inspiration he drew from his dreams—a marvelous construction that still cannot be used for anything, in which there was no place for anything except the wheelbarrow that he had used to transport his materials, that he shed light on finally only by giving it the name *The Ideal Palace.* One can see how concrete irrationality in architecture has attempted since that time to break through all its limits (the case of the mailman Cheval is surely far from being unique), and the severe criticism that we have received in this field since that time is doubtless not the last word on the subject, since just yesterday it was said that in the Swiss Pavilion of the Cité Universitaire in Paris, a building that outwardly answers all the conditions of rationality and coldness that anyone could want in recent years since it is the work of Le Corbusier, there was going to be a hall with "irrationally wavy" *(sic)* walls, and there were plans, moreover, to use them to hang photographic enlargements of microscopic animals and details of small animals. It thus seems that the form of art that blossomed in the magnificent church, all in vegetables and crustaceans, in Barcelona is now preparing its revenge and that the irrepressible human need, coming to light in our era as in no other, to extend what was long held to be the prerogatives of poetry to the other arts will soon get the better of certain routine resistances seeking to hide them-

selves behind the pretended demands that a building be useful.

Just as poetry, as I have said, tends more and more to
pattern the behavior of the other arts on its own personal behavior, to be reflected upon them, we must expect poetry for its
part to remedy that which constitutes its relative inadequacy in
relation to each of these other arts. It is at a disadvantage
compared to painting and sculpture as regards the expression
of sensible reality and the precision of external forms; it is at a
disadvantage compared to music as regards the immediate,
pervading, uncriticizable communication of feeling. We know,
in particular, what expedients the completely new awareness
of this latter inferiority certain poets of the last century were
reduced to, poets who, under the pretext of verbal instrumen-
tation, thought they could subordinate sense to sound and
thereby often exposed themselves to putting together only the
empty carapaces of words. The fundamental error of such an
attitude resides, in my opinion, in the underestimation of the
primordial virtue of poetic language: above all else this
language must be universal. If we have never ceased to maintain, with Lautréamont, that *poetry must be created by everyone,* if this aphorism is, indeed, the one that we have wanted
more than any other to engrave on the façade of the Surrealist
edifice, it goes without saying that for us it implies an indispensable counterpart: *poetry must be understood by everyone.* For
the love of heaven let us not work toward the raising of the
barrier between languages. "Thus," Hegel also wrote, "it is a
matter of indifference whether a poetic work be read or recited.
Such a work may also be translated, without essential alteration,
in a foreign language and even in prose poems. The relationships between sounds may also be totally changed." The error
of Mallarmé and some symbolists will nonetheless have had the
salutary effect of provoking a general mistrust of that which, up
to their day, had constituted the accessory accidental element
wrongly held to be the indispensable guidon and brake of poetic
art, that is to say, those combinations that are completely exterior, such as meter, rhythm, rhymes. The deliberate abandonment of these worn-out combinations that had become arbitrary
obliged poetry to fill the gap that they had left, and we know
that this necessity, even before Mallarmé, gave us the finest
part of Rimbaud's *Illuminations,* and Lautréamont's *Chants de
Maldoror,* as well as almost everything that deserves being considered poetry since that time. Verbal harmony, of course,

profited immediately thereby, and once again, moreover, the cause of universal language, to which poets are attached in a revolutionary way because of their particular dissidence, is no longer betrayed. But poetry's inclination to become dependent upon music at this point in its evolution nonetheless remains symptomatic. Apollinaire's desire later to express himself in his *Calligrammes* in a form that would be poetic and plastic at the same time was equally symptomatic, and his original intention of putting these sorts of poems together under the title *Et moi aussi je suis peintre* is even more so. In this respect it is important to emphasize that the temptation experienced by poets has proved to be much more enduring: it also possessed Mallarmé, as his last poem, *Un coup de dés jamais n'abolira le hasard,* bears striking witness, and it has remained, I believe, very strong down to our own time. Thus I for my part believe today in the possibility and the great interest of the experiment that consists of incorporating objects, ordinary or not, within a poem, or more exactly of composing a poem in which visual elements take their place between the words without ever duplicating them. It seems to me that the reader-spectator may receive quite a novel sensation, one that is exceptionally disturbing and complex, as a result of the play of words with these elements, namable or not. To aid the systematic derangement of all the senses, a derangement recommended by Rimbaud and continuously made the order of the day by the Surrealists, it is my opinion that we must not hesitate to *bewilder sensation*— and such an undertaking might well have this result.

But we have said that poetry simultaneously seeks first by its own means and secondly by new means to be as precise as the sensible forms. However interesting new means on the order of the one that I have just given an example of may be to consider, they require one not to have recourse to them until after one has acquired a very clear idea of the means proper to poetry and has sought to profit as much as possible from these means. Now on what conditions, even in Hegel's time, could there be poetry? It was necessary (1) that the subject be conceived neither in the form of *rational* or *speculative* thought, nor in the form of feeling that paralyzed language, nor with the precision of sensible objects; (2) that on entering the imagination it shed the particularities and accidentals that destroyed its *unity* and shed the relative dependence of these parts; (3) that imagination remain free and shape everything that it conceived as an independent world. As we shall see these commandments were already of a nature so impossible to formulate precisely that one cannot help but notice that it is around them that the whole battle of poetry was waged in the last century.

I have already pointed out in *Misère de la poésie* in 1930 that because it obeyed the necessity of further escaping the form of real or speculative thought, the subject in poetry a century ago could already be held to be merely indifferent, and since that time it has ceased being able to be posed *a priori*. It ceased being able to be posed *a priori* in 1869, when Lautréamont flung down in *Maldoror* the unforgettable sentence: "A man or a stone or a tree will begin the fourth song." The interdependence of the parts of poetic discourse, for its part, has been endlessly attacked and undermined in all sorts of ways: as early as 1875 Rimbaud titles his last poem "Dream," an absolute triumph of pantheistic delirium, in which the marvelous is married without obstacle to the trivial and which remains the quintessence of the most mysterious scenes in the dramas of Elizabethan times and of the second Faust:

DREAM

Someone is hungry in the barracks-room
That is true . . .

Emanations, explosions,
A genius: I am Gruyère
Lefebvre: Keller!
The genius: I am Brie!
The soldiers carve on their bread:
    Such is life!
The genius: I am Roquefort!
—That'll be the death of us . . .
—I am Gruyère
And Brie . . . Etc. . . .

Waltz

They've put me and Lefebvre together . . . etc. . . !

Apollinaire later mixes times and places as he pleases, and in his turn attempts to make the detail of the poem as ambiguous as possible, to situate it in relation to a series of details, of incidents that purely and simply happen to coincide with it, so as to blur more and more the real events that may have been the determining factors in the making of the poem. And thus in the ultramodern framework of the *Poète assassiné,* monks clearing the forest of Malverne make their appearance "in another time"; and this is the very characteristic beginning of one of his loveliest poems:

THE MUSICIAN FROM SAINT-MERRY

I finally have the right to greet beings I do
   not know
.   .   .   .
On the twenty-first of the month of May, 1913
The ferryman of the dead and the deathdealers
   of Saint-Merry
Millions of flies bared a splendor
When a man without eyes without a nose and
   without ears
Leaving Sébasto entered the rue Aubry-le-Boucher
.   .   .   .
Then elsewhere
What time will a train leave for Paris

At this moment
The pigeons of the Spice Islands were fertilizing
   nutmegs
At the same time
Catholic mission of Boma what have you done with
   the sculptor
.   .   .   .
In another quarter
Compete then, poet, with the labels of perfume
   manufacturers
.   .   .   .
In short o laughers you haven't got much out
   of men
And you have barely extracted a little grease
   from their misery
.   .   .   .

The man who links Rimbaud and Apollinaire, in this last respect as in so many others, is Jarry, who is also the first poet who is steeped in the teachings of Lautréamont, and in whom the struggle between the two forces which by turn tended to dominate art in the Romantic era was fought and suddenly became crucial: the force that made the accidents of the outer world a matter of interest on the one hand, and on the other hand the force that made the caprices of personality a matter of interest. The intimate interpenetration of these two tendencies, which more or less alternate in Lautréamont, in Jarry's case ends in the triumph of *objective humor,* which is their dialectical resolution. Willy-nilly, all poetry after him had to pass through this new category, which in its turn will fuse with another so as to be able to be surmounted. Here, as an example of pure objective humor, is a poem by Jarry:

FABLE

A can of corned-beef, on a chain like a lorgnette
Saw a lobster pass by which resembled it like
   a brother.
It was protected by a thick shell
On which it was written that inside, like the can
   of corned-beef, it was boneless,
(Boneless and economical);
And underneath its curled-up tail
It apparently was hiding a key to open it.
Smitten with love, the sedentary corned-beef
Declared to the little live self-propelling can
That if it were willing to acclimate itself
Next to it in earthly shop windows,
It would be decorated with a number of gold medals.

I was saying that objective humor today still has almost all its value as a means of communication, and, in fact, there is not a single outstanding work in these last few years that does not turn out to more or less bear its imprint. I will here propose the names of Marcel Duchamp and Raymond Roussel, and after them those of Jacques Vaché and Jacques Rigaud, who went so far as to try to codify this sort of humor. The whole futurist movement, the whole Dada movement can claim it as their essential characteristic. To deny that it is a durable moment of poetry would be to deny the validity of history. In my opinion it would be far more profitable to seek out the new category that objective humor is called upon to fuse with so as to cease to be itself in art. The study of the poetry of the last few years leads one, moreover, to believe that it is undergoing an eclipse.

I have spoken of the call that Apollinaire heard on several occasions, and that led him to make the poetic event spring forth from a sheaf of completely fortuitous circumstances, all seized upon by chance; it is particularly noticeable in what has been called his conversation-poems.

MONDAY ON THE RUE CHRISTINE

The mother of the concierge and the concierge will
    overlook everything
If you're a man, you'll come with me tonight
One guy would have to hold the door open, that's all
While the other one went upstairs

Three lighted gaslights
The owner of the place is a consumptive
When you've finished we'll play a game of jaquet
An orchestra leader who has a sore throat
When you come to Tunis I'll give you some kif to smoke

That seems to rhyme just fine.

Piles of saucers flowers a calendar
Bim bam boom
I owe 300 damned francs to my landlady
I would rather cut off my—that's exacty right—
    than give them to her
. . . .

This call seems to correspond to a renewal of activity as regards one of the constituent elements of objective humor: the contemplation of nature in its accidental forms, to the detriment of subjective humor, its other ingredient, which is itself a consequence of the need of the personality to attain the highest possible degree of independence. This call, I was saying, even though it was still obscure in the case of Apollinaire, has become more urgent after him, thanks especially to the appeal to automatism that, as you know, was the fundamental procedure of Surrealism. The practice of psychic automatism in every field came to enlarge considerably the field of the arbitrary close at hand. Now, and this is the capital point, after examining the question, there was a violent tendency to deny that this arbitrariness was really arbitrary. The attention that on every occasion I have, for my part, attempted to call to certain disturbing facts, to certain overwhelming coincidences in works such as *Nadja, Les Vases communiquants,* and in other later reports has raised, with an acuteness that is completely new, the problem of *objective chance,* or in other words that sort of chance that shows man, in a way that is still very mysterious, a necessity that escapes him, even though he experiences it as a vital necessity. This still almost unexplored region of objective chance at this juncture is, I believe, the region in which it is most worth our while to carry on our research. It is just on the border of that region in which Dali has chosen to pursue his paranoiac-critical activity. Elsewhere it is the locus of manifestations so exciting for the mind, and a place where there filters in a light so close to being able to be considered that of revelation that objective humor for the moment is dashing itself to pieces against its steep walls. *Today's poetry finds itself face to face with this capital contradiction, and therefore the whole secret of its movement is its need to resolve this contradiction.*

It is necessary, we said finally, for the poetic imagination to remain free. The poet, whose role it is to express himself in a more and more highly evolved social state, must recapture the concrete vitality that logical habits of thought are about to cause him to lose. To this end he must dig the trench that separated poetry from prose even deeper; he has for that purpose one tool, and one tool only, capable of boring deeper and deeper, and that is the *image,* and among all type of images, *metaphor.* The poetic nothingness of the so-called classical centuries is the consequence of the infrequent and timid recourse to this marvelous instrument. I beg permission to cite Hegel one last time: "These images borrowed from nature, although they are inappropriate for representing thought, can be fashioned with deep feeling, with a particular richness of intuition, or with a brilliant play of humor; and this tendency may develop to the point of endlessly spurring poetry on to ever new inventions." The poetic imagination has a mortal enemy in prosaic thought; and today more than ever it is necessary to recall that it has two others, historical narration and rhetoric. For it to remain free is, in effect, for it to be by definition released from fidelity to circumstances, and especially from the *dizzying* circumstances of history; it is equally not to be concerned about pleasing or convincing, and unlike rhetoric it is to appear to be free of any sort of practical end.

I shall read three poems in which to me the deep feeling, the richness of intuition, and the brilliant play of humor have been brought in our time to the highest degree of perfection.

THE MASTERS
by Paul Eluard

At the height of the spasms of laughter
In a lead washtub
How comfortable to have
The wings of a dog
Which has a live bird in its mouth
Are you going to make darkness fall
So as to keep that sober look on your face
Or are you going to give in to us
There is grease on the ceiling
Saliva on the window panes
The light is horrible.

O night lost pearl
Blind point of fall where sorrow slaves away

SPEAK TO ME
by Benjamin Péret

Black of smoke animal black black black
agreed to meet each other between two monuments to
    the dead
that can pass for my ears
where the echo of your ghost voice of sea-mica
repeats your name indefinitely
that on the contrary so resembles an eclipse of the sun
that when you look at me I believe myself to be
a lark's foot in a glacier whose door you would open

in the hope of seeing a swallow of burning petrol escape
    from it
but from the lark's foot a stream of flaming petrol will
    gush out
if you wish it
as a swallow
wishes for the hour of summer so as to play the music of
    storms
and manufactures it like a fly
who dreams of a spider web of sugar
in an eye glass
sometimes as blue as a falling star reflected by an eye
sometimes as green as a spring oozing from a clock

DANDLED BROCHURE
by Salvador Dali

Brochure perditure
while unjustly refusing
a cup
an ordinary Portuguese cup
that today is manufactured
in a tableware factory
for the form of a cup
resembles
a soft municipal Arab antinomy
mounted on the tip of the surrounding countryside
like the look of my beautiful Gala
the look of my beautiful Gala
the smell of a liter
like the epithelial tissue of my beautiful Gala
her farcical lamplighter tissue

    yes I'll repeat it a thousand times

Brochure perditure
while unjustly refusing
a cup
an ordinary Portuguese cup
that today is manufactured
in a tableware factory
for the form of a cup
resembles
a soft municipal Arab antinomy
mounted on the tip of the surrounding countryside

like the look of my beautiful Gala
the look of my beautiful Gala
the smell of a liter
like the epithelial tissue of my beautiful Gala
her farcical lamplighter tissue

yes I'll repeat it a thousand times

I have spoken at too great length of the conditions within which the poetic problem presents itself over and over again in the course of history and the reasons that allow one to maintain that Surrealism today constitutes the only worthwhile solution of this problem to be able to discuss the plastic problem as fully within the limits of this lecture. A good number of the preceding remarks, moreover, might be applied to this field. However, to the very degree that the Surrealist artist has the privilege of attaining the precision of the definite forms of a really visible object, to the very degree that one must take into account the fact that he is acting directly on the material world, I believe it necessary to be more specific here and to first of all make short work of certain objections regarding the so-called idealism that our conception is said to risk falling into. As I go along, I shall try to provide a brief sketch of Surrealist procedures in the plastic arts.

You are doubtless familiar with the fundamental criticism that Marx and Engels leveled at the materialism of the eighteenth century: (1) The conception of the early materialists was "mechanistic"; (2) it was metaphysical (because of the anti-dialectical nature of their philosophy); (3) it did not exclude all idealism, for idealism still existed "at the top" in the domain of social science (because it had no knowledge of historical materialism). On all other points, of course, Marx and Engels agree with the early materialists.

Similarly, Surrealism, in its own domain, has little difficulty designating the "limits" that restricted not only the means of expression but also the thought of realist writers and artists, justifying the historical necessity for it to eliminate these limits, and seeing to it that at the end of such an undertaking there will be no divergence between it and the old realism as regards the recognition of the real and the assertion that the real is all-powerful. Contrary to the insinuations of certain of its detractors, it is easy, as we shall see, to demonstrate that of all the specifically intellectual movements that have succeeded each other up to our day, Surrealism is the only one to have armed itself against any inclination toward idealist fantasy, the only one to have thought out the art of definitely settling its accounts with "fideism"* beforehand.

If it so happens that two spiritual ways of going about things that on first sight are as different as the preceding two present such a parallelism and pursue such a common end, if only in a negative way, then it is all too evident that the line of argument that tends to maintain that the one is opposed to the other, and that they are imcompatible from the revolutionary point of view, cannot help but collapse miserably.

Now in the modern period, painting for example, up until the last few years, concerned itself almost uniquely with expressing the obvious relationships that exist between the perception of the outside world and the *ego*. The expression of this relationship proved to be less and less satisfactory, more and more disappointing, as it turned in circles and found itself increasingly prevented from enlarging, and even more so, by definition, from getting to the bottom of man's "perception-consciousness" system. As it was put forward at this juncture it was, in fact, a closed system in which the most interesting possibilities of reaction on the part of the artist had long been exhausted, and which allowed nothing to exist except an extravagant concern to deify the external object, a concern that the work of many a great so-called "realist" painter bears the mark of. Photography was to deal it a decisive blow by mechanizing to the extreme the plastic mode of representation. Because it did not accept the necessity of engaging in a struggle with photography that was discouraging even before it was begun, it was necessary for painting to beat a retreat so as to take up an impregnable position behind *the necessity of expressing inner perception visually*. It must be admitted that painting thereby found itself forced to take possession of a terrain that lay fallow. But I cannot emphasize too strongly the fact that this place of exile was the only one left to it. It remains to be seen what this soil promised and to what extent that promise was kept from this moment on.

*Fideism: "a doctrine substituting faith for science, or, by extension, attributing a certain importance to faith" (Lenin).

By the very fact that the image of the exterior object was caught mechanically, in conditions that produced a resemblance that was immediately satisfying and that, moreover, was indefinitely perfectible, the representation of this object was to cease to appear to be an end for the painter. (Movies were to bring about a similar revolution in sculpture.)

The only domain left for the artist to exploit became that of *pure mental representation,* such as it extends beyond that of true perception without for all that being identical with the hallucinatory domain. But here it must be recognized that lines of separation are badly drawn, that every attempt to draw sharp lines becomes a matter to be quarreled over. The important thing is that recourse to mental representation (outside of the physical presence of the object) furnishes, as Freud has said, "sensations related to processes unfolding in the most diverse, and even the deepest layers of the psychic mechanism." In art the necessarily more and more systematic search for these sensations works toward the abolition of the *ego* by the *id,* and consequently it endeavors to make the pleasure principle hold clearer and clearer sway over the reality principle. This search tends more and more to liberate instinctive impulses, to break down the barrier that civilized man faces, a barrier that primitive people and children do not experience. Given, on the one hand, the general disruption of sensibility that it brings on (through the communication of quite large psychic charges to the elements of the perception-consciousness system), and the impossibility of regression to the preceding stage on the other hand, the import of such an attitude is socially incalculable.

Is this to say that the reality of the exterior world has become something not to be relied on by the artist who is forced to draw the elements of his specific intervention from inner perception? To maintain this would be proof of a great poverty of ideas. In the mental domain no more than in the physical, it is quite clear that there can be no question of "spontaneous generation." The creations of the Surrealist painters that seem to be most free can naturally come into being only through their return to "visual residues" stemming from perception of the outside world. It is only in the work of regrouping these disorganized elements that their claim to recognition at once expresses both its individual and its collective nature. The possible genius of these painters stems less from the novelty of the materials that they work with, which is always relative, than from the more or less great initiative they give proof of when it comes to exploiting these materials.

Thus the whole technical effort of Surrealism, from its very beginning up to the present day, has consisted in multiplying the ways to penetrate the deepest layers of the mental. "I say that we must be *seers*, make ourselves seers": for us it has only been a question of discovering the means to apply this watchword of Rimbaud's. In the first rank of those of these means whose effectiveness has been fully proved in the last few years is *psychic automatism* in all its forms (the painter is offered a world of possibilities that goes from pure and simple abandon to graphic impulse and the fixing of dream-images through trompe-l'oeil), as well as the paranoiac-critical activity defined by Salvador Dali as "a spontaneous method of irrational knowledge based on the critical and systematic objectification of delirious associations and interpretations."

> It is through a clearly paranoiac process [Dali says], that it has been possible to obtain a double image, that is to say the representation of an object which, without the least figurative or anatomical modification, is at the same time the representation of another object that is absolutely different, one that also is free of any type of deformation or abnormality that would reveal some sort of artificial arrangement.
>
> Obtaining such a double image has been made possible thanks to the violence of paranoiac thought which has slyly and skillfully used the necessary quantity of pretexts, coincidences, etc., exploiting them so as to cause the appearance of the second image which, in this case, takes the place of the obsessive idea.
>
> The double image (for example, the image of a horse that is at the same time the image of a woman) can be prolonged, continuing the paranoiac process, the existence of another obsessive idea then being enough to cause a third image to appear (the image of a lion, for example) and so on until a number of images, limited only by the degree of paranoiac capacity of thought, converge.

We also know what a decisive role the "collages" and "frottages" of Max Ernst have played in the creation of the particular view of things that we are here considering. I shall let him tell you about them:

> The research on the mechanism of inspiration that has been fervently pursued by the Surrealists has led to the discovery of certain procedures of a poetic nature that are capable of removing the elaboration of the plastic work from the domain of the so-called conscious faculties.

These means (of bewitching reason, taste, and conscious will) have resulted in the rigorous application of the definition of Surrealism to drawing, to painting, and even in a certain degree to photography: these procedures, some of which, collage in particular, were employed before the advent of Surrealism, but were systematized and modified by Surrealism, have allowed certain artists to set down stupefying photographs of their thought and their desires on paper or canvas.

Having been called upon to characterize the procedure which was the first to surprise us and put us on the track of several others, I am tempted to consider this procedure to be the exploitation of the fortuitous meeting of two distant realities on an inappropriate plane *(this is said as a paraphrase and a generalization of Lautréamont's famous phrase: "As beautiful as the fortuitous meeting of a sewing machine and an umbrella on an operating table", or, to use a shorter term,* the cultivation of the effects of a systematic bewildering . . .

This procedure, which has been used, modified, and systematized by the Surrealists, both painters and poets, as they went along, has led to one surprise after another since its discovery. Among the finest results that they have been called upon to extract from it, there must be mentioned the creation of what they have called Surrealist objects.

A ready-made reality, whose naive purpose seems to have been fixed once and for all (an umbrella), finding itself suddenly in the presence of another very distant and no less absurd reality (a sewing machine), in a place where both must feel out of their element) *(on an operating table) will, by this very fact, escape its naive purpose and lose its identity; because of the detour through what is relative, it will pass from absolute falseness to a new absolute that is true and poetic: the umbrella and the sewing machine will make love. The way this procedure works seems to me to be revealed in this very simple example. A complete transmutation followed by a pure act such as love will necessarily be produced every time that the given facts*—the coupling of two realities which apparently cannot be coupled on a plane which apparently is not appropriate to them—*render conditions favorable.*

I must also speak of another procedure that I have been led to use through the direct influence of the specific details concerning the mechanism of inspiration to be found in the Manifesto of Surrealism. *In my personal evolution this procedure, which is based on nothing other than the* intensification of the irritability of the faculties of the mind *and which with regard to its technical side I would like to call* frottage, *has perhaps played a greater role than* collage, *from which in my opinion it really does not differ fundamentally.*

Taking as my point of departure a childhood memory in which a mahogany veneer panel opposite my bed had played the role of optical stimulus for a vision while I was half asleep, and finding myself in an inn at the seashore on a rainy day, I was struck by the way that my eyes were obsessively irritated by the ceiling, whose cracks had been accentuated by many cleanings. I then decided to question the symbolism of this obsession, and to aid my reflective and hallucinatory faculties, I got a series of designs out of the boards by randomly covering them with sheets of paper that I began rubbing with a lead pencil. I emphasize the fact that the designs thus obtained progressively lose—through a series of suggestions and transmutations that occur spontaneously, as happens with hypnagogic visions—the character of the material (wood) being questioned and take on the appearance of images of an unexpected preciseness and probably of such a nature as to reveal the prime cause of the obsession or to produce a simulacrum of this cause. My curiosity being aroused and struck with amazement, I came to use the same method to question all sorts of materials that happened to enter my visual field: leaves and their veins, the raveled edges of a piece of sacking, the knife-strokes of a "modern" painting, a thread unwound from a spool of thread, etc. I put together the first results obtained by this process of rubbing under the title Histoire naturelle, *from* Mer, *and* Pluie, *to* Eve, *the only one that still exists. Later, by restricting my own active participation more and more so as to thereby enlarge the active part of the faculties of the mind, I came to be present* like a spectator *at the birth of pictures such as* Femmes traversant une rivière en criant; Vision provoquée par les mots: le pèrè immobile; Homme marchant sur l'eau, prenant par la main une jeune fille et en bousculant une autre; Vision provoquée par une ficelle que j'ai trouvée sur ma table; Vision provoquée par une feuille de buvard; *etc.*

The *Surrealist object,* such as it has been defined by Salvador Dali—"an object which lends itself to a minimum of mechanical functions and is based on phantoms and representations liable to be provoked by the realization of unconscious acts"—cannot fail to appear to be the concrete synthesis of this body of preoccupations. I shall limit myself to recalling that construction of them was envisaged, as Dali again notes:

. . . following the mobile and mute object, Giacometti's ball, an object that already posed all the essential terms of the preceding definition but kept within the means proper to sculpture. Objects with a symbolic function leave no room for formal preoccupations. Corresponding to clearly defined erotic fantasies and desires, they depend only on the amorous imagination of each person and are extra-plastic.

It is important to remember, moreover, the considerable part that Marcel Duchamp had in the elaboration of such objects. I have emphasized* the capital role played in this respect by

*Cf. "Phare de la mariée," *Minotaure,* no. 6; reprinted in *Le Surréalisme et la peinture* (New York: Brentano's, 1945.)

"ready-mades" (manufactured objects promoted to the dignity of art objects by the choice of the artist), which were Duchamp's almost exclusive means of self-expression from 1914 on.

As early as September 1924, in the *Introduction au discours sur le peu de réalité*, I proposed the creation of "certain of those objects that one approaches only in dreams and that appear to be just as indefensible from the standpoint of their utility as from the standpoint of the pleasure they afford":

> *Thus one night not long ago [I wrote], "I got my hands on a rather curious book in my sleep, in an open air market out toward Saint-Malo. The spine of this book was formed by a wooden gnome with an Assyrian-style white beard which came down to its feet. The statuette was of normal thickness and yet it in no way interfered with turning the pages of the book, which were made of thick black wool. I hastened to acquire it, and when I woke up I regretted not finding it near me. It would be relatively easy to re-create it. I should like to put a few objects of this sort in circulation, for their fate seems to me to be eminently problematical and disturbing. . . .*
>
> *Who knows—perhaps I would thereby help to ruin those concrete trophies that are so detestable, and throw greater discredit on "reasonable" beings and objects. There would be cleverly constructed machines that would have no use; minutely detailed maps of immense cities would be drawn up, cities which, however many we are, we would feel forever incapable of founding, but which would at least classify present and future capitals. Absurd, highly perfected automata, which would do nothing the way anyone else does, would be responsible for giving us a correct idea of action.*

It is easy, in this regard, to measure how far we have come today.

The predetermination of the goal man is to attain, if this goal is on the order of knowledge, and the rational adaptation of the means for reaching this goal would be enough to defend it against all accusations of mysticism. We say that the art of imitation (of places, of scenes, of external objects) has had its day and that the artistic problem today consists of making mental representation more and more objectively precise through the voluntary exercise of imagination and memory (it being understood that only the perception of the outside world has permitted the involuntary acquisition of the materials which mental representation is called up to use). The greatest benefit that Surrealism has gotten out of this sort of operation is the fact that we have succeeded in *dialectically* reconciling these two terms—perception and representation—that are so violently contradictory for the adult man, and the fact that we have thrown a bridge over the abyss that separated them. Surrealist painting and construction have now permitted the organization of perceptions with an objective tendency around subjective elements. These perceptions, through their very tendency to assert themselves as objective perceptions are of such a nature as to be bewildering and revolutionary, in the sense that they urgently call for something to answer them in outer reality. It may be predicted that in large measure this something *will be.*

PROLEGOMENA
TO A THIRD
SURREALIST MANIFESTO
OR NOT
(1942)

Doubtless there is too much north *in me for me ever to be a man to pledge his whole allegiance to anything. In my own eyes this north is made up of both natural granite fortifications and fog. Though I am only too likely to demand everything of a creature I consider beautiful, I am far from granting the same credit to those abstract constructions that go by the name of systems. In the face of them my ardor cools, and it is clear that love no longer spurs me on. I've been seduced, of course, but never to the extent that I hide from myself the* fallible point *in what* a man like me holds to be true. *This fallible point, even though it is not necessarily situated on the line traced for me by the original teacher during his lifetime, always appears to me to be located somewhere along the prolongation of this line through other men. The greater the power of this man, the more he is limited by the inertia resulting from the veneration that he will inspire in some and by the tireless activity of others who will employ the most devious means to ruin him. Aside from these two causes of degeneration, there is also the fact that every great idea is perhaps subject to being seriously altered the instant that it enters into* *contact with the mass of humanity, where it is made to come to terms with minds of a completely different stature than that of the mind it came from originally. There is ample proof of this, in modern times, in the impudence with which the most notorious charlatans and fakes have claimed kinship with the principles of Robespierre and Saint-Just, in the splitting of Hegelian doctrine between zealots of the right and zealots of the left, in the monumental quarrels within Marxism, in the stupefying confidence with which Catholics and reactionaries are endeavoring to put Rimbaud in their bag of tricks. Closer still to us, the death of Freud is enough to render the future of psychoanalytic ideas uncertain, and threatens once again to turn an exemplary instrument of liberation into an instrument of oppression. The evils that are always the price of favor, of renown, lie in wait even for Surrealism, though it has been in existence for twenty years. The precautions taken to safeguard the inner integrity of this movement—which generally are regarded as being much too severe—have not precluded the raving false witness of an Aragon, nor the picaresque sort of imposture of the Neo-Falangist bedside-table Avida Dollars.* Surrealism is already far from being able to cover everything that is undertaken in its name, openly or not, from the most unfathomable "teas" of Tokyo to the rain-streaked windows of Fifth Avenue, even though Japan and America are at war. What is being done in any given direction bears little resemblance to what was wanted. Even the most outstanding men must put up with passing away not so much with a halo as with a great cloud of dust trailing behind them.*

So long as men have not become aware of their condition—and I mean not only their social condition but also their condition as men and its extreme precariousness: a ridicu-

---

*An anagram for Salvador Dali.—*Tr.*

lous life-span in relation to the species' field of action such as the mind believes it encompasses, the more or less secret submission of oneself to a very few simple instincts, the power to think, naturally, but a power which is grossly overrated, a power, furthermore, that falls victim to routine, that society is careful to channel in predefined directions where it can keep an eye on it, and, moreover, a power that is ceaselessly set off against a power not to think (by oneself), or to think badly (alone or, far more preferably, with others) that is fully its equal; so long as men stubbornly insist on lying to themselves; so long as they will not take into account the ephemeral and the eternal, the unreasonable and the reasonable that possess them, the *unique* that is jealously preserved within them and its enthusiastic diffusion in the *crowd;* so long as people in the West fall heir to a taste for risk-taking in the hope of bettering things, and others in the East fall heir to a carefully nurtured indifference; so long as some people exploit others without even enjoying it appreciably—among them money is a common tyrant—among them money is like a snake that bites its own tail and a bomb fuse; so long as one knows nothing while pretending to know everything, the Bible in one hand and Lenin in the other; so long as voyeurs manage to take the place of seers in the darkness of the night, and so long as . . . (I can't pin it down to one single thing, since I am the last person in the world to know everything; there are several other *so long ases* that could be mentioned) it isn't worth the trouble to speak out, and still less worth the trouble for people to oppose each other, and still less worth the trouble to love without contradicting everything that is not love, and still less worth the trouble of dying and (except in spring, I still dream of youth, of *trees in bloom,* all this being scandalously disparaged, disparaged that is by old men; I dream of the magnificent workings of chance in the streets, even in New York) still less worth the trouble of living. *There is*—I think of this fine optimistic formula of gratitude that is found again and again in Apollinaire's last poems: there is the marvelous young woman who at this very minute, beneath the shadow of her lashes, is walking round the great ruined chalk boxes of South America, one of whose glances would call into question the very meaning of belligerence; there are the New Guineans, in the front boxes in this war, the New Guineans whose art has always captivated certain of us much more than Egyptian or Roman art—intent on the spectacle offered them in the sky—forgive them, the only thing they had all to themselves was three hundred species of birds of paradise—it appears that they "whoop it up" with barely enough arrows tipped with curare for white men and yellow men; there are new secret societies that attempt to define themselves in repeated secret meetings, at twilight in seaports; there is my friend Aimé Césaire, black and magnetic, who is writing the poems we need today, in Martinique, having made a break with all the catchwords of Eluard and others. There are also the heads of leaders which have just barely appeared above ground, and failing to see anything except their hair, everyone asks what sort of grass this is that will win out, that will overcome the sempiternal "fear of changing only to see the same thing happen all over again." These heads are beginning to sprout somewhere in the world—so keep turning tirelessly round and round in all directions. Nobody knows for sure *who* these leaders are, where they are going to come from, what they mean historically—and perhaps it would be asking too much to expect them to know themselves. But they cannot help but exist already: in the present turmoil, in the face of the unprecedented seriousness of this crisis that is social as well as religious and economic, it would be a mistake to conceive of them as products of a system that we are thoroughly acquainted with. There is no doubt that they are coming from some horizon that is a matter of conjecture: still they will have had to *make their own* several closely related programs for making demands, programs which parties up to now have wanted to have nothing to do with—or we will soon fall back into barbarism. Not only must the exploitation of man by man cease, but also the exploitation of man by the so-called "God" of absurd and exasperating memory. The problem of the relations between men and women must be gone over from top to bottom, with no trace of hypocrisy and in such a manner as to brook no delay. Man must pass, bag and baggage, to the side of man. No more weaknesses, no more childish behavior, no more ideas of indignity, no more torpor, no more lounging about, no more putting flowers on tombs, no more civics lessons between two gym classes, no more tolerance, no more snakes-in-the-grass!

Parties: what is, what is not *in the party line.* But what if my own line, that admittedly twists and turns, passes through Heraclitus, Abelard, Eckhardt, Retz, Rousseau, Swift, Sade, Lewis, Arnim, Lautréamont, Engels, Jarry, and a few others? From them I have constructed a system of coordinates for my own use, a system that stands up to the test of my own personal experience and therefore appears to me to include some of tomorrow's chances.

A SHORT PROPHETIC INTERLUDE

In a short while acrobats are going to come, in tights spangled with an unknown color, the only color to date which absorbs both sunlight and moonlight at the same time. This color will be called freedom and the sky will break out all its blue and black oriflammes, for a com-

pletely favorable wind will have arisen for the first time and those who are there will realize that they have just set sail and that all preceding so-called voyages were only a trap. And people will watch alienated thought and the atrocious jousts of our time with the look of commiseration mingled with repugnance of the captain of the brig Argus *as he picked up the survivors of the* Raft of the Medusa. *And everyone will be astonished at being able to look down without vertigo into the upper chasms guarded by a dragon who turned out to be made of nothing but chains once more light was shed on him. Here they are; they are already at the very top. They have cast the ladder away; nothing is holding them back now. On an oblique carpet, more imponderable than a beam of light, those who were the sibyls come toward us. From the stem that they form with their almond-green robes ripped on stones and their disheveled hair the great sparkling rose-window emerges, swaying weightlessly, the flower of true life blossoming at last. All previous motivations are immediately derided, the place is free, ideally free. The point of honor shifts with the speed of a comet that simultaneously describes these two lines: the dance for the choosing of the being of the other sex, the parade in full view of the mysterious gallery of newcomers to whom man believes he owes an accounting after his death. Aside from this, I see no duties for him. An ear of grain that must be caught on the wing detaches itself from the bouquet of fireworks: it is the chance, the unique adventure, that one assures himself was written nowhere in the depths of books, nor in the gaze of old sailors who now reckon the breeze only from their benches on shore. And what worth is there in any submission to what one has not decreed oneself? Man must flee this ridiculous web that has been spun around him: so-called present reality with the prospect of a future reality that is hardly better. Each full minute bears within itself the negation of centuries of limping, broken history. Those to whom it is given to make these eight flamelike traceries circle above us can do so only with pure sap.*

All present systems can reasonably be considered to be nothing but tools on the carpenter's workbench. This carpenter is *you*. Unless you have gone stark raving mad, you will not try to make do without all these tools except one, and to stand up for the plane to the point of declaring that the use of hammers is wrong and wicked. This, however, is exactly what happens every time a sectarian of such and such a persuasion flatters himself that he can explain the French or Russian revolution by "hatred of the father" (in this case the deposed sovereign) or the work of Mallarmé by the "relations between classes" in his time. With no eclecticism whatsoever, one ought to be permitted to have recourse to that instrument of knowledge that seems the most adequate in each circumstance. All that is needed, moreover, is a sudden convulsion of this globe, such as the one we are going through today, for there to be called into question again, if not the necessity, then at least the adequacy of the optional modes of knowledge and manipulation of reality which have attracted man during the most recent period of history. In proof of this I need only point to the anxious desire that has overcome, one by one, minds which are very dissimilar but nonetheless figure among today's most lucid and daring—Bataille, Caillois, Duthuit, Masson, Mabille, Léonora Carrington, Ernst, Etiemble, Péret, Calas, Séligman, Hénein—the anxious desire, as I was saying, to furnish a prompt reply to the question: "What should one think of the postulate that 'there is no society without a social myth'? in what measure can we choose or adopt, and *impose,* a myth fostering the society that we judge to be desirable?" But I might also note a certain return to the study of the philosophy of the Middle Ages as well as of the "accursed" sciences (with which a tacit contact has always been maintained through the intermediary of "accursed" poetry) which has been taking place during this war. I would also have to mention, finally, the sort of ultimatum delivered, if only in their heart of hearts, to their own rationalist system by many of those who continue to militate for the transformation of the world but make this transformation depend solely on the overturning of world economic conditions: very well then, system, you have me in your power, I gave myself to you body and soul, but nothing that you promised has come about yet. Mind what you're about. What you would have me believe is inevitable is still not in sight and may even appear to have been persistently thwarted. If this war and the many chances that it offers you to live up to your promise were to be *in vain,* I should be forced to admit that there is something a bit presumptuous about you, or for all anybody knows, something basically wrong with you that I can no longer hide from myself. In like manner poor mortals once prided themselves on having put the devil in his place, which made him decide, they say, to finally show himself in person.

The fact remains, moreover, that at the end of twenty years I find myself obliged, as I did in my youth, to take a public stand against every kind of conformism and in so doing attack as well a Surrealist conformism that is all too obvious. Too many paintings, in particular, come upon the scene today all decked out in what cost the innumerable followers of Chirico, of Picasso, of Ernst, of Masson, of Miró, of Tanguy (and tomorrow of Matta) absolutely nothing, followers who are ignorant of the fact that there is no great expedition in art which is not undertaken *at the risk of one's life,* that the road to take is obviously not the one with guard rails along its edge, and that each artist must take up the search for the *Golden Fleece* all by himself.

In 1942 more than ever the *opposition* must be strengthened at its very base. All ideas that win out hasten to their downfall. Man must be absolutely convinced that once there has been general consent on a given subject, individual resistance is the only key to the prison. But this resistance must be *informed* and subtle. By instinct I will contradict a *unanimous* vote by any assembly that will not take it upon itself to contradict the vote of a larger assembly, but by the same instinct I will give my vote to those who are *climbing higher,* what with every new program tending to the greater emancipation of man and not yet having been tested by the facts. Considering the historical process, where it is fully understood that truth shows itself only so as to laugh up its sleeve and never be grasped, I am on the side of this minority that is endlessly renewable and acts like a lever: my greatest ambition would be to allow its theoretical import to be indefinitely transmissible after I am gone.

THE RETURN OF FATHER DUCHESNE

Father Duchesne is in damned fine spirits! Whichever way he turns, mentally or physically, skunks are queens of the walk! These gentlemen in uniforms of old garbage peelings on the terraces of Paris cafés, the triumphant return of Cistercians and Trappists who were forced to get on the train with a kick in the ass, the waiting in line in alphabetical order early in the morning in the suburbs in the hope of getting fifty grams of horses' lungs, and then hav-

ing to start all over again around noon for two Jerusalem artichokes—while with money you can keep on stuffing your face at Lapérouse without a ration card, the Republic having been sent to the smelter so that symbolically your very best effort comes back to spit in your face, all this beneath the supposedly providential eye of a guy with a frozen moustache who is brushing off a necktie of vomit in the shadow—you have to admit that that's not bad! But, what the hell, we'll manage, we'll manage, we'll still manage. I don't know if you're familiar with that fine striped cloth that sells for three sous a meter, it's even free when it rains, that the sansculottes rolled their genitals up in with the sound of the sea. It hasn't been worn much recently, but what the hell, it's coming back in style, it's even going to be terribly fashionable again, God is making us little brothers at present, it's going to come back with the sound of the sea. And I'm going to sweep these scrapings from the porte de Saint-Ouen to the porte de Vanves, and I promise you that this time they're not going to shut me up in the name of the Supreme Being and that all this won't come about according to very strict rules and that the time has come to refuse to swallow this whole mess of books by good-for-nothing bastards who urge you to stay at home and not pay any attention to how hungry you are. But what the hell, look at the street—it's rather curious, rather ambiguous, rather well-guarded, yet it's going to be yours, it's magnificent!

Since universal intelligence has doubtless never been bestowed on man and since universal knowledge in any case is no longer granted him, it is best to have all sorts of reservations about the genius's claim that he has solved questions that go beyond his field of investigation and therefore are not within his competence. The great mathematician displays no particular grandeur in the act of putting on his slippers and burying himself in his newspaper. All we shall ask of him is to talk about mathematics at certain fixed hours. There are no human shoulders that can bear the burden of omniscience. People once claimed that omniscience was an attribute of "God," and since man was supposedly made "in His image" he was only too often urged to lay claim to this omniscience. These two pieces of nonsense must both be done away with at once. Nothing that has been established or decreed by man can be considered to be definite and intangible, and still less become the object of a cult if that cult requires that one yield to some antecedent divinized will. These reservations naturally do not prejudge the *enlightened* forms of willing dependence and respect.

In this regard, there now being nothing to keep me from letting my mind wander where it will, taking no notice of the accusations of mysticism that are sure to be brought against me, I think it would not be a bad idea, as a start, to convince man that he is not necessarily the *king* of creation that he prides himself on being. This idea at least allows me to see certain perspectives that weigh something on the balance-scales of poetry, a fact which confers on this idea, willy-nilly, a remote sort of effectiveness.

The brand of rationalist thought that is the most self-possessed, the most penetrating, the most apt to overcome all the obstacles in the field to which it is applied has always seemed to me to tolerate the strangest kind of self-indulgence outside this field. My surprise at this always crystallizes around a conversation I had with a man whose mind was exceptionally wide-ranging and powerful. It was in Pátzcuaro, Mexico: I shall always see us walking back and forth along the gallery overlooking a flowering patio from which there rose the cry of mocking birds from twenty cages. The fine nervous hand that had controlled some of the greatest events of our time was relaxing by petting a dog wandering about around us. He spoke of dogs, and I noticed that his language became less precise, his thought less exacting than it usually was. He let himself be carried away by his love, went so far as to attribute natural goodness to an animal, and even spoke, as everyone else does, of devotion. I tried at this juncture to get it across to him that there is doubtless something arbitrary about attributing to animals feelings which have no discernible sense unless they apply to man, since they would lead one to hold that the mosquito is knowingly cruel and the crayfish deliberately backward. It became clear that he was offended at having to go along with my line of argument: he insisted—and this weakness becomes poignant as I look back on it, because of the tragic fate men doubtless have in store for him in return for his total gift of himself to their cause—that the dog felt *friendship* for him, in every sense of the word.

But I persist in believing that this anthropomorphic view of the animal world betrays a regrettable facile way of thinking. I see nothing wrong with opening the windows on the broadest utopian landscape in order to make this animal world understandable. An era such as the one we are living in can tolerate any and all departures for voyages à la Cyrano de Bergerac, à la Gulliver, so long as the aim of these eras is the defiance of all conventional ways of thinking, a defiance that we obviously lack. And the great possibility that we may get somewhere, after certain detours we will have had to make even in a country more reasonable than the one we are leaving, is not excluded on the voyage that I am inviting you on today.

THE GREAT TRANSPARENT ONES

Man is perhaps not the center, the cynosure of the universe. One can go so far as to believe that there exists above him, on the animal scale, beings whose behavior is as strange to him as his may be to the mayfly or the whale. Nothing necessarily stands in the way of these creatures' being able to completely escape man's sensory system of references through a camouflage of whatever sort one cares to imagine, though the possibility of such a camouflage is posited only by the theory of forms *and the study of mimetic animals. There is no doubt that there is ample room for speculation here, even though this idea tends to place man in the same modest conditions of interpretation of his own universe as the child who is pleased to form his conception of an ant from its underside just after he's kicked over an anthill. In considering disturbances such as cyclones, in the face of which man is powerless to be anything but a victim or a witness, or those such as war, notoriously inadequate versions of which are set forth, it would not be impossible, in the course of a vast work over which the most daring sort of induction should never cease to preside, to approximate the structure and the constitution of such hypothetical beings (which mysteriously reveal themselves to us when we are afraid and when we are conscious of the workings of chance) to the point where they become credible.*

I think it necessary to point out that I am not departing appreciably from Novalis's testimony: "In reality we live in an animal whose parasites we are. The constitution of this animal determines ours and vice versa," and that I am only agreeing with a thought of William James's:

"Who knows whether, in nature, we do not occupy just as small a place alongside beings whose existence we do not suspect as our cats and dogs that live with us in our homes?" Even learned men do not all contradict this view of things: "Perhaps there circle round about us beings built on the same plan as we are, but different, men for example whose albumins are straight," said Emile Duclaux, a former director of the Pasteur Institute (1840-1904).

A new myth? Must these beings be convinced that they result from a mirage or must they be given a chance to show themselves?

ON SURREALISM
IN ITS
LIVING WORKS
(1953)

It is a matter of common knowledge today that Surrealism, as an organized movement, was born of a far-reaching operation having to do with language. In this regard it cannot be repeated too often that in the minds of their authors the products of free association or automatic writing that Surrealism brought forth in the beginning had nothing to do with any aesthetic criterion. As soon as the vanity of certain of these authors allowed such a criterion to take hold—which did not take long—the operation was put in a false light, and to top it all off the "state of grace" that made it possible was lost.

What was it all about then? Nothing less than the rediscovery of the secret of a language whose elements would then cease to float like jetsam on the surface of a dead sea. To do this it was essential to wrest these elements away from their increasingly narrow utilitarian usage, this being the only way to emancipate them and restore all their power. This need to counteract ruthlessly the depreciation of language, a need which was felt in France by Lautréamont, Rimbaud, Mallarmé, and at the same time in England by Lewis Carroll, has not ceased to be just as imperative since that time, as is proved by experiments of quite unequal interest, ranging from the "words set free" of Futurism to the very relative spontaneity of "Dada," the exuberant "plays on words" more or less related to the "phonetic cabal" or the "language of the birds" (Jean-Pierre Brisset, Raymond Roussel, Marcel Duchamp, Robert Desnos) and the outbreak of a "revolution of the word" (James Joyce, e. e. cummings, Henri Michaux) which was bound to lead to nothing but "Lettrism." The evolution of the plastic arts was to reflect the same disquiet.

Although they are evidence of a common desire to take up arms against the tyranny of a thoroughly debased language, procedures such as the "automatic writing" that began Surrealism and the "inner monologue" in Joyce's system are radically different at base. That is to say, underlying them are two modes of apprehension of the world that are different in every particular. In opposition to the illusory stream of conscious associations, Joyce will present a flux and try to make it gush forth from all directions, a flux that in the last analysis tends to be the closest possible *imitation* of life (by means of which he keeps himself within the framework of *art,* falls once again into *novelistic* illusion, and fails to avoid being placed in the long line of naturalists and expressionists). Much more modestly when one first looks at it, over and against this same conscious current "pure psychic automatism," which is the guiding principle of Surrealism, will set the flow from a spring that one need only go search for fairly deep down within oneself, a flow whose course one cannot try to direct, for if one does it is sure to dry up immediately. Before Surrealism the only things that would give any notion of the intensity of light from this source were certain infiltrations that people didn't notice, such as phrases described as "half asleep" or "waking." The decisive act of Surrealism was to show that they flow along continuously. The experiment proved that very few neologisms show up, and that this continual flow brought about neither syntactic dismemberment nor disintegration of vocabulary.

This is obviously quite a different project from the one that was close, for example, to Joyce's heart. It is no longer a question of making the free association of ideas *serve* for the elaboration of a *literary* work that tends to outdo preceding works by its daring, but at the same time is a work whose recourse to polyphonic, polysemantic, and other inspirations presupposes a constant return to the arbitrary. The whole point, for Surrealism, was to convince ourselves that we had got our hands on the "prime matter" (in the alchemical sense) of language. After that, we knew *where* to get it, and it goes without saying that we had no interest in reproducing it to the point of satiety; this is said for the benefit of those who are surprised that among us the *practice* of automatic writing was abandoned so quickly. It has often been said heretofore that our coming face to face with the products of this writing focused the projector on the region where desire arises unconstrained, a region which is also that where myths take wing. Not enough attention has been paid to the meaning and the scope of the operation which tended to bring language back to true life: in other words, rather than go back from the thing signified to the sign that lives on after it (which, moreover, would prove to be impossible), it is better to go back in one leap to the birth of that which signifies.

The spirit that makes such an operation possible and even conceivable is none other than that which has always moved occult philosophy: according to this spirit, from the fact that expression is at the origin of everything, it follows that "the name must *germinate,* so to speak, or otherwise it is false." The principal contribution of Surrealism, in poetry as in the plastic arts, is to have so exalted this germination that everything other than it seems laughable.

As has been proved to me after the fact, the definition of Surrealism given in the first Manifesto merely "retouches" a great traditional saying concerning the necessity of "breaking through the drumhead of reasoning reason and looking at the hole," a procedure which will lead to the clarification of symbols that were once mysterious.

Unlike the various disciplines which claim that they guide us along this path and allow us to forge ahead on it, Surrealism has never been tempted to hide from itself the element of glittering fascination in man's love for woman. It was all the less tempted to do so by the very fact that its first investigations, as we have seen, led them into a country where desire was king. Where poetry was concerned, it also marked the culmination of a long line of speculation, which apparently goes back to the middle of the eighteenth century, tending to give women a greater and greater share in things. From the ruins of the Christian religion, which came into being within Pascal's lifetime, there sprang—not without "hell" dogging its footsteps in Sade, in Laclos, in Monk Lewis—a completely different conception of woman, who now represents man's greatest chance and demands, in the opinion of Goethe toward the end of his life, that man consider her the keystone of the edifice. This idea follows a path, albeit a very rough one, that leads through German and French romanticism (Novalis, Hölderlin, Kleist, Nerval, the followers of Saint-Simon, Vigny, Stendhal, Baudelaire). But despite the assaults that it underwent at the end of the nineteenth century (Huysmans, Jarry), it comes down to us with everything that might still make it obscure decanted out of it, so to speak, and the bearer of its own pure light. From that point Surrealism needed only to go back even further than I have said—

to the letters of Héloise or the Portuguese Nun—in order
to discover how wondrous the stars that spangled its *heart
line* were. From the lyrical point of view at which it placed
itself, it could not fail to notice that most of the highlights
of man's struggle to rise above his condition lay along this
line, and thus a chain reaction from one to the other provoked veritable *transport*s of emotion. It was woman who
in the end reaped the glory, whether her name was Sophie
von Kuhn, Diotima, Kâtchen von Heilbronn, Aurélia,
Mina de Wanghel, the "black" Venus or the "white" one,
or the Eva of Vigny's "Maison du Berger."

The object of these remarks is to make the reader
understand the Surrealist attitude toward *the human,* an
attitude that far too long has been held to be rather negative. In Surrealism, woman is to be loved and honored as
the great promise, a promise that still exists even after it
has been kept. The sign she bears as the Chosen One,
which is there only for a *single individual* to read (each
of us must discover it for himself), suffices to make short
work of the charge that there is a soul-body dualism. At
this stage it is absolutely true that carnal love is at one with
spiritual love. Their reciprocal attraction must be strong
enough to bring about perfect unity, at once organic and
psychic, through their being absolutely complementary. It
is not our intention, certainly, to deny that great obstacles
stand in the way of accomplishing this. Provided, however,
that we have remained worthy of seeking it, that is to say
provided we have not corrupted within ourselves the notion of such a love at its very source, if only out of spite,
nothing in life can prevail against our continuing thirst
for it. Bitter failures in this direction (most often attributable to social arbitrariness, which generally severely
limits the range of choices and makes the united couple
a target for all the forces of division working against it *from
the outside*) cannot discourage us from following this very
path. It is essential, here more than anywhere else, to un-

dertake the reconstruction of the *primordial Androgyne* that all traditions tell us of, and its supremely desirable, and *tangible,* incarnation within ourselves.

From this point of view, it was to be expected that sexual desire—which up to that time was more or less repressed in an anxiety-ridden or a guilt-ridden conscience because of taboos—should prove to be (in the last analysis misleadingly) the dizzying and invaluable "world on this side of eternity" in whose endless purlieus human dreams have built all "worlds beyond."

It need merely be pointed out that here Surrealism deliberately departs from most traditional doctrines, according to which carnal love is a mirage, and passionate love a deplorable intoxication by astral light, insofar as this latter love is said to be prefigured in the serpent of Genesis. Provided that this love corresponds in every particular to the word *passionate,* that is to say presupposes *election* in all the rigor of that term, it opens the gates of a world where by definition it can no longer be a question of evil, of a fall, or of sin.

The attitude of Surrealism toward nature is governed above all by its initial conception of the poetic "image." It is common knowledge that Surrealism saw in it the means of obtaining, most often under conditions of complete relaxation of the mind rather than complete concentration, certain incandescent flashes linking two elements of reality belonging to categories that are so far removed from each other that reason would fail to connect them and that require a momentary suspension of the critical attitude in order for them to be brought together. From the moment that one has come upon its mode of generation and become conscious of its inexhaustible resources, this extraordinary network of sparks leads the mind to have a less opaque image of the world and of itself. The mind then proves to itself, fragmentarily of course, but at least *by itself,* that "everything above is like everything below" and everything inside is like everything outside. The world thereupon seems to be like a cryptogram which remains indecipherable only so long as one is not thoroughly familiar with the gymnastics that permit one to pass at will from one piece of apparatus to another. It cannot be emphasized too strongly that the metaphor, which enjoys every freedom in Surrealism, leaves far behind the sort of (prefabricated) analogy that Charles Fourier and his disciple Alphonse Toussenel attempted to promote in France. Although both concur in honoring the system of "correspondences," the same distance separates them as separates the high-flying from the earthbound.* It should be understood that it is not a question of increasing one's speed and agility in a vain spirit of improving one's technique, but rather of becoming the master of the one and only conductive electricity so that the relationships that one wishes to establish may truly be of some consequence.

As for the core of the problem, which is that of the relationship between the human mind and the sensory world, Surrealism is here of the same mind as such thinkers as Louis-Claude de Saint-Martin and Schopenhauer, in the sense that it believes, as they did, that we must "seek to understand nature through ourselves and not ourselves through nature." This does not lead, however, to its sharing in any way the opinion that man enjoys absolute superiority over all other beings, or, put another way, that man is the world's crowning achievement—which is the most unjustifiable sort of postulate and the most arrant abuse that anthromorphism can be charged with. Its position on the matter, rather, is doubtless the same as Gérard de Nerval's, as expressed in the famous sonnet

---

*Even though admittedly Fourier uses it naively and illustrates it with examples that are usually dismaying, his theory of "the analogy of the passions or hieroglyphic table of human passions" abounds in strokes of genius.

"Vers Dorés." As regards other creatures whose desires and sufferings he is less and less capable of appreciating the farther down he goes on the scale he has constructed, man must, in all humility, use the little that he knows about himself to reconnoiter what surrounds him.* The most effective means he has of doing this is *poetic* intuition. This intuition, finally unleashed by Surrealism, seeks not only to assimilate all known forms but also boldly to create new forms—that is to say, to be in a position to embrace all the structures of the world, manifested or not. It alone provides the thread that can put us back on the road of Gnosis as knowledge of suprasensible Reality, "invisibly visible in an eternal mystery."

*In this regard no one has put it better or more definitively than René Guénon in his book *Les Etats multiples de l'être:* it is absurd to believe that "the human state occupies a privileged place in the whole of universal Existence, or that it is distinguished metaphysically from other states by the possession of some prerogative or other. In reality this human state is a state of manifestation like any other, and merely one among an indefinite number of others; in the hierarchy of degrees of Existence, it is situated in the place assigned it by its very nature, that is to say, by the limitations of the conditions that define it, and this place confers on it neither superiority nor absolute inferiority. If we must on occasion consider this state in particular, it is only because, being the state in which we in fact find ourselves, it thereby acquires for us, but for us alone, a special importance; this is merely a very relative and contingent point of view, that of the individuals that we are in our present mode of manifestation." Moreover, we have not borrowed this opinion from Guénon, because it has always seemed to us to fall under the head of elementary good sense (though on this point good sense may be the most unfairly divided thing in the world).

Ann Arbor Paperbacks

Waddell, *The Desert Fathers*
Erasmus, *The Praise of Folly*
Donne, *Devotions*
Malthus, *Population: The First Essay*
Berdyaev, *The Origin of Russian Communism*
Einhard, *The Life of Charlemagne*
Edwards, *The Nature of True Virtue*
Gilson, *Héloïse and Abélard*
Aristotle, *Metaphysics*
Kant, *Education*
Boulding, *The Image*
Duckett, *The Gateway to the Middle Ages* (3 vols.): *Italy; France and Britain; Monasticism*
Bowditch and Ramsland, *Voices of the Industrial Revolution*
Luxemburg, *The Russian Revolution and Leninism or Marxism?*
Rexroth, *Poems from the Greek Anthology*
Zoshchenko, *Scenes from the Bathhouse*
Thrupp, *The Merchant Class of Medieval London*
Procopius, *Secret History*
Adcock, *Roman Political Ideas and Practice*
Swanson, *The Birth of the Gods*
Xenophon, *The March Up Country*
Trotsky, *The New Course*
Buchanan and Tullock, *The Calculus of Consent*
Hobson, *Imperialism*
Pobedonostsev, *Reflections of a Russian Statesman*
Kinietz, *The Indians of the Western Great Lakes 1615–1760*
Bromage, *Writing for Business*
Lurie, *Mountain Wolf Woman, Sister of Crashing Thunder*
Leonard, *Baroque Times in Old Mexico*
Meier, *Negro Thought in America, 1880–1915*
Burke, *The Philosophy of Edmund Burke*
Michelet, *Joan of Arc*
Conze, *Buddhist Thought in India*
Arberry, *Aspects of Islamic Civilization*
Chesnutt, *The Wife of His Youth and Other Stories*
Gross, *Sound and Form in Modern Poetry*
Zola, *The Masterpiece*
Chesnutt, *The Marrow of Tradition*
Aristophanes, *Four Comedies*
Aristophanes, *Three Comedies*

Chesnutt, *The Conjure Woman*
Duckett, *Carolingian Portraits*
Rapoport and Chammah, *Prisoner's Dilemma*
Aristotle, *Poetics*
Peattie, *The View from the Barrio*
Duckett, *Death and Life in the Tenth Century*
Langford, *Galileo, Science and the Church*
McNaughton, *The Taoist Vision*
Anderson, *Matthew Arnold and the Classical Tradition*
Milio, *9226 Kercheval*
Weisheipl, *The Development of Physical Theory in the Middle Ages*
Breton, *Manifestoes of Surrealism*
Gershman, *The Surrealist Revolution in France*
Lester, *Theravada Buddhism in Southeast Asia*
Scholz, *Carolingian Chronicles*
Marković, *From Affluence to Praxis*
Wik, *Henry Ford and Grass-roots America*
Sahlins and Service, *Evolution and Culture*
Wickham, *Early Medieval Italy*
Waddell, *The Wandering Scholars*
Rosenberg, *Bolshevik Visions* (2 parts in 2 vols.)
Mannoni, *Prospero and Caliban*
Aron, *Democracy and Totalitarianism*
Shy, *A People Numerous and Armed*
Taylor, *Roman Voting Assemblies*
Goodfield, *An Imagined World*
Hesiod, *The Works and Days; Theogony; The Shield of Herakles*
Raverat, *Period Piece*
Lamming, *In the Castle of My Skin*
Fisher, *The Conjure-Man Dies*
Strayer, *The Albigensian Crusades*
Lamming, *The Pleasures of Exile*
Lamming, *Natives of My Person*
Glaspell, *Lifted Masks and Other Works*
Wolff, *Aesthetics and the Sociology of Art*
Grand, *The Heavenly Twins*
Cornford, *The Origin of Attic Comedy*
Allen, *Wolves of Minong*
Brathwaite, *Roots*
Fisher, *The Walls of Jericho*
Lamming, *The Emigrants*
Loudon, *The Mummy!*
Kemble and Butler Leigh, *Principles and Privilege*
Thomas, *Out of Time*